D

35655

710

D1357190

THE PUBLIC SCHOOLS

THE
PUBLIC SCHOOLS

An Historical Survey

By

BRIAN GARDNER

WITH A FOREWORD BY
LORD BUTLER

HAMISH HAMILTON
LONDON

First published in Great Britain, 1973
by Hamish Hamilton Ltd.
90 Great Russell Street London W.C.1

Copyright © 1973 by Brian Gardner

SBN 241 02337 8

Printed in Great Britain by
Western Printing Services Ltd., Bristo

Of all things in the world there is nothing, always excepting a good mother, so worthy of honour as a good school.

—RUDYARD KIPLING

CONTENTS

LIST OF ILLUSTRATIONS

FOREWORD

by LORD BUTLER

IT would be an unwise man who attempted to write a long foreword to this book on Public Schools. The same man would be equally ungenerous not to praise the extraordinary wealth of historical detail which the book contains about independent schools of almost every type, not all of which fall easily under the definition of Public Schools. It is because of this wealth of detail that comment is really superfluous. The details of the founding of almost every independent school are found in these pages together with elaborate accounts of the distinguished people who have been present at the schools and it would be mere repetition to enumerate these, whether they are de Quincey, C. S. Forester or anyone else. The writer must have taken infinite trouble to verify every fact and detail about the masters, boys and curricula. All is set out here.

No attempt is made to deal with the problem of the Public Schools, that is a solution to their difficulties in the modern age of the wealth tax and social change. Indeed the chapter on the twentieth century is the shortest of all and merely makes reference to the abortive attempts made under my education settlement to solve the problems through the Fleming Committee and the unfulfilled suggestions of the Newsom Committee at a later date quite recently. I was informed by Sir Will Spens, forty years ago, that there was no solution to the Public Schools problem and it is probably wise for this book to adhere to the details of history rather than the mists of the future. It would, however, be intriguing if the author, after concluding his mammoth essay in research, which he describes as a historical survey, were to turn his attention to what may be the future of some of these ancient foundations.

King's School, Canterbury, is given the prize as the oldest school and reference is made to Somerset Maugham's far from flattering descriptions of life there, as also those of Horace Walpole. In the chapter inscribed 'Early Schools', there are great encomia about Winchester and Eton, together with the most dazzling account of the distinguished persons who have been at these two schools. It is rather interesting that in his historical method the author, once he gets his teeth into a school like Winchester, does not stop at William of Wykeham but goes through with the success of the school in later days. This method is employed in relation to all schools mentioned in detail in the survey. It is really as well when one reads the list of those who have been in public schools, given in a table at the end of the book, and who have been Prime Minister, Home Secretary or Foreign Secretary, to realise that there are many who are listed in the introduction on page 4 as never having been to a Public School. These include Dickens, Lister, Rhodes, Constable, Gainsborough, Adam Smith, Henry Moore, Bertrand Russell and Disraeli, although in *Coningsby* Disraeli gives a skit on Eton. The author is keen to show that the Public School is not a harbour of privilege and I think he succeeds. It is, however, interesting to note that most of the foundations of these great schools made sufficient provision for paupers and poor scholars. While there are not so many paupers left in the country there are plenty of poor scholars and it would do no harm if some of the ancient foundations returned to their original articles by including a greater number of entrants from the public system.

Schools which are given particular attention are Manchester Grammar, Tonbridge founded by the Skinners, and in modern times Millfield. But no school is underdone. There is an impressive bibliography which shows the extent of the research of the author, who manages to compress into a short space this vast historical collection of names, dates and figures. I certainly would regard the book as being an important one on the shelf of any headmaster and would expect it to appeal to a wide public of readers because of its common sense and lack of snobbishness of which the Public Schools are often accused.

INTRODUCTION

JOHN DANCY has written: 'There are few subjects on which more irrational and extreme views are held' than the public schools. Perhaps this is because few people have a clear idea—if tested—as to what they mean by a public school. This is not surprising because in law they hardly exist. There is no such thing. There are independent boys' schools, partly-independent boys' schools and state schools. I have cast my net widely in the first two pools. It is not enough to say that the public schools are the members of the Headmasters' Conference (membership two hundred), as the conference itself has always known well. It is a conference of men, not of schools, and they represent all types of schools, including, for many years, state schools. Neither is the Association of Governing Bodies of Public Schools (membership 250) an entirely satisfactory guide, although it is a more complete and better one than the Headmasters' Conference.

As good a definition as any is that found in *A Guide to English Schools* (Pelican, 1969): 'Independent, Direct Grant, or other secondary school, controlled by a governing body created by some statute, scheme, or trust deed.' This would presumably include voluntary aided schools. All independent or semi-independent grammar schools are public schools. They are, practically speaking, the same thing. The main difference, dating from the end of the last century, was a reputation, based on snobbery. The only difference between Portsmouth Grammar School and, say, Brentwood, is that the former has the words 'Grammar School'. Bedford and Rugby dropped the words years ago: Manchester and Leeds retain them. As Robin Davis well puts it in *The Grammar School*: 'The plain fact is that they are grammar schools, some good, some less good, some boarding, some day schools, and the relevant distinction between these and other grammar schools is that they have adequate funds and endowments to remain independent of the state while the others, less well endowed, have accepted state aid in one form or

I

another ... the term "public school" is historically accidental and
romantically misleading. .... For me these schools are independent
grammar schools.' What then is a grammar school? 'Foundation
and subsidy by private—later too by corporate but non-state—
initiative, an academic curriculum and, till 1944, recognition of
parental involvement and responsibility by charging fees.' All pre-
Victorian boys' secondary schools have a common history: monastery schools, choir schools, chantry schools, reformation schools,
privately endowed schools, City livery schools, religious schools.
The term 'public school' evolved, quite legitimately, to distinguish
these foundations from private schools that had sprung up by the
late eighteenth century to offer a broader curriculum than the older
foundations, tied by their statutes. The new, Victorian, schools
sought the cachet of being a 'public school' while enjoying a greater
freedom. By the end of the century some of the old foundations
could not keep up with this social race, or did not want to, or were
prohibited from raising their fees: they became the artificially
separated Grammar Schools. It is worth noting that many of these
endowments were of great nobility of intent, and many of them were
betrayed during the nineteenth century under the aegis of the
Charity Commissioners (although undoubtedly the schools needed
reviving). By the end of the nineteenth century there was another
completely spurious notion: that to be a public school a school had
for some reason to be a boarding school. Even A. F. Leach, the
acknowledged expert on the subject, wrote: 'It is an endowed
Grammar School, which is wholly or almost wholly a boarding
school for the wealthier classes.' This idea faded away during the
present century. Now public schools are generally seen as something
rather different: independent secondary schools of special reputation. There are about 33,000 schools in England and Wales, of
which some three thousand are independent and 320 Direct Grant.
There are about half a million pupils at independent schools, some
90,000 of them boy boarders. The state now has many boarding
schools of its own (e.g. Ottershaw, Wymondham, Brighton, Hove
and Sussex G.S., Swanage G.S., Brockenhurst G.S., the Duke's
G.S., Alnwick, Brewood G.S., Queen Elizabeth's, Kirby Lonsdale,
Dawlish, Okehampton G.S.). It subsidises others, not only directly
or through the Local Education Authority, but by sending some
twenty thousand boys to public schools. The state-owned Cooks
Scholastic Service provides help with boarding-school problems.

Some old endowed boarding schools have thrived as never before since accepting voluntary aid. Others, like Sir Roger Manwood's, have become boarding schools on public school lines for the first time in their history since accepting L.E.A. control.

Another misconception about the public schools is that they are an old-established element of British society. This is not the case. They have existed, as we know them, for about a century-and-a-half. The only schools that have *always* been public schools in the modern sense are Eton and Winchester.

A further misconception is that they are the cause of self-perpetuating social privilege. In the first place, many parents who desire to send their boys to them were not educated at them themselves. The social intake at them is wider than ever before because wealth is more widely distributed than ever before. In 1963 (the latest figures available) at least 27 per cent of fathers with sons at boarding H.M.C. schools did not go to H.M.C. schools themselves, and for independent day H.M.C. schools the figure was 40 per cent. Secondly, many of our most eminent socialists—Laski, Harold Wilson—have sent their sons to them. The Labour M.P. for Eton and Slough has said: 'Never be deceived that one buys a better education; one buys advantage and a privileged position in society; that is what the public school system is all about.' It would be difficult to be more muddleheaded. The idea that people are paying large sums of money—it will soon be £5,000—and making great sacrifices in order to gain for their children privileged places in society is based on a cynical view of human nature. It may have applied a hundred years ago: but then there was no state secondary education. What parents are doing is seeking a good—a really good—education for their children. The public schools are better placed educationally. About twenty per cent more pupils gain A-levels in three subjects than at state schools. In 1969, there were 930 open awards at Oxford and Cambridge: five went to pupils at comprehensive schools.* The only satisfactory way of abolishing the public schools is to make the state system as good, if not better, in which case no parents in their right mind would want to pay such vast sums to obtain independent education over and above what they would already be paying for education in tax. It is a prime duty of any and every parent to get the best education he can for his children—not only for the children's sake but also for society's. It is evident

* In 1972 there were 772,612 pupils at comprehensive schools.

that this point has not been lost on the many Labour M.P.s who have sent their sons to public schools. Nevertheless, the Labour Government of 1970 was about to abolish the Direct Grant system and to force about half the independent schools into the state system when it fell from power. 'The independent schools would be given fair warning that unless they could prove that there was a need for them, which couldn't be met within the State system, then they wouldn't get a licence and they couldn't function. It would be forbidden.'*

Privilege? Most of our greatest men have done without it: arguably our greatest novelist (Dickens), man of medicine (Lister), imperialist (Rhodes), artist (Constable), portrait painter (Gainsborough), engineer (Brunel), economist (Adam Smith), lyric poet (Wordsworth), journalist (Northcliffe), sculptor (Moore), actor (Irving), industrialist (Nuffield), modern philisopher (Russell), modern architect (Lutyens), hero (Scott of the Antarctic), bacteriologist (Fleming), nineteenth-century premier (Beaconsfield), consul (Milner), composer (Elgar), Victorian military heroes (Roberts and Kitchener), prophet (H. G. Wells) and cricketer (Grace) all managed to get on all right without public school education. Privilege from schools can be confused with inherited privilege, a very different thing. The absurdly over-bearing and ill-mannered style affected by some who were at these schools, and which has been such a curse to their reputation, is more likely to have been developed under middle-class family tutelage than at hardy schools. There is certainly no encouragement of privilege in the schools themselves. Charles Dickens, who sent his eldest son to Eton, said in 1864: 'As far as I know, nowhere in the country is there so complete an absence of servility to mere rank [i.e. social], to mere position, to mere riches, as in a public school. A boy there is always what his abilities or his personal qualities make him.' However— whether privilege or not—there is no doubt that in this century the public schools have dominated the scene, so far as their products are concerned (q.v. Appendix 8†).

Whether the world of Smith minor, the tuck-shop, fags, and old-

* Edward Short, Secretary of State for Education, 1968–70, *Where*, April 1971.

† For the years 1900–71, the first time, so far as I know, that such a survey has been done from a wide selection of activities. A previous survey for the years 1837–97 was made by the researcher A. H. H. Maclean (pages 206–7).

school ties has much longer to last is very dubious. Whatever authority decides to do, the schools will change themselves, and are changing, to answer a demand in a very different age. That the demand is as great as ever is shown by the unexpected rise in preparatory school numbers, which virtually exist for the public schools. The independent and partly-independent boys' schools and the remaining county secondary schools, in their new joint stance vis-à-vis the comprehensives, are closer than ever before. But some schools may well rue their stubborn refusal to come to terms with the framework of state education, with its emphasis on ages other than thirteen, in particular the retention of the Common Entrance examination. Some schools, like Oundle, St. Lawrence and Sevenoaks, have made special provision for entry from the state system; others, like Leighton Park, have done everything to encourage such entry. The actual Conference of the headmasters itself has for many years now contributed little of note.

The growth of public schools in Scotland and Ireland ran parallel to that in England in the nineteenth century, and in a few cases much earlier. It is a phenomenon which has also spread abroad, most notably to Australia (which has its Cranbrook, Haileybury and St. Paul's), New Zealand, South Africa and the Argentine. But such schools are all too often unfortunate caricatures of the originals. The myth that Scotland has hardly known the phenomenon—and then only as a weak mission from the south—does not square with the facts.* For centuries the Royal High School held much the same position as Winchester, for instance. The public schools are well-entrenched north of the border.

This book—the first history of the public schools of Great Britain and Ireland—has been written primarily from many individual school histories, the assistance of which I gratefully acknowledge, from general educational histories, from standard reference works, from personal research, and from prospectuses. If the quoted memories seem weighted on the critical side, it is not planned that way. It is a remarkable thing how many people who write books have unpleasant memories of their school-days. Although each school is treated separately, it is done so in the framework of history, and it is hoped that the thread of the development of the public schools can be followed in this way. As well as the works listed in the

* About one in every twenty-third school-child in Scotland is at an independent school.

bibliography, I am grateful to the headmasters or staff of the following: Chatham House Grammar School, Coleraine Academical Institution, Confederation of British Industry, Collyer's School, Godolphin and Latymer, Grocers' Company, Huish's Grammar School, King Edward's, Witley, Owen's School, Reading Blue Coat School, the Royal High School, Old Rutlishians Association, Simon Langton Grammar School, St. Brendan's College, Sexey's School, United Westminster Schools, and Wymondham College. I am grateful to the following for the permission to quote: William Heinemann Ltd. for W. Somerset Maugham's *Of Human Bondage*; Secker and Warburg Ltd. for Compton Mackenzie's *Sinister Street*; Butterworth and Co. for Winston Churchill's *My Early Life*; and Constable and Co. for Bruce Marshall's *George Brown's Schooldays*; and to Sir Robert Birley for his many helpful comments.

1

ANCIENT SCHOOLS

THE origin of that remarkable institution, the British public school, is as old as Christian society in these islands: older, indeed, than Parliament itself, which from time to time threatens to abolish it. Although many schools were founded in the following centuries, the oldest public schools today are those which have developed from the ecclesiastical schools of the Middle Ages. The cathedral, monastery and church schools were either 'grammar', i.e. Latin-teaching, or song schools, which provided only a primary education; it is some of the former which have survived to the present day as 'public schools'. The cathedrals were the centres of academic life, and the secular clergy, rather than the monks, undertook the teaching of boys in Latin, which was the key to learning and to religion. What direct connection such 'grammar' schools have with the cathedral and abbey schools which we know today is not always clear. In some cases entire centuries pass with no word or record of the school, when there may indeed have been no school at all; but a few contemporary schools claim a continuous history from the seventh century. It may be that some historians would not accept all of these claims without strong reservations. A few such schools, on the other hand, with restraint, state the year of their foundation from later times, where there can be no doubt as to continuity: such schools as Durham, King's, Peterborough, Sherborne and Westminster.

The question as to which is the oldest public school is one that has caused some contention among the rivals. On paper, St. Peter's, York, would appear to have the best claim. But following the logic of the 'cathedral school' approach, The King's School, Canterbury, must be the victor, Augustine having founded the cathedral there in 598. King's, Rochester, also has a good claim, but here again, if it is assumed that the cathedrals had schools from their foundation, or soon after it, then it cannot be older than King's, Canterbury.

The King's School, Canterbury, is said to have been founded in

about the year 600. There is a possibility of a school existing in
Canterbury back to Roman times. Not a great deal is known of the
early history of the school, but, as at other Christian centres, two
sorts of school probably developed: a grammar school and a choir
school. In many cathedral cities, these two have long since combined, the grammar school attending to the education of the choir
boys, but at Canterbury, where the two foundations were combined
for several centuries, the distinction again exists. The history of the
school evidently remained unbroken at the Reformation, because
when Henry VIII refounded it in 1541 the same headmaster, Twyne,
was retained. The school then became known as the King's School.
It was to consist of 'fifty boys, poor and destitute of the help of their
friends, to be maintained out of the possessions of the church, of
native genius as far as may be and apt to learn'. Boys were expected
to have some basic knowledge of reading and writing at entry; it
was expressly stated in the statutes that if they could not keep up
with the work, they were to be expelled. This regime seems to have
had good effect, for King's, Canterbury, has produced many distinguished men since then, including Thomas Linacre, founder of
the Royal College of Physicians, Christopher Marlowe, William
Harvey, the discoverer of blood circulation, Lord Tenterden, Lord
Chief Justice, John Tradescant, donor of the Ashmolean Museum,
Walter Pater, essayist, Sir Carol Reed, and writers Patrick Leigh
Fermor, Edward Lucie-Smith, Alaric Jacob and Basil Collier. The
King's School has turned out two famous English novelists—W.
Somerset Maugham and Sir Hugh Walpole, whose mutual admira-
tion, it seems, was less than warm. Somerset Maugham did not
spend the happiest days of his life at the school, but, in a contra-
diction that is familiar to public-school men, he lived to become
fond of it; he became, indeed, a munificent benefactor.

Maugham wrote at length of his old school in *Of Human Bondage*,
calling it 'The King's School at Tercanbury'. He wrote: 'The masters
had no patience with modern ideas of education, which they read of
sometimes in *The Times* or *The Guardian*, and hoped fervently that
King's School would remain true to its old traditions. The dead
languages were taught with such thoroughness that an old boy
seldom thought of Homer or Virgil in after life without a qualm of
boredom; and though in the common room at dinner one or two
bolder spirits suggested that mathematics were of increasing importance, the general feeling was that they were a less noble study

than the classics. Neither German nor chemistry was taught, and French only by the form-masters; they could keep order better than a foreigner, and, since they knew the grammar better than any Frenchman, it seemed unimportant that none of them could have got a cup of coffee in the restaurant at Boulogne unless the waiter had known a little English. Geography was taught chiefly by making boys draw maps, and this was a favourite occupation, especially when the country dealt with was mountainous.' During Maugham's time the school, which had previously concentrated on Kent, and had turned out numerous country vicars, began to attract boarders from London' 'We've rather gone out of our way to avoid the contamination of boys from London,' one of the masters in the novel says. Maugham's headmaster has a clear vision of his task. 'Of course, schools are made for the average,' he says. 'The holes are all round, and whatever shape the pegs are they must wedge in somehow'—perhaps the most succinct lines ever written about the late Victorian public schools. When he leaves King's School, Maugham's hero does so with mixed feelings. 'Philip thought occasionally of the King's School at Tercanbury, and laughed to himself as he remembered what at some particular moment of the day they were doing. Now and then he dreamed that he was there still, and it gave him an extraordinary satisfaction, on awaking, to realise that he was [not].'

Hugh Walpole, who was also a benefactor to the school, was ten years Maugham's junior. He wrote two notable public school novels, *Mr. Perrin and Mr. Traill*, and *Jeremy at Crale*. Bearing in mind the importance cathedral cities play in his work, it is interesting to note that he also spent a short time at Durham School. In *Jeremy*, Walpole gave a poignant portrait of departure for boarding school for the first time. Chapter XII of that book has something in it for everyone who has ever left home for public school:

'His father called him into the study. He gave him ten shillings and a new prayer-book. Jeremy knew that he was trying to come close to him and be a friend of a new kind to him.

'He heard in a distance such words as ". . . a new world, full of trial and temptation. God sees us. . . . Work at your Latin . . . cricket and football . . . prayers every night. . . ." But he could feel no emotion, nothing but terror lest some sudden stupid emotional scene should occur. Nothing occurred. He kissed his father and went.

'Then, quite suddenly, just as he came down in his hat and coat and heard that the cab was there, his restraint melted; he was free and impulsive and natural. He kissed Mary, telling her: "You have my toy village. I'd like you to—Yes, rather. I mean it." '

Under Canon Shirley, headmaster 1935–62, the desire for expansion noted by Maugham in the previous century was greatly increased. Shirley, one of the notable headmasters of the first half of the twentieth century, turned a minor public school into a great one. He had previously been headmaster at Worksop College. Owing to the inevitable constriction and lack of space, his was a difficult task, and a considerable achievement. King's, Canterbury, is still closely associated with the greatest of English cathedrals. The Dean is the chairman of the board of governors, and the school is part of the cathedral foundation. School services are held in the cathedral. The houses and classrooms are in the precincts, splendidly situated in a series of quadrangles beneath the towering grey walls of the cathedral—Mint Yard, Green Court, Palace Court, and the Oaks.

King's School, Rochester, has also made a claim to be the oldest school in the land. This claim is based on a statement by the Venerable Bede, who referred in 631 to a school founded by Sigbert, who 'presided over the kingdom of the East English'. There is reason to believe this may have been in Rochester. However, the present school has a good claim to be descended directly from the cathedral grammar school of the seventh century (the cathedral was founded by St. Augustine in 604). The school was reconstituted in 1542 by Henry VIII, after whom, as other cathedral schools, it is named. It was the scene of a *cause célèbre* in the nineteenth century when Robert Whiston, headmaster, was dismissed when he petitioned the Dean and Chapter of the cathedral for increased finances for the school. He took the matter to court, was vindicated, and was reinstated in 1852. Today the school is still governed by the Dean and Chapter, and aims 'to provide a public school education at a moderate cost'. The cathedral is used each day for worship. The buildings are beside the cathedral precinct, and close to the castle and other historic edifices of this old English town. The school still provides the cathedral choir, and well over a quarter of the boys are boarders, in houses overlooking the Paddock (the playing fields), the Vines or the precincts.

Unlike its two ancient rivals in Kent, St. Peter's, York, was obliged to leave the vicinity of its religious foundation in the mid-nineteenth century, in order to find much-needed space. It is situated on the outskirts of York.

St. Peter's claims, as does King's, Canterbury, to have existed in Romano-British times. It may well have begun with the beginnings of the great Minster, the Cathedral of St. Peter, in the early seventh century, or even before. If, as has recently been suggested after an examination of the Minster records, it was in existence in the sixth century, then it has an excellent claim to be the oldest school in Britain. Headmasters of the school can be traced back to the early six-hundreds. The school was attended by the sons of noblemen from all over northern England, and its fame spread to Europe; one headmaster, Alcuin, was sent for by Charlemagne to establish a similar school at Aix. Alcuin had been a boy at the school himself. He wrote of the headmaster in his day, one Albert: 'To some he diligently gave the art of the use of grammar, pouring into others the streams of rhetoric. These he polished on the grindstone of law, those he taught to sing in Aeonian chant . . . others the aforesaid master caused to know the harmony of the sky and the sun, the labours of the moon, the five belts of the heavens, the seven wandering stars, their rising and their setting, the tides and earthquakes, the natures of men, cattle, birds and wild beasts, the divers kinds of numbers and various figures . . . and especially doth he unveil the mysteries of Holy Scripture. . . . Whatever youths he saw of remarkable intelligence, he got hold of them, taught them, fed them, cherished them.' A broad education for one man to administer—but much the same could have been said, and was said, by former pupils of Dr. Arnold of Rugby, more than a thousand years later. Alcuin told his former masters: 'You brought me to man's estate with whippings of fatherly discipline and made me strong with the learning of sacred rules.' Such a description would have been considered apt for a Victorian public school, as well as an Anglo-Saxon one. The school seems to have had strong Roman tendencies in the sixteenth and early seventeenth centuries; no fewer than four of the Gunpowder Plot conspirators had been educated at the school, including Guy Fawkes himself. Sir Thomas Herbert, who accompanied Charles I to his execution, had also been at St. Peter's. Over the years it was known as the York Free School and York Grammar School.

St. Peter's was bedevilled by problems of space for several

centuries. From very early days it accepted boarders, but there was often the problem of where to house them. The precincts were limited and the Minster itself made increasing demands for space over the ages. In 1730, the school moved to a disused church near by. It revived under the headmastership of Stephen Creyk, who had known Arnold at Oxford. In 1844, the school moved to Clifton on the outskirts of York, taking over the prepossessing buildings of a rival school, which the Dean and Chapter bought out. In the twentieth century St. Peter's came to occupy in the north much the same standing and position as King's, Canterbury in the south. It has long been associated with Yorkshire sport, and two recent captains of the county, A. B. Sellers and N. W. D. Yardley, attended St. Peter's. Other old boys are C. Northcote Parkinson, of 'Parkinson's Law', Christopher Hill, historian, and Professor E. W. Gilbert, geographer. The Dean of York is still, *ex officio*, the chairman of the governors. An unusual aspect of St. Peter's is that day boys are encouraged to spend all day until night-time, including Sundays, with the boarders.

According to the latest findings Warwick School probably began in the year 914. It is another survivor of about three hundred 'grammar schools' which existed before the Reformation. It was, of course, a church school, under the wing of St. Mary of Warwick, with irrefutable documentary evidence back to the reign of Edward the Confessor. Henry VIII refounded the school as a Protestant institution in 1545. Soon afterwards it was moved to the Earl of Leicester's Hospital (early schools were often associated with hospitals). It moved again in 1571. The school declined until, during the nineteenth century, the only playground was the churchyard. Numbers were low. But it was reconstituted in 1875, under the Endowed Schools Acts, and completely new buildings were put up towards the end of the century. Boarders are accommodated in the School House. The Lord Lieutenant of Warwickshire and the Mayor of Warwick are *ex officio* governors of the school.

St. Alban's School probably dates from about 948, although there may have been an earlier school in Roman times. The present school is another survivor of the old church grammar school, having close connections with the old abbey and monastery. During the unruly middle ages an underground passage was built connecting school and monastery. Towards the end of the thirteenth century it was ordained that the poorest sixteen scholars should pay no fees, but the remainder were to be fee-payers 'according to ancient custom'. Students were forbidden 'to carry arms in school or out'. The school appears to have been one of the leading places of education in England, and it had an early library. There seems to have been a short gap after the closing of the monastery in 1539, but the school was soon in operation again, the control being in the hands of the laity, although for the next two hundred years and more classes still were held in the Lady Chapel. One of its patrons, Sir Nicholas Bacon (father of Francis, who may have briefly attended the school), obtained a 'wine charter' by which the school benefited from the sale of wine licences. By 1578 there is a reference to sport— archery—in the statutes. The school declined, like so many others in the eighteenth century. It is now centred on the monastery gate-house, to which it moved in 1871, with grounds stretching down to the River Ver. The town is represented by the Mayor of St. Albans on the board of governors. It is claimed that the only English Pope, Nicholas Breakspear (Pope Adrian IV), who was born near St. Albans, attended the school about 1110. The early English chronicler, Thomas Walsingham, was also educated there.

The ecclesiastical grammar school at Ely, now King's School, Ely, probably has existed since 970. Over a hundred years before that there may well have been a school at the monastery, but this was ended when the Danes destroyed the place in 870. The Benedictine school at Ely was as famous as the school at York, and attracted the children of the aristocracy. Edward the Confessor received some primary education there. The abbots of Ely were men of considerable importance in the land, and their school was well attended by boarders from all parts. Afterwards the school declined, but it was refounded by Henry VIII in 1541 as both choir and 'grammar' school, a position it holds to the present day. The school flourished after the Reformation; one account says there were over three hundred scholars there in the sixteenth century. The importance of the abbots faded; they were replaced by the town bailiffs, who virtually governed town and school until 1850. The constitution of the school was last revised by the Ministry of Education in 1963. About two-thirds of the boys are boarders. The Dean is the chairman of the governors.

King's, Ely, is justly proud of its buildings, which are some of the oldest school premises in Britain, many of them of architectural importance. Part of the School House dates from the reign of Edward

III. The school library is housed in a Norman structure. The school chapel, restored in the nineteenth century, is one of the finest examples of the decorated style in England. The Assembly Room, over the gateway of the old monastery, dates from the reign of Richard III. The dining-hall has been in use since the fourteenth century. King's, Ely, has found expansion difficult, like other cathedral schools, but although it is some thousand years old, it is in the van of public school education; in 1970 it admitted twenty-four girls.

Reading School was probably already founded by 1125, when Henry I instituted the abbey there. It was endowed in 1485 and survived the dissolution of the abbey in 1539; it was re-endowed by Queen Elizabeth and Archbishop Laud, an old boy, who left £20 a year to the headmaster. Another pupil was Sir Thomas White, who founded St. John's College, Oxford, and kept two closed scholarships there for boys leaving the school. The school moved from the centre of the town to its site on the southern side in 1871. Reading has accommodated boarders since the eighteenth century and there are now three houses for them. The Rt. Rev. B. C. Butler, former Abbot of Downside, John Minton, the artist, and John and Roy Boulting, the film directors, are old boys.

Wells Cathedral School, founded in 1140 or before, is a school which languished for centuries in its own small community, playing a useful part there until very recent times. The song and grammar schools at Wells cathedral combined after the Reformation. It remained a small, local school until the late nineteen-twenties. Expansion in recent years, under the Quilter family, has brought it to the position of being the largest completely independent cathedral school in the country, about half the students being boarders. The school holds 'a belief that to grow up in the atmosphere and beauty of this cathedral city of Wells in the lovely buildings which the school possesses must leave a good and lasting impression on a boy's whole being'. Houses and buildings are close to the magnificent cathedral, many of them medieval. A major redevelopment of the school, including the introduction of girl pupils, took place in the late nineteen-sixties and early seventies. The present headmaster believes it 'right for the future that while there should be every opportunity for boys and girls to develop separately and according to their own individual interests, they should, from an early age, be members of the same community and learn to work together. I accept that young people mature earlier than used to be the case.' The Dean and Chapter are on the board of governors. Also founded in 1140 was Bristol Cathedral School, originally the grammar school of the abbey. A day school, it was refounded under Henry VIII in 1542.

Derby School was founded in 1160 by the Bishop of Lichfield, and was refounded in 1554, but a school was probably in existence even before 1159. Huntingdon Grammar School, attended by Oliver Cromwell and once part of the Hospital of St. John, dates from about the same time. Carlisle Grammar School, associated with the cathedral, began not later than 1170, and was refounded in 1541. Lincoln School, founded about 1190 or before, no longer caters for the choir boys, unlike Wells Cathedral School. Originally there were two schools, one associated with the cathedral, the other with the town authorities. These were combined in 1583, but the school again divided along similar lines in the nineteenth century. Norwich School may date from the same time, the earliest mentions being in the mid-thirteenth century. It was refounded by Edward VI in 1547 and has been on its present site in the Cathedral Close since about 1553. The school chapel dates from 1316. There are now three boarding houses, School House, Old Palace and Daynes. The school has the unusual history of being an old cathedral grammar school which receives support from a merchant company. Company connections with public schools normally date from the sixteenth century, but the Worshipful Company of Dyers' interest in Norwich School dates from 1949. The company has three representatives on the board of governors and has provided several grants for buildings. The cathedral choristers are still educated at the school.*

The Royal Grammar School, Worcester, founded ante 1290, has had civic rather than cathedral connections from the earliest times. The school moved from its ancient site in 1968 to more spacious accommodation. It retains its connection with the corporation, and has one boarding house. Beverley Grammar School, Yorkshire, and St. Bartholemew's, Newbury, are other extremely old schools; the latter is said to have been founded originally in the reign of King John, and the former is even older. One of the oldest schools in the country not in a cathedral city is Abingdon School. It may even be of pre-Norman origin. An early mention is in 1372, when there was

* Sir Edward Coke, Lord Nelson, Raja Brooke, George Borrow, and Lord Blake are old boys.

a dispute between the clergy of two parishes as to which should minister to the school, and thus be entitled to the emoluments. In 1563 the school was re-endowed by John Roysse, a mercer of London, and the present school really dates from that foundation. The first scholar at the new school, one Thomas Tesdale, lived to become another great benefactor, providing for six scholarships at Oxford; four of these scholarships are still tenable at Pembroke College. The school has been on its present site, on the outskirts of Abingdon, since 1870. Roysse's schoolroom in the town centre is now part of the corporation buildings. The mayor, the Recorder and the local M.P. are all on the governing board, retaining the strong local connections, although since 1953 there have been four boarding houses.

2

EARLY SCHOOLS

THE fourteenth century was not an active time for the foundation of schools, and few have survived to modern times. It is chiefly important as the time when grammar stopped being taught through Norman French and schools began to be conducted in English. One of the schools which has survived is Bablake School, Coventry, originally part of a monastic college, founded in 1344. It was revived after the dissolution of the monasteries, under control of the city, and was directly connected with the cathedral. Three years later, in 1563, it was given financial aid by Thomas Wheatley (the school still uses his arms), and it has played an important role in Coventry ever since. Towards the end of the last century it absorbed the other local schools, the 'Gift Schools'. Of the seventeen governors today, fourteen are representative, mostly from the city. The school has developed into a large day school, receiving over eight hundred boys.

Hereford Cathedral School gives its foundation as 'ante 1384', the date of the first real evidence of the existence of the school, a letter from the Bishop to one Richard Cornwalls: 'Seeing that by old custom the appointment and control of the Master of the Grammar School in the City of Hereford belongs to the office of the Chancellor of the Cathedral, and that we have repeatedly required and urged the chancellor and his Proctor to provide an adequate master for our school, and that they have expressly refused to comply with our request, to the prejudice of Holy Church and grave injury of the scholars who require instruction, we therefore, having regard to your fitness for such an office, and having by careful enquiry tested your character and learning, do hereby by virtue of our episcopal authority appoint you to have the rule and discipline of the Grammar School with birch and rod as is customary for one year only from the issue of the present commission.' It is certain, therefore, that a school had been in existence long before this at Hereford, and it could claim to have been founded in the seventh century, with the cathedral. There was an Olde Schole Street in Hereford in the thirteenth century. For two hundred years after this letter, practically nothing is known of the school. In 1583 it received emoluments from Elizabeth, and more from Charles I in 1637. During the Civil War the town was defended by an old scholar, Colonel Fitzwilliam Coningsby, and it seems likely that he used the pupils of the school to steal out of the town to set fire to the be-siegers' works. In 1665 the fees were 'five shillings entrance, and twenty shillings per annum for the sons of all free cyttyzens of the said citty, saveing only such as are poore and are unable soe to doe, who are to pay five shillings for entrance and to be left to their owne will for the rest. And as for foreigners, the schoolmaster is left to his own discretion for compounding with them for his salary.' The school has had various accommodation, once being taken over almost entirely as a home for beggars; its present site, near cathedral and river, dates from 1876. The school has been somewhat limited by restrictions of space; there are now some three hundred and sixty boys, of whom more than one in three are boarders. The choristers are boarded and educated at the school, and there is a short school service in the cathedral each morning. An interesting fact of this ancient school in the former capital of Mercia is that its first re-corded old boys' reunion was at the Green Dragon Hotel, in Here-ford, as far back as 1801, well before such gatherings were normal elsewhere.

Two extremely old grammar schools on the east coast, Grimsby Grammar School and Hull Grammar School, also date from this century; the former was founded sometime before 1329 and the latter in approximately 1331. The poet Andrew Marvell went to Hull Grammar School, where his father was headmaster. In the early days the boys were taught by the chantry priest of Holy Trinity. There is a mention of Doncaster Grammar School in 1351 and of Ripon School in 1354. The Royal Grammar School, Lancaster, one of the greatest schools of the north, was refounded in 1469, but a grammar school had existed in Lancaster at least two hundred years earlier. Its refounding in the fifteenth century was largely through an endowment from one John Gardner. This very old school still takes boarders.

*

Winchester College was founded in 1382, although it did not open until some years later. The founder was William of Wykeham, a

building entrepreneur. He was responsible for much of the construction of Windsor Castle, at the personal invitation of Edward
III, having already made a reputation at Winchester. His successful
building operations and personal charm made him a favourite at
court, and he became the Bishop of Winchester and Lord Chancellor. He died at the age of eighty.

Wykeham's educational plans were extremely elaborate for their
day. His scholars were first to be educated at his new school at
Winchester, from whence they would transfer to a New College at
Oxford, also founded by himself. The main object was to supply
qualified persons for the church. New College was completed first
and the work was then completed on 'Sainte Marie College of
Wynchester'. Wykeham's buildings for the school, carefully planned
for educational purposes, were easily the finest for any school in the
country up till that time, and assured for it an important place in
educational affairs for centuries to come. There had been nothing
like it before. It was seven years from the laying of the foundation
stone before the school was ready to open, which it did on 28 March
1394. Independent as it was of a cathedral or church, indeed with
its own chapel more grand than most churches, the school was a
great novelty in its day, and William of Wykeham is a most important figure in the history of our education.

The foundation consisted of a Warden, ten Fellows, a Headmaster, an usher (or second master), three chaplains, three lay
clerks, seventy scholars and sixteen choristers for the college chapel,
'queristers' as they were called at Winchester (now 'quiristers'). Ten
'commoners' (i.e. fee-payers) were also allowed to live in the college,
nothing being said as to the numbers of student commoners living
outside the college. The government of the foundation is still much
the same after some six hundred years. The Warden is comparable to
the chairman of the board of governors at other schools, and there
are now a sub-warden and eleven fellows, acting more or less as
governors. The importance of the Warden has declined in the day-
to-day affairs of the school, as compared to that of the headmaster.
There is still some distinction between scholars and commoners
although the latter now, of course, make up most of the school.

At first teaching was restricted to 'grammar', i.e. Latin, as at other
schools, with religious instruction. As for school clothing, an outfit
for two brothers in 1395 refers to '5¾ yards of russet cloth for summer
wear 8s. 7d., 2 sets of fur for winter wear 4s.', and twenty-four pairs

of shoes. Before the end of the first year all scholars had to have their heads shaved, a duty performed by the porter. The inventory of the Porter's Lodge in 1413 included three basins, six shaving cloths and four razors. After three hundred years, this practice was still operating. A boy wrote home in April 1682: 'When I was with you at London you was Speaken Concerning my heare being shaved of and my wearing a periwig which then I was very much Against it but Everybody here admires [wonders] that I will not have it Cut and say that it is the worst head of heare that Ever they saw therefore if you please I will have it Cut off here: here is a man which sells Good periwigs if you will be please to let me know what price you are willing to bestoo on own. My chamber fellow will Cut of his heare this Spring; a many of my Sholefellows doe weare periwigs And I am willing to weare one if you are willing, not Else. Nothing shall be done without your Consent.'

From an early time the school at Winchester was well known, and occupied much the same position as a major public school does today. It was often visited by royalty, most monarchs going to see the place during their reigns. Henry VI made several visits, and he studied its working previous to the foundation of Eton. After Agincourt, the college received one of the French prisoners to be installed as cook. Towards the end of the fifteenth century the curriculum was changed by the inclusion of Greek. The college, like Eton, survived the Reformation without interruption, being treated much the same as Oxford and Cambridge colleges. During the Civil War, Winchester steered a careful course with friends on both sides; two prominent Cromwellians, Nathaniel Fiennes and Nicholas Love, were Wykehamists, as former pupils were already called.

By 1650 the routine was as follows: '5.0 a.m., get up, sing a Latin psalm in chambers; 5.30–6.0, Chapel; 6.0–9.0, school; 9.0, breakfast; 9.30–11.0, private study; 11.0–12.0, school; 12.0, dinner; 1.0–3.30, school; 3.30, beer; 4.0–5.0, school; 5.0, prayers; 6.0, supper; 6.30–7.45, toy-time; 8.0, chapel; 8.15, chambers, bed.' Despite this rigorous regime, the college never had much trouble in attracting commoners, except during the Jacobite times, when Winchester was suspected of having Jacobite leanings. In 1734 there were 123 commoners, but in 1751 there were only eight; by 1780 they were again over a hundred. The harsh regime, no doubt had much to do with the two revolutions in 1793 and 1818. The first, at a time of general unrest among the young, was ostensibly because of

the punishment of the whole college when it went off to listen to a
militia band in the Cathedral Close. The revolt lasted several days;
the students shut themselves in and used cobblestones as missiles
when the staff attempted to regain possession. The affair ended with
the expulsion of thirty-seven, including two future generals and a
bishop. The second revolt was more easily dealt with. The authorities promised the boys no less than two weeks' holiday if they would
abandon their stronghold; on doing so, the surprised boys found
themselves surrounded by a posse of soldiers with fixed bayonets.
This betrayal ended in the expulsion of twenty sadly disillusioned
boys, including a future Lord Chancellor and Sir Alexander Malet,
the diplomat, who not surprisingly sent his son to Eton.

In the nineteenth century the school progressed under three
great headmasters: Dr. Goddard, 1793–1809; Dr. Moberly, 1836–
66; and Dr. George Ridding, 1866–84. The latter found 173 commoners and left 337, having expanded the college by the purchase of
a number of boarding houses near by. The Victorian idea of the
public school was largely formulated by these men; they produced
several headmasters, both from the pupils and staff, who took the
Winchester system to other schools, although changing it to their
fashion, most notably Thomas Arnold. (The lack of any movement
worth mentioning of masters from Eton to Winchester over a long
period of years is difficult to avoid noticing.) They were followed by
M. J. Rendall, a master from 1887 to 1924, and headmaster from
1911. Among the facets thought essential to nineteenth-century
public school education, which largely emanated from Winchester,
was the obsession with Greek (although Winchester was, perversely
enough, one of the first to relax in this direction), harsh discipline
and the respect for old customs, traditions and use of a private
language. On the other hand, Winchester retained characteristics of
its own: it became difficult to gain admission, and it retains to this
day its own entrance examination in preference to the Common
Entrance, and consequently there has long been a lower percentage
of the sons of old boys at the school than at, say, Eton; it had
buildings which few if any could rival; it believed in communal life
rather than in the comparative privacy which developed at Eton and
under Thring at Uppingham; it had, again unlike other schools, an
aversion to ceremony and display; and it could be that it never quite
attached the same importance to games as elsewhere. In October
1908, *The Wykehamist* recorded: 'Winchester College is probably

the most conservative institution in the world. Any change of any importance is made with immense difficulty, usually after a prodigious lapse of time, and in the teeth of furious opposition.'

For some centuries there was the custom of walking the 'Hills', where there was a playground; this lasted from at least 1460 to 1868. But during the nineteenth century organised games, including the college's own form of football, developed, and sports fields were acquired; cricket, rowing, football and court games were played. In 1825 Winchester began playing Eton and Harrow at Lord's Cricket Ground, the first school matches to be played there (two years before the Oxford and Cambridge match began there). But Winchester abandoned these matches at Lords in 1854, Dr. Moberly giving way to the protestations of parents, who complained of the temptations to which their sons were exposed in London. This caused an uproar among Wykehamists, and several irate articles were written about the matter. In remembrance of this, the cricket eleven at Winchester was referred to as 'Lord's'. R. Townsend Warner, in his *Winchester*, published in 1900, declared: 'Unquestionably, if Winchester undertakes any other public school match besides that against Eton, it ought if possible to be a revival of the Harrow match rather than one against any other school, but the authorities at present feel that the distraction of one school match is enough.' He went on: 'The only survival now to be seen of the presence of Winchester at Lord's is in the dark-blue-and-white-striped cap of the Harrow eleven, Winchester having been victorious in a match played against Harrow for the right to wear a plain dark-blue cap, which has been the Winchester eleven colour since 1851. In earlier days top hats were worn.' Notable cricketers produced by Winchester are Douglas Jardine, the aloof England skipper, who coolly introduced 'bodyline' bowling to the terror of Australians, and the brothers G. H. G. and A. P. Doggart.

By 1900 the total annual school fees, for board and tuition, were £112, which was by no means little. (Seventy-two years later they had risen to £867.) In the 250 years since 1650, getting-up time had advanced an hour-and-a-quarter to 6.15. A cold bath was taken instead of the washing of hands and face. But 'toy-time', 7.0–8.30 p.m., survived, as did two daily attendances at Chapel. Senior boys did not go to bed until 10.30.

Winchester retains its academic traditions and is proud of the Wykehamist 'type', who is said to be a reticent sort of person with a

respect for scholarship (presumably in contrast to Eton). Dr.
Moberly described the Wykehamist, over a hundred years ago, as a
man 'not of a very showy kind'. Moberly also said (to the parlia-
mentary commission of 1861): 'Every school of this size has a
definite character, and gives a peculiar stamp to its pupils; and I
could, with more or less distinctness, characterize the pupils of the
public schools of England by the particular stamp or mint-work they
bear.' Wykehamists use their reticence, real or feigned, to explain
the curious fact that, despite its eminent position of six centuries,
the school produced hardly anyone of note till the mid-nineteenth
century; they claim that numerous bishops, judges and dons were
sound, but did not become famous because they were not 'showy'.
Certainly Winchester cannot claim the men of distinction, prior to
1800, who have received posterity's attention that other schools can,
such as Christ's Hospital, the Royal High School, King's, Canterbury, King's, Grantham, St. Paul's, Magdalen College School and
Westminster. It is strange that Winchester has produced only one
prime minister. Disraeli was a near-miss—however he chose Eton
for his fictional hero in *Coningsby*, one of the wittiest accounts of life
at Eton by a non-Etonian. One of the choicest and most pertinent
remarks about Wykehamists was made by an Etonian Labour
cabinet minister, Lord Longford: 'When an Etonian Cabinet
Minister comes into office, he expects to find a Wykehamist civil
servant running the Department.'

In 1901 there was a positive sensation at Winchester when the
first headmaster not to have been a Wykehamist since 1454 was
appointed. The school motto is perhaps the most famous of all
public school mottoes: 'Manners makyth Man.' The critics of
Winchester point out that intellectual arrogance does not easily
blend with manners, especially in the old meaning of that word, and
Wykehamists have sometimes proved irritating to their contemporaries. An annual old boys' dinner, probably the first of its kind, was
begun in 1758; it was held for about half a century at the Crown and
Anchor in the Strand. A Winchester Club was established at
Oxford in 1867, the connection with New College having always
survived, and the club lasted till the beginning of this century. Old
boys who should be mentioned, who may or may not have something
of the Wykehamist about them, are: Sydney Smith (who was head
boy), Matthew Arnold (for a short time, before he went to Rugby;
he was said to shudder in after life every time he heard Winchester

mentioned), Sir C. A. Pearson (founder of St. Dunstan's), H. A. L. Fisher, historian, Sir Edward Grey, Arnold Toynbee, Field-Marshal Earl Wavell, George Mallory, the mountaineer, Air Chief Marshal Lord Dowding, Sir Charles Oman, historian, Lord Swinton, Sir William Hayter, Hugh Gaitskell, Lord Eccles, Lord Clark, the art historian, Sir Patrick Reilly, John Sparrow, Warden of All Souls, F. W. Paish, economist, Charles Madge, sociologist, Sir Stafford Cripps, William Empson, poet, Marshal of the R.A.F. Viscount Portal, A. P. Herbert, Field-Marshal Sir Francis Festing, Dermot Morrah, writer on royal affairs, William Whitelaw, Douglas Jay, Sir Geoffrey Howe, Robert Conquest, authority on Soviet history, Judges Danckwerts and Roskill, J. C. Dancy, headmaster of Lancing and Marlborough, Nicholas Wollaston, the author, Professor M. R. D. Foot, Mark Bonham-Carter, P. W. Milligan, chairman of Lloyds, Christopher Dilke and Thomas Hinde, authors, Sir Oswald Mosley and D. N. Pritt. Those who have conformed rather less are Nicholas Monsarrat, perhaps the best novelist of the Second World War, and Cecil King, the newspaperman, both of whom have recorded their detestation of Winchester. Cecil King has written: 'I hated almost every day of my time at Winchester. I am not a conformist and Winchester was a very conformist institution, so my approach to becoming a Wykehamist was not suitably reverential. . . . The day I left Winchester my house-master said good-bye and that it was doubtless a very sad day for me. I said it was the happiest day of my life. He said I would come to think of my time at Winchester very differently. I said I was sure I would not. Though, naturally, I have had unhappy days since then, it is true, as I thought at the time, that nothing afterwards could ever be so bad as Winchester.'

For many years the most popular song at Winchester was a lament entitled 'Domum'. Not only did it contain no praise of the college, it did not even have an allusion to the place. The chorus went as follows:

> Domum, domum, dulce domum,
> Domum, domum, dulce domum,
> Dulce, dulce, dulce domum,
> Dulce domum reconemus!

*

Ipswich School, which was probably founded around the same time as Winchester, has quite different origins. Ipswich was already a prosperous town and port, and the local grammar school came into being through the interest of the townspeople themselves rather than from any one benefactor, as at Winchester, or as an appendage to an ecclesiastical foundation, as had been almost universal until that time. It is probable that the citizens were impressed by Norwich already having its own school. The school's first-known endowment, by Richard Felaw, was not until 1483: 'the said master for tyme beying shall receyve and take alle children born and dwellyng within the said Town of Yppyswich comyng to the seid scole, frely without takyng off any thyng for ther techyng Except childyrein of such persons as have lands and tenements to the yerely value of [twenty shillings] or ellys goods to the valew of [twenty pounds] to be solde'. The school received charters from Henry VIII and Elizabeth, and prospered with the town. During the eighteenth century Ipswich School continued to thrive, one of the few that did so. It already recruited its numbers from all Suffolk, as well as from the town. For eighty years in that century there were only three headmasters.

An advertisement for a headmaster at Ipswich School, in 1843, gave his annual salary as £118 6s. 8d. 'The Headmaster's residence, which is well situated, will be free of rent, rates and tolls, is capable of accommodating from thirty Boarders, and will be kept in repair at the expense of the Corporation.' New buildings were taken over in 1852, replacing the old one which had accommodated pupils for many generations since 1565. From 1858 to 1894 there were two headmasters, Rev. H. A. Holden and Rev. F. H. Browne. Browne had been second master at Reading School, and he brought a new influx to Ipswich in the shape of most of the staff of Reading and no less than forty-three boys from that school (the movement of some pupils with a transferring master was fairly common practice). Browne was a good headmaster and revitalised the school in the Arnoldian concept. In five years he almost quadrupled the number of boys. But his ambition to make Ipswich a leading public school independent of the town naturally brought him into conflict with the governors, as also happened with his successor when the school became more closely associated with the local education authorities. By the time A. K. Watson became headmaster in 1906, the first layman to do so since 1608, the emoluments of the post had increased to £700. During the inter-war period the school achieved

Browne's wish at last and became a recognised public school. One distinctive feature of Ipswich was that boys wore black coats and pin-striped trousers from 1919 until recent times. The school was refused a Direct Grant in 1945, but the crisis which ensued, as so often in the history of the public schools, only brought about a determination to survive which in turn led to greater prosperity. The school became, and still is, completely independent, thanks largely to a hastily formed society, The Friends of Ipswich School, which established an endowment fund. The most famous former pupil is Cardinal Wolsey, who was almost certainly a pupil, but nevertheless attempted to set up a rival establishment to take over the old school (it survived only two years).*

The history of Ipswich School, one of the best school histories, concludes with words that apply more generally when it recalls— 'the steady boom of Chapel bell, the sound of sawing in the carpenter's shop and the muffled shouts from the Swimming Bath—the murmur that spreads through the Big School before the first and last Roll Call of the term—the stifling heat of Speech Days—those few summer afternoons when even the shade under the limes was not enough to defy the heat, and the drone of the motor mower set you nodding in the classrooms—the delayed excitement of the Steeplechase—the ragged line of spectators at a School Match on a wintry day, even the bored or resentful roused time and again to a "Play up, Scho-o-l!" ' A remarkable aspect of public school-days is that there seems always to have been during them a succession of fine summers.

With Oswestry School we return to an early foundation due to a particular benefactor. It was founded by David Holbache, a lawyer, in 1407. The trustees were Lords and Burgesses of the town of Oswestry, and the school is of particular interest in that it was free of all ecclesiastical connections, being a Free Grammar School for sons of Burgesses. Oswestry is one of the earliest surviving secular foundations, although Ipswich is almost certainly older. Although overshadowed by its neighbour, Shrewsbury, the school has continued to serve its community over the centuries; but it was not until the headships of Dr. James Donne, 1796–1833, and his son, the Rev. Stephen Donne, 1833–60, that it achieved wider fame.

* Others: Sir George Adam Wood, who commanded the gunners at Waterloo, Rear-Admiral Sir Philip Vere Broke, Charles Keene, the illustrator, Sir Henry Rider Haggard and Sir Francis Shipway, the authority on anaesthetics.

Oswestry provided several men prominent in the history of the East India Company, including, among others, Sir Richard Jenkins, chairman of the company, and Lieutenant-General Colin Mackenzie. Other famous old boys are Colonel Frederick Burnaby, the Victorian adventurer, and Dr. Thomas Bray, founder of the S.P.C.K.

Durham School was certainly in existence long before the fifteenth century, but it is usually dated from 1414, when it was re-founded. In its early years it appears to have been a typical cathedral grammar school. In 1414 the school was reconstituted by Cardinal Langley; he appointed a master to 'instruct all willing to learn or study under him, the poor indeed freely for the love of God, if they or their parents humbly ask for it, but taking from those who by themselves or their friends were willing to pay the moderate fees accustomed to be paid in other schools of grammar'. At the Reformation the control of the school passed, in 1541, from monastery to cathedral, and the choir school was incorporated; but the same headmaster remained (the choir school is now a separate preparatory school). The school has been governed by the Dean and Chapter continuously since that year. As at many other schools, it was found exceedingly difficult to find men sufficiently educated to teach the boys. Not all the masters at the school seem to have been dedicated, for a clergyman wrote: 'First in the morning at six o'clock, the Grammar School and Song School, with all the servants of the House, resort to Prayers in the Church: which exercise continueth almost half an hour. . . . Because we lack an able schoolmaster, I bestow daily three or four hours in teaching the youth.' For over two hundred years Durham School was in the buildings put up by Langley on Palace Green; it later moved to another building on the same green. It moved to its present magnificent site, above the Wear, with the great cathedral looming across, in 1842. The short-list for the first new headmaster in the new buildings consisted of Edward Thring and Henry Holden, headmaster of Uppingham. Holden got the job and Thring took his place at Uppingham, where he became one of the most influential headmasters in British education. Canon H. K. Luce was headmaster from 1932 to 1958. The school has remained at a modest size. Candidates for admission now are encouraged from the state system as well as from preparatory schools. Christopher Smart, the poet, and R. S. Surtees, author of the incomparable Jorrocks sporting novels, were educated at Durham.

An early lay foundation is Sevenoaks School, founded in 1418.

The founder was Sir William Sevenoke, who is said to have started life as a foundling discovered in the streets of the town; as was the custom, he took the name of the place as his own. He became a grocer in London, prospered and became Alderman of the Tower Ward, Warden of the Grocer's Company, was knighted, and became a friend of Henry V. He was Mayor of the City in 1418–19, the predecessor of Dick Whittington. Sevenoke was a well-known reformer and philanthropist of his day. He made several useful reforms in the City. In his home town he founded almshouses and a school, facing each other, at the top of Sevenoaks Hill. The foundation was a thank-offering for his share in the victory at Agincourt. Sevenoaks School has the unique distinction of being mentioned in Shakespeare (*Henry VI*, Part Two, Act IV, Scene VIII). The school was refounded by Elizabeth in 1560, when the master was instructed to teach 'according to the methods used in the school of St. Paul's in London'. For a long time the school was known as Queen Elizabeth's Free Grammar School. The school was governed by 'The Wardens and four Assistants of the Town and Parish of Sevenoaks'. In a statute of 1574 they required their successors to choose for the master 'one honest and mete man, sufficiently learned and expert in grammar, not being in Holy Orders, to teach grammer in the school'. This was at a time when teaching was starting as a profession distinct from the clergy. The school hours were: summer 6.0 till 11.0 in the morning and 1.0 to 5.0 in the afternoon. In 1718 the school sold its property in London and a fine new building was erected by Lord Burlington (now a boarding house), but it remained a small country-town grammar school until the twentieth century. It is really only since the Second World War that Sevenoaks has achieved its reputation, under the headships of L. C. Taylor, himself an Old Sennockian, 1954–68, and Dr. M. G. Hinton (who resigned in 1971 to become headmaster of a comprehensive). Benefactions, appeals and the interest of the Company of Tobacco Pipemakers and Blenders have all helped the school. In recent years it has become a pioneer in the educational sphere so far as public schools are concerned. There is a Parents' Association and a scheme in which parents and boys combine in various activities; there are exchanges with schools in Paris, including a common Anglo-French form with a French school; an 'international centre' for sixth-formers contains two-thirds of boys from overseas; a voluntary service unit, run jointly with state schools in Sevenoaks, involves the boys in 'the problems of the elderly, of young people in trouble, of the physically and mentally handicapped'; boarders are allowed home every week-end. In all these fields, Sevenoaks has been a leader. No old public school has made greater efforts to change the traditional character of the public school to fit the second half of the twentieth century, while retaining the best of the old ways. Another interesting innovation is the annual appointment of a Lord Attlee Fellowship, in honour of the prime minister. 'The purpose of the Fellowship is to contribute to the vitality of the school by bringing masters and boys into contact with a practising artist or scientist or with those doing, or able notably to contribute to, interesting new developments in teaching.' At present the value of the Fellowship is £1,000. The school adjoins Knole Park, and the Lords of the Manor of Knole, the Sackville family, are hereditary governors.

*

The next school to be founded was the greatest in British, and indeed in European, history—Eton College. School historians have claimed that other places were pre-eminent at periods of history since the fifteenth century, but such periods must have been short indeed. Eton has been one of the leading schools in England since the year of its foundation, apart from a few years in the reign of Edward IV. Henry VI, who founded it, would have been satisfied with nothing less. Perhaps impressed by Winchester, he wanted to found an even greater school, not without glory to himself. Many schools claim royal connections, often in their names, but in not a few cases the monarch in question never saw them and took little, if any, interest in them. Only one school had the honour of a reigning sovereign taking the most detailed interest in its every facet, in its foundation and in its development, planning much of it himself: that school is Eton. From the start, therefore, it was in an unusual and privileged position. Henry wrote: 'That the same school as it surpasses all other such grammar schools, whatsoever of our kingdom in the affluence and the pre-excellence of its foundation, so it may excel all other grammar schools, as it ought, in the prerogative of its name, and be named therefore the King's General School, and be called the lady, mother and mistress of all other grammar schools.' He gave the school certain properties, including open land of 'sixty-four acres between Charing Cross and Hay Hill and ninety-four acres in the north field opposite'—this includes what is today

Leicester Square, Piccadilly and part of Mayfair; had Eton retained this property it would have been rich indeed, but unfortunately some ninety years later Henry VIII realised the prospective value of the land and obliged the college to exchange it for other property. Like Wykeham, Henry VI gave detailed instructions for the buildings, which were to be grander than those at Winchester. The King laid the foundation stone of the magnificent chapel in 1441 (the actual day is uncertain); other buildings followed, and although the first boys were admitted in 1443, building continued with few interruptions for another fifty years. After 1461 there was no building for eight years.

The original foundation, in 1441, was for a provost, ten priests, four clerks, six choristers, a schoolmaster, twenty-five 'poor and needy scholars', and twenty-five poor men. However, this did not seem quite grand enough, and with the foundation of King's College, Cambridge, in 1441, which was to take scholars from Eton as New College, Oxford, took from Winchester, the foundation was enlarged, the poor men being reduced, but the number of scholars being increased to seventy. Provision was also made for fee-payers, who were to be the sons of rich or noble parents, and it was in this direction that Eton College expanded. Edward IV, Henry's successor, was antagonistic towards the college, and removed a large part of the endowment.

Henry had taken another enthusiastic educationist, William of Waynflete, from Winchester, to be master at Eton. He was followed by other Wykehamists, although the grammar used at Eton was that devised at Magdalen College School.

During the seventeenth century, corruption, which had been growing for some time, became infamous. A surplus revenue was arranged and much of it went to the provost himself (Henry's second foundation having provided for a provost and ten fellows as at Winchester). But the college remained well patronised by the wealthy and the nobility. George III took a close interest in Eton and became a great favourite there if not elsewhere in the country. The King used to visit the school and talk to the boys informally when staying at Windsor; he knew, of course, many of the boys' parents.

The college had always been divided between 'Collegers' (King's Scholars) and Oppidans (fee-payers). The latter lived in reasonable comfort in surrounding houses, run by 'dames', often bringing their own tutors until well into the nineteenth century. The life of the Collegers, on the other hand, was, by most accounts, quite hideous. The Collegers lived and slept in Long Chamber, into which masters seldom dared to enter. Unlike Oppidans, who dressed much as they wanted, Collegers had to wear short trousers until the mid-nineteenth century. Their diet was unvarying: mutton, bread and beer. The mutton bones were used as bait for the rats which infested Long Chamber; the rats were caught in the boys' stockings and then banged to death. Bullying, or rather torturing, was commonplace in Long Chamber; new boys in particular were expected to suffer devilish humiliations. The fittest survived; others were removed by their parents, ran away, or found the money to buy themselves a bolt hole in the town. There were no proper washing facilities, the windows were usually broken, food was scanty, and sometimes there were not enough beds for all the inmates. Lord Chatham declared he 'scarce observed a boy who was not cowed for life at Eton'. A semblance of discipline was only kept by frequent, almost frenzied, application of the birch. By the end of the nineteenth century conditions had improved, as had also the financial abuses. A select committee under Lord Brougham examined Eton and Winchester, in 1818, and found that the wishes of the founders had been disregarded at both places, and that these abuses had been 'dictated more by a regard to the interests of the Fellows than that of the Scholars'. In his *Education*, published in 1861, Herbert Spencer declared, 'The discipline which boys meet with at Eton, Winchester and Harrow, etc., is much worse than that of adult life.' The foundation was completely revised in the eighteen-seventies. King's College, Cambridge, was to open its endowments to Oppidans and some to non-Etonians. Collegers were to be less discriminated against at school. The new constitution provided for the Provost, a kind of chairman of the governors, to be appointed by the Crown, and the Provost of King's College to be *ex officio* a Fellow. The number of Collegers today remains the same at seventy, but the scholarship does not always cover the full amount of the fees; the standard at the examination is extremely high. The fee for Oppidans seems to be approaching £1,000 a year with a certain inevitability. Every Oppidan has his own room in one of the twenty-five houses. The majority of boys still are the sons of Etonians.

The college has long dominated the town. The chapel was also the parish church until 1854. The buildings overshadow the narrow streets, through which boys are constantly passing. If there were any doubt as to the importance of the place in the minds of new boys, it would soon be dispelled. The situation, surroundings and buildings are all of a singular elegance and beauty, but in a fortuitous and very English scheme. There are a number of Eton traditions which have lasted to the present day, including the celebrations of 4 June (George III's birthday), which was once the start of the English season, the Wall Game, in which generations of Collegers and Oppidans have been able to work off their private complexes about each other in a private and purposefully incomprehensible game, and the exclusive society of Pop, founded in 1811, which traditionally rejects too obvious candidates, including royalty.

Although at Eton itself rowing has usually been considered the smartest sport, for most of the nineteenth century, and the first half of the twentieth century, the greatest tradition in the public's mind concerning Eton was the Harrow cricket match at Lord's. This almost tribal ceremony was of the greatest fascination to newspapers throughout the period. The first match was played in 1805, on the original Lord's ground, and with few interruptions from 1825 on. By 1863 'carriages were five or six deep all round the ground, and besides that a ring of some 8,000 spectators'. One of the most famous matches was five years later, when C. I. Thornton (Eton) drove a ball straight over the pavilion, a feat very rarely accomplished in the history of the ground. Lord Harris, later captain of England, wrote: 'I was in with him at the time. He had just previously hit one against the old armoury, and one over D Block, and when he followed these big hits—very big for a boy—by that astounding drive over the pavilion I thought it was all right for Eton.' And so it was. But Eton's greatest era in the history of the fixture was in the period between the wars, when Harrow did not win a single match until 1939, on which occasion there were 'unprecedented' scenes after the game. It was the match at Lord's which best expressed the intense rivalry between the two schools. The fixture proving a success, other schools were invited to play at Lord's, and a kind of élitism developed at cricket between the 'Lord's' schools and the rest. A match between the Lord's schools and the remainder, begun in 1913, lasted until a few years ago. Apart from Winchester, which, as we have seen, abandoned its Lord's match early on, the eight other Lord's schools, in seniority of their first appearance, were: Marlborough and Rugby, Cheltenham and Haileybury, Clifton and

1a. Winchester

1b. Schoolroom, Winchester, 1861

2a. William of Wykeham

2b. Richard Busby

3a. Eton. An 18th-century view

3b. Eton. School Yard, showing the statue of the founder, Henry VI

4.   John Colet

Tonbridge, Beaumont and Oratory. Other schools which have made at least one appearance at Lord's are: Berkhamsted, Bishop's Stortford, Charterhouse, Rossall, Sherborne, Stowe and Westminster.

The possibilities of quotation about Eton are almost endless. I would like to quote two peers, very different men, but recognisably Etonian: Lord Curzon and Lord Berners. They give something of Eton's flavour, at any rate from the Oppidan point of view, which whether loved or, much less often, detested, haunts for the remainder of their lives all those who have tasted it. Curzon, Viceroy of India when still in his thirties, and later Foreign Secretary, enjoyed Eton immensely, although at least one of his masters considered him a 'brainless ass with no talent'. He was there in the eighteen-sixties. 'I was a confirmed cutter of names in desks and if an opportunity came to make a joke at the expense of one of the masters I was always leader. . . . Out of school I carried my indiscipline or independence to a pitch that was never suspected of so hard-working and orthodox a student as I was. I made it a point of honour to attend Ascot Races every year, not because I cared in the least for racing but because it was forbidden. . . . Another of my somewhat daring eccentricities was that I had a zinc lining made for the bottom of my oak bureau, in which I used to keep a stock of claret and champagne . . . [it] was to me a happy and glorious time, perhaps the happiest and most glorious that it will ever be given me to enjoy.' Parents of Etonians have not always gone through agonies of separation from their children. Curzon's mother came to see him only once, and his father not at all. In one letter Curzon's father warned him not to 'get puffed up. And do not celebrate your success by wearing your hair long and wrapped round your ears. You know what I mean and I do detest long hair'.

Lord Berners, a notable dilettante in the arts, wrote one of the best of all books on life at Eton, *A Distant Prospect* (a title taken from Thomas Gray's poem on Eton). He was there at the turn of the century. 'During my first days at Eton I had to concentrate on learning the various regulations of the school. They were mostly of a negative order. You were not supposed to walk on one side of the High Street, to turn down the collar of your change coat, to furl up your umbrella, to button the bottom button of your waistcoat. . . . Many of the rules seemed unreasonable, and their origins dated from so far back that they had long been forgotten. But if you didn't wish to involve yourself in trouble or expose yourself to ridicule they had to be rigidly observed . . . we were roused by a bell at six o'clock every morning both summer and winter. At Eton a boy's maid came and tapped on the door—just as at home—in summer at six-thirty, in winter at seven o'clock. Early school was about half an hour later. Coffee and biscuits were provided in the houses. . . . Chapel lasted for about half an hour, and after this spiritual fortification there was school till half-past ten, and again from eleven till twelve. The two-hours interval that followed was known as "after twelve", and it was generally spent in Pupil-room. Pupil-room, facetiously termed Puppy-hole, was a class devoted to the study of the Classics . . . luncheon (or dinner as it was called) was at two o'clock. At Mr. Oxney's house the food was not very good. . . . In the afternoon there was school lasting from a quarter to three till half-past, and again from five till six. "Lock-up", the curfew hour, when we were shut up in our houses for the night, varied with the seasons. In the winter it followed immediately after the last school. In the summer it was nine. . . . I passed a good deal of my time in the streets or in the playing fields, bathing or going on the river, frequenting the sock-shops [food shops] when I had money to spend. Later, when I had acquired a little more confidence, I used to go out sketching. This had to be surreptitiously, as in those days it was a form of "slacking" that aroused contempt and hostility. . . . It was only at the moment of leaving Eton that I realized to the full my deep attachment to the place, to its buildings, its fields and trees, the river, the surrounding town with the great Castle dominating the horizon, a conglomeration steeped in the romance of bygone centuries. I knew now how much I loved Eton at all times, at all seasons; the summer sunshine on the playing fields and the river, the bathing at Cuckoo Weir and Athens, the winter fogs and rain that had so often rescued me from football, the walls and cloisters mysterious in lamplight, the darkness of the lanes and passages as one returned in the dusk from out-lying classrooms, and, to descend to more material things, the strawberries-and-cream in the sock-shops and the hot buns at Little Brown's in the mornings before early school. . . . In so far as my education was concerned, I had learned nothing, less than nothing, a minus quantity. I had lost what little knowledge I had of foreign languages. In history, geography and science I had been confused rather than instructed. I left Eton with a distaste for the Classics and, what was more serious, a distaste for work itself.'

Some of the most eminent Etonians have been Collegers, no doubt spurred on by memories of distant humiliations. A list of distinguished Etonians would be so long that it is not practicable. No other school approaches the contribution that Old Etonians have made, but this is particularly so in politics. Over a third of our prime ministers, eighteen in all, have come from Eton (the greatest Etonian politician not to become prime minister was Charles James Fox). They include Walpole (a Colleger), Chatham (who disliked it and kept his son William Pitt away), Canning, Wellington, Salisbury, Gladstone and Balfour. In any other country such a proportion of the nation's leaders from the same school would have been the cause of an official enquiry long since; in Britain it is accepted that Eton has been the best school for budding politicians, not so much through any 'network' but more that Etonians are well fitted for the political arena. Harold Macmillan said, 'Mr. Attlee had three Etonians in his Cabinet. I have six. Things are twice as good under the Conservatives.' He was preceded by Anthony Eden and followed as prime minister by Sir Alec Douglas-Home, who played a famous innings for Eton at the Lord's match. The college has been well represented in all parties, although in the past Eton was considered generally Tory, while Harrow was Whig. Three of the last four leaders of the Liberal Party have been Etonians. Hugh Dalton, the socialist Chancellor of the Exchequer, was an Etonian. Other Labour Etonians are Lords Longford and Campbell. Of Conservatives in recent times, apart from prime ministers, one should mention, among virtually countless others, Lord Halifax, Lord Norwich (Duff Cooper), Sir Nevile Henderson, those two stalwarts of the Second World War, Lord Chandos and Oliver Stanley, and the Marquess of Salisbury, Viscount Amory, Viscount Head, Lord Crathorne, Lords Carrington, Boothby, Hailsham and Balneil, Sir Christopher Soames, Sir Harry Legge-Bourke, Duncan Sandys, Anthony Nutting, Julian Amery, Sir Edward Boyle, Lord O'Neill (prime minister of Northern Ireland), Richard Sharples, Anthony Kershaw, Airey Neave (head of M.I.9 in the war), Ian Gilmour and John Peyton.

In other activities, Eton's record is more comparable to that of a few of the other great schools, although still extremely formidable. Still confining oneself to recent times, the college produced the following great commanders of the First World War: Field-Marshal Viscount Plumer, Field-Marshal Viscount Byng, General Lord

Rawlinson and General Sir Hubert Gough. In the Second World War there were, among others, General Sir Frank Messervy, commander at Kohima, and Lieut-General Sir Oliver Leese, C. in-C. Allied Land Forces S.E. Asia, 1944–45. Among economists there have been Nassau Senior, Lord Keynes (a Colleger) and Sir Dennis Robertson. Bankers include Montagu Norman and Lord Cromer. In science, Sir Julian Huxley was at Eton. The composer Philip Heseltine (Peter Warlock) was an Etonian. In literature there have been Gray, Shelley, Algernon Swinburne, who had a highly successful academic career at the college, Julian Grenfell, Osbert Sitwell (who disliked the place, and later wrote: 'I avoided passing through Eton itself, so much did it depress my spirit'), George Orwell (a Colleger, significantly perhaps), Sir Desmond MacCarthy, Lord David Cecil, Aldous Huxley, Robert Bridges, Anthony Powell, Cyril Connolly, Christopher Hollis, Peter and Ian Fleming, Andrew Sinclair, Tom Stacey, Michael Holroyd and Jeremy Sandford. In journalism there have been Geoffrey Dawson, the Earl of Arran, Lord Hartwell, Sir Christopher Chancellor, David Astor, Randolph Churchill and John Mander.

Lord Snowdon and the Hon. Angus Ogilvy were both at Eton. Other Etonians of recent times who should be mentioned are Lord Caccia, Monsignor Ronald Knox, John Cobb, the first man ever to achieve 400 m.p.h. on land, Sir Gerald Kelly, Alan Dawnay, who destroyed the Hejaz railway in the First World War, the Earl of Harewood, Lord Gladwyn, Sir Humphrey Gibbs, Sir Con O'Neill, Lord Redcliffe-Maud, Lord Dilhorne, Alastair Buchan, Brian Young, headmaster of Charterhouse and director-general of I.T.A., Sir Fitzroy Maclean, Ludovic Kennedy, and Humphrey Lyttleton, Britain's greatest jazz musician. A typically mixed bag. Guy Burgess was an Oppidan; the headmaster wrote of him, 'It is refreshing to find one who is really well read and who can become enthusiastic or have something to say about most things. . . . He should do very well.' In contrast to Winchester, no obvious Eton type exists, except in so far as they seem to be opposite to Wykehamists in most things; they are mostly marked by an uncomplicated enjoyment of living and a sense of duty. Captain Oates of the Antarctic was an O.E., but so was Beau Brummell. Christopher Hollis, the author of the definitive modern history of the place, has written: 'There is something to be said for tolerating such a place as Eton and something to be said for not tolerating it, but the only reason for tolerating it is that in a too conformist world it is well to have somewhere where people are given the opportunity and taught the courage not to conform.'

Despite the presence of some forward-looking headmasters of recent years, including Sir Robert Birley and Anthony Chenevix-Trench (who made the fascinating move to Fettes), Eton remains much the same. It is extremely well entrenched in English society, and efforts to uproot it are likely to prove exhausting. In some form or other it will survive, although it may not play such a vital role in political life as in the past. Most people will be glad to see it continue. It is not a hot-house academically, but it has over the centuries served the nation well. Besides, contrary to what a few politicians believe, the British people, who expect, and usually get, a sense of responsibility from inherited privilege, rather like Eton.

*

With the last quarter of the fifteenth century we come to another of the great educationists of this time. We have already seen how William Waynflete was an early provost at Wykeham's college at Winchester, and then began the foundation of Eton for Henry VI. He now determined to found a college of his own. This he did in 1448, founding Magdalen College, Oxford; beside the college he founded a school where youths could learn their grammar before entering the college proper. Waynflete, already Bishop of Winchester, became Lord Chancellor of England and one of the most powerful men in the land. His college was completed in 1480. Waynflete had a miraculous ability of keeping on good terms with royalty through several reigns, and through the Wars of the Roses. Soon after its opening he received at his college Edward IV, and two years later Richard III. Magdalen College School soon gained a high reputation. The choir school of the college was originally separate from the grammar school, although the two joined sometime in the nineteenth century. In 1483 Magdalen College gained control of an ancient endowment at Brackley, Northamptonshire; this became a chantry, and in 1549 a grammar school controlled by the college. It is also known as Magdalen College School.

The pay of the first headmaster of Magdalen College School, Oxford, was £10 a year. Magdalen School's early fame was due to the new invention of printing, which made possible the spread of the teaching methods used at the school. Masters at other schools, including many of the most famous, were instructed to use the text-books devised by the grammarians of Magdalen College School, notably John Anwykyll, the first headmaster, John Holt, John Stanbridge, William Lily and Robert Whittington. But while printing was being developed, Latin grammar was still learnt by systems of oral transmission, the best-known method being that of Stanbridge of Magdalen School. The statutes of Manchester Grammar School required the teaching of grammar to be taught according to Stan-bridge's method, which was famous throughout the country. Thomas Wolsey, later Cardinal, was a master at the school, and he may just have been a pupil there also after leaving Ipswich, as were Lily and Whittington. The grammar of Lily, who became the first head-master of St. Paul's, was still in use in public schools in the nine-teenth century. It has been claimed that Sir Thomas More may have been an early pupil, and William Tyndale, translator of the Bible, was also at the school. From early on there were two ushers as well as a headmaster, a most unusual arrangement, and one which reveals the popularity of the school. In the sixteenth century, within the space of about a dozen years, Magdalen College School produced one archbishop and five bishops, as well as Thomas Whythorne, the Elizabethan songwriter. William Camden, the historian, was a pupil soon afterwards. But towards the end of the sixteenth century the school lost its pre-eminence, although it continued to produce famous men in the academic world, including Thomas Hobbes and Lord Clarendon. During the eighteenth century the school was almost in eclipse, and suffered with the decline of Oxford. However, one of the principal architects of the revival of Oxford, Dr. John Parsons, Master of Balliol at the beginning of the nineteenth century, was an old boy of the school. The turning point came after a cele-brated lawsuit, in which the Town Clerk of Oxford endeavoured to have the school made into a free grammar school for Oxford boys (at the time only choristers had free education). He was out to abolish the custom by which the Fellows divided the surplus reven-ues among themselves. Litigation dragged on for several years, and in the end the Town Clerk lost his case. But the college had been embarrassed and it made immediate and effective efforts to improve the school. Another old boy, J. E. Millard, headmaster 1846–64, re-established the fortunes of the school, in a new building (now the college library). The school began again to turn out a stream of scholars. The main winter sport was hockey, and Magdalen College

School was probably the first to play the game. Millard said: 'They also in the playground practise during the cold weather an excellent game resembling the ancient Golf and the Scottish Shinty, but by the Oxonians called Bung and Hockey, being played with a bung and a hooked stick called a hockey. The players are divided into two parties and the object of each is to strike the bung to the wall or boundary defended by the opposite party.'

In 1894 the present boarding-house, School House, with its garden sloping down to the Cherwell, was opened. And the remainder of the school buildings, across the bridge from the college, all moved to an adjoining site in 1928. After the First World War well over half the boys were boarders, but now about one in seven is a boarder. A large assembly hall was completed in 1966. The playing-fields, approached by a bridge from School House, on an island between two branches of the river, have a prospect of Magdalen Tower, with Christ Church Meadow seen through the surrounding chestnuts, poplars and willows. The second master of the school, which is still governed by the President and Fellows of Magdalen College, is called Usher, as has been the custom for nearly five hundred years. In the same tradition, the headmaster is the Master (of whom there have been only six since 1888). R. K. Davis, 1930–44, wrote: 'The comparative smallness of the school, which encourages intimacy among its members and favours personal development; the blending of varied elements in its composition; the beauty of its playing fields and of its general setting, and even the sense of rather heroic striving to compete with larger and wealthier schools. All these, upon a background of long history, combine to produce a very distinctive character, to which all but the dullest boys are in a greater or less degree susceptible. I have never known a school with a more lovable atmosphere.' It is a school which has produced few, if any, full generals or admirals in its five hundred years, but has turned out numerous bishops and not a few headmasters; however, Major-General T. B. L. Churchill, the commando leader of the Second World War, was a pupil. Distinguished old boys in modern times include J. R. Green, the first historian to achieve mass readership, E. B. Elliott, mathematician, Sir George Bonner, jurist, Sir Edgeworth David, the first man to reach the South Magnetic Pole, Sir Raymond Unwin, architect and planner of the garden suburbs, Sir Richard Winstedt, orientalist, Sir Basil Blackwell and, on the stage, Ivor Novello and Sir Felix Aylmer. In 1972, the College considered handing the school over to the local authorities, or going completely independent.

With Magdalen College School, and from it the spread of new methods of teaching Latin grammar, we come to the end of the schools founded in the fifteenth century. With the continuation of the ecclesiastical grammar schools and the establishment in a few decades of schools founded by individuals, notably Henry VI, William of Wykeham and Waynflete, for an academic élite intended for university colleges similarly founded, the basis of public school education had been laid.

3.

THE REFORMATION

THE sixteenth century was the most active period in English education until modern times. The activity began with the reign of
Henry VIII. Little happened educationally under Henry VII; but
a few schools were established, including Stockport Grammar
School, founded by Sir Edward Shea in 1487, Haverfordwest
Grammar School (1488) and Loughborough Grammar School
(1496). In Scotland, the education already established in the high
schools continued less disturbed, and sometimes survived the
closure of religious houses; an act had already been passed in
Scotland, in 1496, requiring householders of means to send their
eldest sons to school in order to 'have perfite Latine'. Thus in
Scotland the supply and demand for secondary education was better
balanced. After the Reformation in Scotland, a royal commission
decreed that every town must have a school and teacher. But in
England the cutting of so many links with Rome made a new basis
for education essential, or English education would almost dis-
appear.

The dissolution of the monasteries, abbeys, chantries and other
religious foundations in the fifteen-thirties and fifteen-forties led to
the closure of most of the grammar schools associated with them,
although some more independent schools, notably Winchester and
Eton, were considered sufficiently important to be expressly ex-
cepted; others, like King's, Canterbury, continued with only
nominal changes. All the wealth from the dissolution of the abbeys
and monasteries went to the king, and most of this he put to warlike
use, building a fleet and constructing defences on the east coast, and
to filling his own coffers; but some of it he put to educational use,
re-founding certain of the closed schools, now independent of their
former ecclesiastical control. This was the first plan for secondary
education in England, but it was not as extensive as the Protestant
Cranmer would have liked. For a long time there were fewer
grammar schools in England than there had been before the

dissolutions. Protestant scholars saw this as a great threat affecting everyone, and leading to the possibility of the English being at a disadvantage in controversies with the Church in Rome. Henry, of course, was not a 'protester'; his quarrel was with the Pope, not with the teachings of Rome. As his reign saw the abolition of more schools than were being founded, he cannot be considered the great educationist which he is sometimes presented to have been. By the time his daughter Elizabeth came to the throne, the Speaker of the House of Commons felt it his duty to point out the lack of schools in the nation, saying that 'at least one hundred were wanting, which before this time had been'. In Herefordshire, for instance, with a population of thirty thousand, there had been seventeen grammar schools before the dissolutions: by the time of Edward VI there were only three or four. The pressure to found, or re-found, more schools was partly to serve the Protestant establishment in England. The schools bearing the names of Henry VIII and Edward VI were not founded by them financially or personally, but they were part of a movement with which the monarchs thought it best to associate themselves to give the new or refounded schools official authority and themselves some credit. The real founding of new schools or the re-establishment of old church schools which had lapsed was often done by private citizens, mostly from the powerful merchant class or by their associations in London, the 'Companies', to whom the Reformation was often a stimulus; such men as Sir William Laxton, grocer (Oundle), Sir John Gresham, mercer (Gresham's), Sir Andrew Judd, skinner (Tonbridge), Sir William Harper, Lord Mayor (Bedford), Richard Platt, brewer (Aldenham), Lawrence Sheriff, grocer (Rugby), and Peter Blundell, merchant (Blundell's). These men were not aristocrats, landed gentry or bishops: they were members of a new class, which we would call the middle class; they were rich, and anxious to contribute to society.

This process of merchant-founding had begun before the breach with Rome. It was considered a suitable charity for men who had made their fortune in London to found a school in their home town. King's, Macclesfield, was founded by the Will of Sir John Percyvall, in 1502. Unusually, it was intended for 'gentlemen's sons and the good men's sons of the town and country hereabouts'. The school had a shaky start, but was re-established under Edward VI in 1552 for the teaching of 'grammatical learning and good manners'. Although it is no longer a free school, it continues to instruct the sons of gentlemen and good men in learning and good manners, there being at present well over a thousand day boys at the school. Queen Elizabeth's, Blackburn, was originally a church school, founded in 1509 by the Earl of Derby. It was broken up at the Reformation, but it was re-founded in Queen Elizabeth's reign by royal charter in 1567. Wolverhampton Grammar School, like Macclesfield, owes its existence to one man—Sir Stephen Jennings, a merchant taylor of London, who founded the school in 1512. It opened in 1515. Until 1784 it was one of the schools under the control of the Merchant Taylors' Company, which still offers an exhibition to Trinity College, Cambridge. The company asked to be and was discharged from the care and management of the school, which is now Voluntary Aided.

The most remarkable of all the re-foundings of schools at this time was that of St. Paul's, in London, which happened before the break with Rome. A modest grammar school belonging to the church was transformed into a major institution directed by the Mercers' Company. John Colet deserves to be remembered with Wykeham and Waynflete. The son of a prosperous mercer who became Lord Mayor of London, he was a priest who became Dean of St. Paul's in 1504. He was a good friend of Erasmus, who deeply influenced him. Four years after becoming Dean, Colet founded a school in 1509 on a small fortune he had inherited from his father. There has been some controversy as to whether this was a re-foundation of the existing grammar school or a completely new establishment; it is a controversey which has become set in semantics. There seems little doubt that Colet's school was completely new, but that it soon replaced the existing school.

The endowment was extremely generous, providing places for 153 free scholars, whereas Winchester and Eton provided for seventy. Colet chose the Mercers' Company as the trustees for his school, being the son of a mercer and having been educated by them; mercers were merchants in textiles and silk, and their association was prosperous and known for its integrity. Colet's statutes for the new school, upon which those of Manchester Grammar School and Merchant Taylors' were later based, are of great interest. The English historian, J. R. Green, wrote that 'the grammar schools of Edward VI and of Elizabeth, in a word the system of middle-class education which by the close of the century had changed the very face of England, were the direct result of Colet's foundation of St.

Paul's'. Colet explained that he was 'desiring nothyng more than the education and bringing uppe of Children in good manners and literature' and that his financial settlements were 'ever to endure'. 'In that Scole shall be first an Hyghe Maister. This Hyghe Maister, in doctrine, learnyne and teachinge, shall directe all the Schole. . . . A man hoole in body, honest and vertuous, and lerned in good and cleane Laten literature, and also in Greke, yf such may be gotten.' Colet also ordered that there should be an Under Master and a Chaplain. The High Master was to have a wage of thirteen shillings and four pence (i.e. one mark) per week, thirty days' annual holiday, and a pension of ten pounds a year. The Under Master was to receive six-and-eight per week, with the same holidays. 'There shall be taught in the Scole, children of all Nations and Contres indiffer-ently . . . but first se that they canne saye the Catechyzon, and also that he can rede and write. . . . In every Forme one principall childe shall be placid in the chayre, President of that forme. The children shall come into the Scole in the Mornynge at Seven of the clocke, both Winter and Somer, and tarye there untyll Eleven, and returne againe at one of the clocke, and departe at Five. . . . As touching in this scale what shall be taught of the Maisters, and learned of the Scolers, it passeth my witte to devyse and determine in particular, but in general to speak and sumewhat to saye my minde I would they were taught always in good literature bothe Laten and Greke.' St. Paul's, therefore, was one of the first schools in the country to introduce Greek. These impressive statutes have been faithfully carried out over the centuries by the trustees, the Mercers' Company, until this day. There are still a High Master, an Under Master, a Chaplain and 153 scholars.

For his first High Master Colet chose the famous grammarian William Lily, a master at and formerly pupil of Magdalen College School. Lily was one of the few men in the country sufficiently versed in Greek to be acceptable to Colet, but he was eminent also in Latin teaching, and was well travelled. Lily remained at St. Paul's for ten years. Colet's school house, facing the cathedral, was described by Erasmus: 'A magnificent structure to which were attached two dwelling-houses for the two several masters.' The school house was divided 'into four chambers. The first, as you enter, contains those who may be called the catechumens whom the Chaplain teaches: but none is admitted who cannot read and write. The second apartment is for those who are taught by the Under

Master. The third is for the boys of the Upper Forms, taught by the High Master. . . . The last apartment is a little chapel for divine service. In the whole school there are no corners or hiding-places; neither a dining nor a sleeping place . . . he that is at the head of the class has a little desk by way of pre-eminence'. Erasmus took a close interest in the new school and he wrote the school prayers and some of the religious tracts on the walls. This building was lost in the Great Fire of 1666, but a new building, still on Colet's old site, was designed and built, with two additional masters' houses, and a play-ground. During all this time St. Paul's was recognised as one of the leading schools in London, reaching its zenith under F. W. Walker, High Master 1877–1905, previously High Master of Manchester Grammar School, which under him had become a fee-paying school. By this time, nearly a hundred years ago, there were seven masters in addition to the three required by the statutes (the High Master's salary being £900). Holidays had increased to six weeks in the summer, four at Christmas and one at Whitsun. The greatest change during Walker's administration was the removal of the school from the very centre of the metropolis, where it had always served the community, to the suburbs. At first the Mercers con-sidered buying the old East India Company College buildings at Haileybury, but eventually erected a large new Gothic struc-ture on land at Hammersmith, to which the school moved in 1884.

Under Walker, St. Paul's was without question the leading school, academically, in England. It has been claimed for him (in the *D.N.B.*) that he raised the standard of public-school education throughout the country. He surrounded himself with a good staff, and his former pupils took most of the prizes at Oxford and Cam-bridge. In 1899 St. Paul's carried off no less than twenty-nine open scholarships at the two universities. When asked what was the secret of his success, Walker replied: 'I walked about'. He knew every boy well, and followed his progress up the school. His assistant masters did not seem put out by Walker's perambulations; one of them said of him: 'No one ever gave a more practical refutation to the theory that school-masters belong to a sedentary profession.' Walker had been a day boy at Rugby, which had instilled in him a dislike of the traditional boarding school, and his boarding houses were merely places where boys lived in the intervals between work. He reacted strongly against the Arnold theory of 'character-building' and believed that boys' characters would take care of themselves if only they were taught to work.

One of the factors that had brought about the move to West London was that Colet's endowment was in considerable surplus. Added to the sale of the old site, the Mercers were now able to establish a school for girls as well. There were various proposals as to the composition of the boys' school, and the matter was finally decided by the Charitable Trusts Act of 1900, under which the original 152 scholarships were retained, the remaining places, nearly five hundred of them, going to fee-payers. The new building was in a busy part of outer London. Compton Mackenzie recalled: 'It was pleasant to be in the only form-room in the whole school that looked out south with a clear view of the playing field. By some incomprehensible process of reasoning it had been decided when the new St. Paul's was built in the 'eighties, to the design of Alfred Waterhouse, that all the classrooms should look north. Why the sight of grass and a groundsman with a roller should have been considered more distracting to the eyes of youth than the red omnibuses rumbling along Hammersmith Road is hard to guess.' The school made its second move in 1968, to more extensive grounds beside the Thames at Barnes. Portraits, panels and other heritages of the past have been moved to the fine modern buildings. Although Colet, unlike Wykeham, saw his school as a day school, the governors have been able to provide two boarding houses for many years, and about one in five of the boys are now boarders.

The list of Old Paulines is a most formidable one, foremost among them being John Milton and the Duke of Marlborough, two of the greatest three or four men to have come from the public schools. There have been long periods when St. Paul's has been to academe what Eton has been to politics. Other great sons of the school's early days are Sir William Paget, Privy Councillor to four sovereigns, John Leland and William Camden, the antiquaries, William Whittaker, champion of the Reformation, two Speakers of the House of Commons, the first Earl of Forfar and the first Duke of Manchester, Roger Cotes, the astronomer, and Samuel Pepys. Pepys must have been an early example of the conventional 'old boy', for his diary is full of references to former school-friends. In 1661 he wrote: 'Up early to Paul's School, it being Apposition Day there. I heard some of their speeches and they were just as school boys used to be, of the seven liberal sciences but I think not so good as ours were in our time.' In the next period came Edward Halley of the comet, Sir Philip Francis, author of the *Letters of Junius*, Charles Barham, author of the *Ingoldsby Legends*, Lord Chancellor Truro and Benjamin Jowett. Under Walker were the writers E. C. Benson, G. K. Chesterton and Sir Compton Mackenzie. Chesterton recalled: 'I was perfectly happy at the bottom of the class. I think the chief impression I produced, on most of the masters and many of the boys, was a pretty well-founded conviction that I was asleep.' He thought Walker 'a very remarkable man. . . . It is he of whom the famous tale is told that, when a fastidious lady wrote to ask him what was the social standing of the boys at his school, he replied, "Madam, so long as your son behaves himself and the fees are paid, no questions will be asked about his social standing".' Four of Chesterton's friends at St. Paul's became Presidents of the Oxford and Cambridge Unions. Sir Compton Mackenzie wrote at great length of St. Paul's ('St. James's') in his novel *Sinister Street*, something of a sensation in its day. '. . . Every Saturday afternoon, when there was a home match, Michael, in rain or wind or pale autumnal sunlight, would take up his position in the crowd of spectators to cheer and shout and urge St. James's to another glorious victory. . . . Those were indeed afternoons of thunderous excitement. Now everybody used to shout—School—Schoo-oo-ol—Schoo—ol! Play up Schoo-oo-ool!' He writes elsewhere of the public-school system, declaring: 'This rigid doctrine setting forth the importance of not letting down the side sets a problem to somebody who may think that the side is wrong, but in nine cases out of ten the man educated at a public school will surrender his private convictions for what he believes to be the value of unity.'

Other Old Pauline writers of modern times include Leonard Woolf, Edward Thomas, Lawrence Binyon (whose *For the Fallen* is quoted on so many school war memorials), Sir B. H. Liddell Hart, Henry Cecil, Ernest Raymond, Eric Newby and Arthur Calder-Marshall. Of economic and political scientists there have been Sir Otto Niemeyer, Sir George Catlin, Sir Isaiah Berlin, G. D. H. Cole, F. R. Salter, Professor Max Beloff and David Butler. Of artists and musicians, Duncan Grant, Paul Nash, Eric Kennington, E. H. Shepard and Dennis Brain. P. G. H. Fender, the scorer of the fastest century in cricket, was an Old Pauline, as was H. H. Garland-Wells, captain of Surrey in the nineteen-thirties. In other fields there are Lord Pearson, judge, the Rev. P. T. B. (Tubby) Clayton, founder

of Toc H, Professor A. M. Low, scientist, Viscount Dawson of
Penn, physician, Sir John Clements, actor, Lord Nathan, politician,
Victor Gollancz, and Sir David Kelly, ambassador to the U.S.S.R.
The school has also produced some distinguished soldiers, foremost
among whom in modern times is Field-Marshal Viscount Montgomery, who for a time had his headquarters at the school (he was
captain of the rugby XV). Other Old Pauline soldiers are Lieut.-
General Sir Humphrey Gale, Deputy Chief of Staff to General
Eisenhower 1942–45, Major-General Sir Frederick Maurice,
military historian, and, by no means least, Major-General R. E.
Urquhart, G.O.C. at Arnhem 1944. Although St. Paul's is obliged,
by statute, to limit its number of non-Christians, some of its most
eminent old boys are Jewish.

If there is a Pauline type, he is both donnish and sporting; not so
fusty as the Wykehamist, less dashing than the Etonian.

*

Far away to the north, on the moors of Yorkshire, another school
was being founded at about the same time, in the village of Giggleswick, outside the small town of Settle. James Carr opened his school
there in 1512, based on a chantry school already in existence for
several years. Chantry schools had come about through the custom
of benefactors founding chantries, which were chapels for particular
prayers, usually for the benefactor and his family; the duties of
chantry priests were therefore not onerous, a fact which was something of a scandal, and some of them were given additional duties
in the form of teaching boys Latin or teaching them singing; many
of the former became grammar schools. James Carr had himself
been the chantry priest of Giggleswick. He now had a two-storey
building put up on half an acre, with the following inscription (in
Latin) over the door: 'Kindly Mother of God, defend James Carr
from ill. For priests and young clerks this house is made in 1512.
Jesus, have mercy upon us. Old men and children praise the name
of the Lord.' Giggleswick was not a rich foundation like St. Paul's,
but from early times it took boarders as well as local boys; they
lodged in houses in the town, a custom continued till the second half
of the nineteenth century. Carr was followed as Master by his
nephew, Richard Carr; the Carr family retained an interest in the
school until the second half of the eighteenth century, John Carr
being Master 1712–44 and George Carr being Usher 1726–55. The

Vicar of Giggleswick managed to get the school refounded in 1553, at the dissolution of the chantry. The school continued quietly to serve the town, with a few boarders, for centuries. A transformation came under the Rev. George Style, headmaster 1869–1904. He found fifty-six boys, of whom eighteen were boarders. There was a staff of two; there could be no more because of the statutes of 1553. The first problem was the private boarding houses, which were, according to a school history published in 1912, 'inadequate and the sanitary arrangements most prejudicial to health'. Boys had enjoyed considerable freedom, not least in frequenting the local public houses. A hostel was built to house the boarders, and soon more were living in the town. Day-boys were still educated free, but this was becoming increasingly difficult. The school came under the general enquiry into endowed schools in the eighteen-sixties, when the commissioner reported: 'It is not too much to hope that it may one day become for the North of England what Rugby is to the Midland district.' An amalgamation with Sedbergh, another endowed school in difficulties, was suggested, but at length it was settled that fees would have to be paid: up to £24 per annum for day-boys, up to £69 for boarders. The local people naturally fought against this proposal vigorously, and with some reason. The school history of 1912 comments: 'They were fighting a losing battle. It was clear that no school could maintain the efficiency of its education without the imposition of fees. . . . For three hundred years and more a grammar school education had been such that by its very breadth it endeavoured to fit men for whatsoever walk in life they intended to adopt. But in the nineteenth century education was becoming more expensive, and the old ideals could not be maintained at the old cost.' These words could apply to many another endowed public school in the late nineteenth century. As a concession to the townspeople, who were not impressed by this sort of argument, the Shute scholarships, which for two centuries had sent poor boys from the school to the universities, were transformed in 1872 to allow local boys to enter the school free. The second major change was the building of new premises, magnificently set high on the moors, with boarding accommodation for 150 boarders, and ninety day-boys. Today, the senior school is about the same size, with 260 boys, fifty of them day-boys (who remain at the school until evening prayers). From former times the most famous old boy of the school is William Paley, the eighteenth-century philosopher and divine; in modern times,

James Agate, the critic, is probably the most celebrated product of the school.

A great day school, Nottingham High School, was founded at about the same time, by a woman, Agnes Mellers, in 1513. This lady, the widow of a rich bell-founder who had twice been Mayor of Nottingham, seems to have been a very determined person. She was anxious to join the growing band of founders of schools, and not only gave a considerable part of her estate for a new school in Nottingham but persuaded her friends to do likewise. The governing of the school was entrusted by Agnes Mellers to the Mayor and Corporation of Nottingham (who are still on the governing body to this day). The first headmaster, chosen by the founder herself, was 'Maister John Smythe, parson'. It was laid down by the founder that a commemoration day should be held each year on 16 June, which was her husband's saint's-day. This wish was not carried out for some centuries, and was only revived in 1923. The school, known as Nottingham Grammar School, was given a charter to continue by Henry VIII, by Philip and Mary, and by Elizabeth. A new site was granted by Edward VI.

The school at Nottingham remained a classical grammar school until 1868, when the name was changed by Act of Parliament to Nottingham High School. In that year it opened in imposing new buildings set between two large open spaces, the Forest and the Arboretum, with a view across the city. The building programme continued for the next decade. Unfortunately the school did not thrive in its new premises. There was a feeling in Nottingham that a classical education was not practical, nor was it what was needed. There was competition from the High Pavement School, which provided a modern education. Nevertheless, there was an outcry when school fees, against the Mellers' statutes, were introduced in 1868. A few free places were available, but in 1882 these numbered only ten. Boarders were also taken, lodging with the headmaster and three other masters for sixteen guineas per annum (double the day-boy fees); this practice was discontinued during the First World War.

Nottingham High School revived under the headmastership of Dr. James Gow, 1885–1901. His was a bold appointment, for Gow was only thirty years old, very young for such a position in those days, and he had no school-teaching experience whatever (the head-masters of four other public schools had applied for the post, including those of Kingswood and King William's College). Gow had been an academic and a barrister. Under him the school was transformed, gaining a great reputation, and the remarkable confidence in him of the governors was rewarded. In four years the numbers in attendance more than doubled. When Gow left for the headmastership of Westminster, it was said of him: 'In regard to Nottingham, he found a mob of schoolboys and left a Public School.' Since Gow, Nottingham High School, still independent, has continued as one of the major day schools in the country. Since the Second World War considerable building has taken place, including, in 1965, a new dining-hall and swimming-pool at a cost of over £160,000. The most illustrious son of the school is D. H. Lawrence, who won a scholarship and rose to the Modern Sixth. He won two prizes in mathematics and left his name, for future generations, carved on a fireplace. The school is mentioned by name in *Sons and Lovers*. When searching for a name for his concupiscent gamekeeper in *Lady Chatterley's Lover*, Lawrence seems to have discovered it in the founding family of his old school.*

The year after the foundation of Nottingham High School another northern school, Pocklington, was started, in 1514, by John Dolman, Canon of St. Paul's. Dolman was undoubtedly influenced by Colet. The school was closely connected with St. John's College, Cambridge, founded three years earlier; Cambridge was becoming the centre of the Reformation in England. It was designed, according to a nineteenth-century source, 'for a fit man sufficiently learned in grammatical science to teach all scholars resorting to Pocklington', a small market town beneath the Yorkshire wolds. It is now a Direct Grant school of over 570 boys, in buildings dating from 1850, including three houses for boarders. The greatest product of Pocklington School is William Wilberforce (in recent years, playwright Tom Stoppard). All Hallow's School, in Devon, may date from this period also, but its foundation is uncertain. It originated as a grammar school in Honiton, but was completely re-established in 1938, when it moved to Rousdon, high up in 350 acres on the coast (with a private beach) above Lyme Regis, from which date it may be said to have become a public school. The school buildings have views of some forty or fifty miles of coast. The new governing

---

* Others: Industrialists John Player and Jesse Boot (Lord Trent), Albert Ball, V.C., greatest World War I air ace, E. A. Abbott, Chaplain to the Queen, R. T. Simpson, England cricketer, Sir Bernard Gilbert.

body includes the Vice-Chancellor of Exeter University and, carrying on an old tradition, the Mayor of Honiton. At present there are about 250 boarders and a few day-boys. In 1969 ten girls were admitted to the sixth form, boarding in the headmaster's house. Sir Richard Woolley, Astronomer Royal, 1956–71, is the most distinguished living old boy.

*

All old public schools were once 'grammar' schools, but most have preferred to drop that appellation. One which retains the same name it has had for centuries is Manchester Grammar School, which has long been one of the most celebrated schools in England, famed for its high academic standards. The grammar school in Manchester was founded in 1515 by Hugh Oldham, a native of Manchester who had become Bishop of Exeter. Oldham helped found Corpus Christi College, Oxford, to which place he contributed a 'greate masse of money', and he ordered that the High Master and usher of his school in Manchester should be appointed by the President of that college; the President still sits on the board of governors (together with the Lord Mayor of Manchester, the Mayor of Salford and the Dean of Manchester). Oldham insisted that the school was to be absolutely free, expanding on the point at some length; in this respect Manchester Grammar School, like so many other endowed schools, dishonoured its founder in the last century. He also wrote: 'There shall be no schollar or infaunt, of what country or shire, soever he be of, being man-child, be refused, except he have some horrible or contagious infirmytie.' The High Master's salary was to be £20 and there were to be twenty days holiday. Oldham seems to have been anxious that his school should be less religiously dominated than others of his time, but he stressed the importance of Latin, as the 'grounde and fountayne of all the other liberall arts and sciences'.

For a long time income for the school came from the profits of corn mills. One of the first pupils was the martyr John Brackford, the Protestant preacher. The school declined in the seventeenth century, and on one occasion there was a revolt, when the boys locked themselves in for a fortnight, holding off the headmaster and authorities with firearms. The Manchester school was revived under William Purnell and Charles Lawson, successively High Masters in the second half of the eighteenth century. The latter is probably best known for the cutting remarks made about him by Thomas de Quincey in his *Confessions of an English Opium-Eater*. Lawson was by then an old man. De Quincey, who went to the school as a boarder from King Edward's, Bath, had a love-hate relationship with his old school, a not unfamiliar attitude. De Quincey recalled his arrival in mid-term thus: 'One of the young men, noticing my state of dejection, brought out some brandy [which] at once reinstalled me in my natural advantages of conversation . . . a question arose naturally out of a remark addressed by one of the boys to myself, implying that perhaps I had intentionally timed my arrival so as to escape the Sunday evening exercise. No, I replied; not at all; what *was* that exercise? Simply an off-hand translation from the little work of Grotius on the Evidences of Christianity. Did I know the book? No, I did not.' De Quincey was impressed by his schoolfellows. 'I have since known many literary men; men whose profession was literature; who were understood to have dedicated themselves to literature. But amongst such men I have found but three or four who had a knowledge which was as near to what I should consider a comprehensive knowledge as really existed amongst those boys collectively.' And there was more that impressed him about the school. 'It was honourable both to the masters and the upper boys, through whom only such a result was possible, that in the school, during my knowledge of it (viz., during the closing years of the eighteenth century and the two opening years of the nineteenth), all punishments, that appealed to the sense of bodily pain, had fallen into disuse; and this at a period long before any public agitation had begun to stir in that direction. How then was discipline maintained? It was maintained through the self-discipline of the senior boys, and through the efficacy of their example, combined with their system of rules.' The boarders at the school, de Quincey says, were 'bound together by links of brotherhood; whereas the day-scholars were disconnected'. However, despite all this, de Quincey wished only to get away. He felt physically confined. 'There was no playground, not the slightest, attached to the school', and 'Mr. Lawson had barred up all avenues from morning to night through which any bodily exercise could be contained'. He added: 'By the old traditional usages of the school, going in at 7.0 a.m., we ought to have been dismissed for breakfast and a full hour's repose at nine. . . . Yet such were the gradual encroachments upon this hour that at length the bells of the collegiate church . . . regularly announced to us, on issuing from the schoolroom, that the bread and milk which composed our simple breakfast must be despatched at a pace fitter for the fowls of the air than students of Grecian philosophy.'

However, this concentration on learning brought the school academic honours. Even today, among public schools, Manchester Grammar School is perhaps less impressed by games than are most others, although trekking and camping have long been a tradition. Nevertheless, in the ten years after the Second World War 350 boys from the school won awards to Oxford or Cambridge and there were 103 Blues among them. In 1931 it moved from Long Millgate, where it had been for 416 years, to the suburbs of the city. But boys continued to come from as far as Cheshire, Derbyshire and Yorkshire, so high was the reputation of Manchester Grammar School. A history records: 'What a blessing it was to be able to run straight from school on to the fields without the half-hour intervention of a drab bus or tram journey.' Manchester takes the cream from a large and populous area, and the school remains among the leaders academically, sending over seventy per cent of its pupils to university. Its reputation was never higher than in the nineteen-fifties, under the High Mastership of Lord James of Rusholme (who took the appointment in his mid-thirties). Manchester has always been the most democratic of schools, drawing its intake from the sons of professional and clerical men and of manual labourers. Lord James once said: 'We probably have a wider social cross-section than anywhere in the Western world.' In recent years, under P. G. Mason, there has been increasing experimentation in teaching methods, particularly in languages and science, and the school has done some pioneering in this respect.*

*

There are four comparable great academic day public schools: Dulwich in the south, King Edward's in the Midlands, Manchester Grammar School in the north and, in Scotland, the Royal High School. The grammar school at Edinburgh had been founded some

* Eminent old boys since de Quincey's time are very numerous, but include Harrison Ainsworth, the novelist, Sir Ernest Barker, political scientist, Lord Sumner, Lord Woolton, Lord Marks, Lord Sieff, Harold Laski, Robert Bolt, Harold Lever and Sir H. Andrew, Permanent Under-Secretary, Department of Education, 1964–70.

time before that in Manchester, but its continuous existence dates from the same era. The grammar schools, or high schools, in Scotland dated from at least the twelfth century, and probably earlier, certainly at Lanark, Linlithgow, Stirling and Perth (which by 1587 had three hundred pupils). Other early grammar schools were at Ayr, Kelso and St. Andrews. But Aberdeen Grammar School has perhaps the best claim for a continuous existence since the mid-thirteenth century. By the fifteenth century there was probably a grammar school in every town in Scotland. After Edinburgh, the richest was probably that at Dundee.

The school at Edinburgh was attached to the abbey of Holyrood, but the first mention of a 'summa schola grammatica', or high school, is in 1505. In April 1519, usually given as the date of the modern foundation, in the reign of Henry VIII's nephew, James V of Scotland, the town council ordered the citizens 'no manner of neighbours or indwellers in the Burgh put their bairns to any school except the principal Grammar School'. In later centuries it was, of course, impossible to honour this provision owing to the expansion of the city, but the school has remained the major day school until present times. In about 1590 the crown granted the school the prefix 'Royal'. Greek was introduced into the curriculum in 1614. The Royal High School passed smoothly through the Reformation, despite the fact that the rector, or headmaster, was 'ane obstinat papeist'; Queen Mary took a personal interest in his retaining the post, but he was eventually replaced by a Protestant, selected by the corporation rather than Holyrood abbey, which from then on lost its authority over the school.

The greatest date in the Royal High School's history is 1827. In that year it moved to its magnificent classical building overlooking the city, most of the cost being met by the council (the remainder coming from subscriptions and from the sale of the former building); the cost was £33,970, an enormous sum for a school at the time. At the same time there was a revision in the course of study, the Royal High School dropping its rigid classical discipline—partly because of competition from other schools in Edinburgh, which were teaching modern subjects. English literature, history, French and geography were introduced in that year; higher mathematics was introduced in 1839, German followed in 1845 and chemistry in 1848. In 1839 the boys unsuccessfully petitioned the city council to suspend Saturday school, but the plea was granted in 1851. In 1851 the college committee of the council declared: 'The Committee think it right to state at the outset that in all their liberations they have kept steadily in view the maintenance of the high character of the School as a classical seminary, and they feel satisfied that this can be done and at the same time additional opportunities afforded to the pupils for the acquisition of other branches of knowledge of a more practical character.' It was the end for the traditional lists, although the school retained a high standard in classics. Prefects, as in some other Scottish schools, are still called Duxes. In 1927, for the first time so far as is known, a boarding house was opened, boys from outside Edinburgh having previously lodged in the city. The school stopped accepting boarders in 1970, and now comes under the City Education Department.

Of the many distinguished former pupils, the most famous is Sir Walter Scott, who was at the Royal High School from 1779–83, and who sent his son there. Scott wrote in his Memoirs: 'There is, from the constitution of the High School, a certain danger not sufficiently attended to. The boys take precedence in their places, as they are called, according to their merit, and it requires a long while, in general, before even a clever boy, if he fall behind the class, or is put into one for which he is not quite ready, can force his way to the situation which his abilities really entitle him to hold. . . . It was the fashion to remain two years [in the Rector's] class, where we read Caesar, and Livy, and Sallust in prose, Virgil, Horace and Terence in verse. I had by this time mastered, in some degree, the difficulties of the language, and began to be sensible of its beauties. This was really gathering grapes from thistles; nor shall I soon forget the swelling of my little pride when the Rector pronounced that, though many of my school-fellows understood the Latin better, Gualterius Scott was behind few in following and enjoying the author's meaning . . . and, though I never made a first-rate Latinist, my school-fellows and, what was of more consequence, I myself considered that I had character for learning to maintain. Dr. Alexander Adam, to whom I owed so much, never failed to remind me of my obligations when I had made some figure in the literary world.' Another notable former pupil, soon after Scott, was Lord Brougham, Lord Chancellor and one of the great Whig politicians. Brougham was more interested in education than almost any other leading politician of his time. A select committee of 1816 disclosed the misuse of the charity funds on which many schools were founded, and was

followed by another enquiry two years later; this led to the establishment of the Charity Commissioners, which in turn oversaw the
change of many ancient free grammar schools into fee-demanding
public schools. Throughout the eighteen-twenties Brougham took
the lead in attempts to improve the educational system, but with
little success except for the first steps towards the founding of
London University. Two other Lord Chancellors from the Royal
High School were Erskine and Loughborough. Throughout the
nineteenth century former pupils dominated the Scottish legal
profession: in the eighteen-fifties ten of the thirteen Scottish judges
were former pupils of the Royal High School.*

One should not pass from Scotland without referring to the other
great day school of the country, Glasgow High School. There is a
mention of a grammar school at Glasgow in 1460. Glasgow was one
of the smaller Scottish burghs, but it was second to receive a university, and between 1523 and 1555 the list of electors of the rector
of Glasgow University contains the name of the master of the
grammar school four times. The High School's greatest moment
was in the early years of this century, when two former pupils were
prime ministers: Sir Henry Campbell-Bannerman and Andrew
Bonar Law. Lord Fleming, who reported on the public schools
between 1942 and 1944, was also at Glasgow High School. Glasgow
High School is now integrated in the education department of the
Corporation of Glasgow.

*

Some schools south of the border fared less well in the Reformation
than those north of it. Among these was King's School, Bruton,
which was founded in 1519 by three prominent Londoners: Richard
Fitzjames, Bishop of London, John Fitzjames, his nephew,
Attorney-General, and their friend, Dr. John Edmunds, Chancellor

* Other notable former pupils: James Boswell, Henry Dundas, Pitt's Secre-
tary of War, and his son Viscount Melville, First Lord of the Admiralty for
fifteen years, Mountstuart Elphinstone, the great governor of Bombay, the ninth
Earl of Dalhousie, governor-general of Canada, William Drummond, poet,
Robert Adam, one of the greatest architects, buried in Westminster Abbey,
Allan Ramsay, portrait painter, Thomas Coutts, banker, John Ruskin, Robert
Hamilton, economist, J. G. Bartholomew, cartographer, Alexander Graham Bell,
inventor of the telephone, Sir Theodore Martin, biographer of Prince Albert,
Sir Archibald Geikie, geologist, Sir Landsborough Thomson, ornithologist, and
Sir David Ross, classical scholar.

of St. Paul's. The master was required to teach Latin, free of charge, in the manner of Magdalen College School or St. Paul's, and was expressly ordered not to teach songs or the English language, which were considered 'petite learning'. The school closed on the dissolution of the monastery (at which the master used the premises for a malt-house). It was not re-opened, as the 'King's' school, until twelve years later. The statutes on this occasion were based on those of Sherborne (themselves based on St. Paul's), which school lent its statutes to Bruton for the fee of sixpence. The first master of the refounded school was John Slade, Master of Magdalen College School, who was, however, only on 'loan' from Oxford. The school was re-organised, by permission of the Chancery Court, in 1859, charging fees and teaching non-classical subjects. Two D. E. Nortons, father and son, were headmasters from 1873 to 1916, and they established Bruton as a modern public school. There are now about 260 boys in the senior school, housed in buildings dating from the foundation of the school onwards, nearly all of them boarders.

Cranbrook School, one of the great schools of Kent, dates from 1520, under the will of John Blubery, who left his handsome mansion to be used as a school. It is still the School House. Cranbrook was re-endowed in 1574 by Simon Lynche as a free grammar school, when it obtained a charter from Queen Elizabeth. It became a fee-payers' school in the nineteenth century. The fee in 1877 was four guineas per annum, the school at that time being still entirely classical. Cranbrook is not a well-endowed school, but it gained a high reputation in this century under C. R. Scott, 1929–60, and J. MacKendall-Carpenter, 1960–70. Like many other schools, Cranbrook's most important developments have occurred in the twentieth century, and no school in the country has a more interesting recent history. It became a Voluntary Aided School under the 1944 Education Act. This meant that the cost of tuition was from then on to be borne by the State and not the parents, although the governors retained the right to appoint the headmaster and teaching staff, and were responsible for existing and new buildings. Cranbrook therefore retained a good measure of autonomy, and the governors of many another public school as ill-endowed as Cranbrook must have watched its progress with interest. Naturally competition to enter the school was heavy and standards of entry became high. It became no longer possible for parents to pay fees for boys who had not reached the required standard. As five of the nine houses are for boarders, this meant that only the boarding fee had to be paid, and thus a public school education could be gained at a very reasonable cost. In the nineteen-sixties the school almost doubled in size, and some £400,000 was spent on improvements. At the end of the decade it was decided to turn the school co-educational, providing secondary education from the age of thirteen for boys and girls in the area who are going to continue their school education for a further five years and for at least as many fee-paying boarders as before. This process is expected to be completed by 1980. Cranbrook may well be a trail-blazer for what nearly all the public schools one day will be like, if they are to be more integrated in the general system. Cranbrook provides, and will continue to do so, with the support of the Kent Education Committee, a modern public school education, in new buildings as well as old, pleasantly placed about in the streets of this attractive old town. It has long been a well-known games school, its traditional opponents, in various sports, including Hurstpierpoint, St. Lawrence, Ardingly, Brighton, Tonbridge, Eastbourne, Dover, and King's, Rochester.*

King's College, Taunton, one of three public schools in this Somerset town, is the successor to another old grammar school, founded in 1522 by Richard Fox, Bishop of Winchester, who also founded Corpus Christi College, Oxford. The most distinguished pupil of its early history was Gilbert Sheldon, Archbishop of Canterbury, 1663–78. King's, Taunton, was one of the few schools which thrived in the eighteenth century. In 1869 the school was moved to its present buildings, to the south of the town, having amalgamated with a private school two years earlier. The school took boarders, but to retain goodwill in the town and to continue its ancient connection nine scholarships for day-boys, and two for boarders, were offered to boys who lived in the borough. It got into debt and, in 1879, the school was bought for £8,000 by Canon Woodard, a rich cleric anxious to promote public schools in England; it became a school of the Woodard Corporation (q.v. Lancing below). Woodard named it King's, after King Alfred.†

---

* Lord Rootes, Sir Reginald Rootes, Canon Collins, Peter West and Air Vice-Marshal Sir John Weston, director of Air Ministry signals in the war, are among the old boys.

† Old boys include Major-General Charles Gordon, of Khartoum, Sir Lionel Whitby, physicist, Dr. Anthony Hemish, radio-astronomer, the Rev. Michael Scott, and Geoffrey Rippon.

Bolton School was founded in 1524 by William Haighe, and was later refounded in 1641 by Robert Lever, in a new building. Bolton was unusual in that it had a wide curriculum for the time. Lever provided for instruction not only in Latin and arithmetic, but also in writing, geography, navigation and French. In 1656 it was united with another local school. By 1880 there were thirty-six free scholars, but the remainder paid only one guinea a quarter. A clause in an act of the reign of George III, relating to Bolton School, had declared that 'As long as there shall be anyone of the Blood, Kindred and Name of the said Robert Lever, the founder, dwelling within the Town or Parish of Bolton aforesaid, or within twenty miles thereof, who shall be deemed fit to be made Governors, they shall respectively be appointed Governors accordingly, in case of vacancy.' This probably referred to a wish of Robert Lever. On the strength of this, in 1898 Sir W. H. Lever, later Lord Leverhulme, was invited to become a governor, being a native of the town (although he had not attended the school). Whether he was, in fact, related to Robert Lever is uncertain. He became a munificent benefactor, providing land, buildings and income from shares in Lever Brothers. A move was made to new buildings in 1965, and there are now over a thousand day-boys in the school.*

The grammar school at Newcastle upon Tyne was yet another school founded at this time by a wealthy merchant. It came into being under the will of Thomas Horsley, in 1525, a former mayor of the town. The school opened some years later. The school was not to be free, but the charge of five shillings quarterly was not prohibitive. In 1600 the school was incorporated as a free grammar school, under a charter of Elizabeth. Seven years later it moved into the buildings of the Hospital of St. Mary the Virgin, an almshouse, with which it merged financially; it remained on this site until 1844. During the late eighteenth century, under the headmastership of Hugh Moises, the Royal Grammar School, Newcastle, gained a great reputation, at a time when education generally was at a low ebb. The school always had close links with the corporation, and for many years the first public function of a newly elected mayor was to visit the school, where he also relinquished his office at the end of his term. It retained its free status in the nineteenth century, but is now a Direct Grant school, charging fees, with a fee-remission scheme. The present headmaster, W. D. Haden, was the last

* Sir Geoffrey Jackson and critic Irving Wardle are among the old boys.

headmaster of Mercers' School, London. The academic standard is extremely high.*

Another northern school, Sedbergh, has derived over the centuries from a chantry school, founded by Roger Lupton, a Canon of Windsor, who became Provost of Eton for thirty-two years. Sedbergh, in Yorkshire, was his native place, and in deciding to remember it in his seventies with a chantry he wrote that his object was 'the maintaining and increase of virtue and learning in Christ's Church', and for his 'soul's health'. The endowment was completed in 1528 and it bound the free grammar chantry school to St. John's College, Cambridge, the Fellows of which were to govern the school. This was done to such purpose that the headmasters, over the centuries, were seldom anything but St. John's men. At the suppression of the chantries, under Henry VIII and Edward VI, the school almost ceased for ever, and only survived because of the efforts of St. John's, which augured, 'if the schools are abolished, the University will perish'. In fact, the school was closed for over a year, but re-opened in 1551 as a lay school, but still connected with St. John's, which retained the right to appoint the headmaster. The costs for the school, still free, were to be found from the proceeds of the suppressed chantries. The twelve governors, who were under the direction of St. John's, were to be local men of 'the more discreet and better inhabitants of the town and parish'. The school served boys from the dales and gained a good reputation. In 1722 Aldenham School advertised that the methods used in teaching Latin and Greek there were 'after the short and most accurate method of Sedbergh School'. But later, between about 1740 and 1875, the school was often in near eclipse. By the time Henry George Day became headmaster, in 1861, Sedbergh was in dire straits. Day had no feeling for the task; he 'had a habit of walking close to a wall or a fence and this caused him to be called an eccentric and wanting in common intelligence'. The school's historian records: 'Mr. Day gave up having boardings in his house for the simple reason that they made his life unbearable.' Sedbergh became a village school, with a few local boys and about four or five boys lodging in houses in

* Former scholars: Nicholas Ridley, sixteenth-century martyr, Mark Akenside, poet, John Brand, antiquary, Admiral Lord Collingwood, who commanded at Trafalgar after Nelson's death, and Lord Eldon, Pitt's Lord Chancellor. In recent times: Sir Henry Wilson Smith, Professor R. J. Scothorne, anatomist, George Gale, editor of the *Spectator*.

the district. In 1866 there were only ten boys at the school. During the enquiries of the Charity Commissioners in the eighteen-sixties no school had a worse report than Sedbergh; the commissioner said, bluntly: 'as to Sedbergh, I despair of putting it into any class at all. In its present state it simply cumbers the ground.'

However, better days were ahead. The school survived these strictures, but was reorganised. The appointment of the headmaster was taken away from St. John's and the governors were given complete control; residence in the parish of Sedbergh was no longer a condition of governorship. Modern subjects were to be taught. Tuition, as well as boarding, fees were established. The first headmaster under the new regime was Frederick Heppenstall, who had just spent ten years at the Perse School, where he had raised the numbers from 100 to 145, had re-established the finances, and had secured a high standard of scholarship. Heppenstall found that the headmaster's house was 'unfit for habitation' and scholarship has 'completely disappeared'. In five years the number of boys increased to ninety-one, new buildings were opened and playing-fields acquired. Sedbergh was fortunate in its headmasters from that time. The school continued to grow in size and reputation under H. G. Hart, C. Lowry (who went on to Tonbridge), F. M. Malim (who went on to Haileybury and Wellington), and W. N. Weech. Sedbergh, with the great advantage of its ideal setting in the hills, became one of the great schools of the north, as it had occasionally promised to do in the past. There are now nearly 450 boys in the school, but only about ten are day-boys.*

The Crypt School, Gloucester, is one of three great schools of that city, the others being the Blue Coat Hospital (founded in 1666 by Sir Thomas Rich) and King's. King's is the successor to the original grammar school of the city, but Crypt is the oldest continuous foundation. The School of St. Mary de Crypt was founded by the will of John Cooke in May 1528. The master, preferably a priest, was to 'say mass every week within the parish church of Christ near

* Former pupils: John Haggarth, who urged for the enquiry into endowed schools, William Craven, Vice-Chancellor of Cambridge University, and Adam Sedgwick, Cambridge geographer (he held the chair at the university for thirty-five years). Those of more recent times: General Sir John Shea, Brendan Bracken, Lord Wakefield, Lord Helsby, former head of the civil service, Lieut.-Colonel F. Spencer Chapman, D. A. Rickards, founder headmaster of Welbeck College, M. S. Mitchell-Innes, cricketer, and historians H. Montgomery Hyde, Philip Woodruff, Noble Frankland and Robert Rhodes-James.

adjoining unto the said free school and have for his stipend yearly
£10'. In 1539, after Cooke's death, the school was endowed by his
widow, Dame Joan Cooke, and it opened in 1540. W. E. Henley
was educated at the Crypt, under T. E. Brown, headmaster in the
late eighteen-fifties (q.v. King William's College below). In the
following year the old ecclesiastical grammar school (King's) was
refounded by Henry VIII, having been extinct since the dissolution
of the monasteries. It was in this year that Gloucester became a see
and a cathedral city, having previously been under Worcester. The
previous grammar school had gained some fame in 1410, when it
had been the subject of a well-known law case; the grammar school
had sought redress against a rival establishment, claiming it had the
only licence; it had been decided that 'to teach youth is a virtuous
and charitable thing to do and helpful to the people for which a man
cannot be punished by our law'. It was therefore apt that Gloucester was, in the second half of the sixteenth century, one of the few
towns which boasted of two good grammar schools. The new
foundation was placed under the control of the Dean and Chapter,
as it still is to this day, and was for long known as the Cathedral
School. The buildings are beside the cathedral and date from the
thirteenth century to science laboratories built in 1967. The main
building was once the Bishop's palace. Nearly a quarter of the boys
are boarders, distributed between three houses in the precincts. The
cathedral choristers are educated at the school.

Another school in this area, founded at about the same time, is
Bristol. It existed, under a lay-master, in 1532, but was refounded in
that year under a charter of Henry VIII, financed by the estates of
St. Bartholomew's Hospital, which it received from Lord de la
Warr, Robert Thorne, and others. The control of the school was
placed with the Corporation of Bristol, from whom it passed to the
Trustees of the Bristol Municipal Charities in 1836, where it remains. Fees, and a boarding house, were introduced in the last
century; in the mid-nineteenth century it was closed, but by 1870
there were thirteen masters. Bristol Grammar School has received
several benefactions in the twentieth century, and it began its
present reputation under Sir Cyril Norwood, 1906-16, one of the
great public school headmasters of this century, who went on to
Marlborough and Harrow. It is now a Direct Grant day school of
about a thousand boys, in buildings adjacent to the university. Old
boys include W. L. Ferrar, mathematician, Lord Gridley and Lord

Franks. Collyer's School, Horsham, was founded by Richard Collyer, a London mercer, in 1532. His will provided for 'threescore scolars', and 'the said scolars to be at noo charge of their scole hire'. Collyer's was placed under the government of the Mercers' Company and was reconstituted in 1889. It still has close links with the Company.

Other cathedral schools founded at the same time as King's, Gloucester, were King's, Worcester, King's, Chester, and King's, Peterborough, the latter two at new cathedrals. King's, Worcester, traces its origin to a cathedral school of the seventh century, but its present existence dates from a charter of Henry VIII in 1541. Provision was made for the education of forty free scholars, to be instructed in Latin and Greek by two masters. The school was reorganised in 1834 as a fee-paying public school, but the Dean and Chapter kept their position on the governing body, and twenty of the original forty King's scholarships were retained. In 1944 King's took over the small cathedral choir school. The school still occupies its splendid original site in the quadrangles around College Green, in the shadow of one of the greatest of all English cathedrals, and its life still centres around the superb fourteenth-century Hall, one of the finest possessions of any school in Britain.

The King's School, Chester, was founded in the same year under the auspices of Henry VIII. Classes were held for over three hundred years in what had been the refectory of the old abbey. By the time it came under the authority of the Endowed Schools Act of 1873, it was still providing free education to twenty-four King's scholars, elected by examination, but its three exhibitions to Oxford and Cambridge had not been awarded 'from time immemorial'. From that date the school recovered, sending many boys to the universities and gaining a reputation in rowing. It is now a Direct Grant day school, in new buildings just outside Chester, but the Bishop is still chairman of the governors. Sir John Vanbrugh is the most famous old boy. King's, Peterborough, also dating from 1541, was a twin foundation. Like Chester and Gloucester, it was also known as the Cathedral School until near the end of the nineteenth century. The school was founded as a grammar school under the new cathedral, the old abbey church. It remained in the precincts until 1885, when the need for expansion brought about the move to its present site in Park Road, in the northern suburbs of the city. Unfortunately, the main playing-fields are about twelve minutes'

5a. St. Paul's, 1816

5b. St. Paul's. The new school at Barnes

6a. King's, Canterbury

6b. Sherborne

7a.   Shrewsbury, 1896

7b.   Drilling the Blue-Coat Boys in the new playground
at Christ's Hospital, 1858

8a. Tonbridge, 1830

8b. Oundle

walk away; a rugger school, King's, Peterborough, plays, among
other schools, Culford, King's, Ely, King's, Grantham, Perse and
Stamford. In 1948 it became a Voluntary Aided school, the governing body consisting of the Dean, the residentiary canons, governors
co-opted by them, and four representatives of the Local Education
Authority. It has, like other Voluntary Aided schools, retained considerable freedom while at the same time being able to offer boarding
education at fees even less than those of Direct Grant schools. Out
of about 460 boys, seventy are boarders, including choristers. In
1970 the boarding fees were £132 per annum.

King's, Peterborough's nearest rival is Stamford School, which
was founded by William Radcliffe in 1532; poor scholars were to be
taught free. It probably opened some years later. By the second half
of the nineteenth century Stamford was still a free grammar school,
catering for about sixty boys. The present chapel was used as the
schoolroom for over three centuries. Stamford is still predominantly
a day school for boys of the town and the surrounding area. Sir
Malcolm Sargent and Sir Michael Tippett were at the school, and
M. J. K. Smith, the cricketer and rugby player, is another old boy.

*

The oldest Irish public school is Kilkenny College. For historical
and political reasons, boarding and grammar schools in Ireland have
been mostly Protestant until recent times. St. John's College,
Kilkenny, was founded in 1538 by the Earl of Ormonde. It is a
classic example of a school benefiting from a patron family. It was
moved to its present site in grounds beside the River Nore, in 1684,
when it was re-endowed by the Duke of Ormonde, and fine Georgian
buildings, still in use, were erected in 1782. The great castle of the
Ormondes stands across the river. The school has produced more
distinguished men than any other school in Ireland, including Dean
Swift, William Congreve, Bishop George Berkeley, the philosopher,
Richard Baldwin, the mysterious Provost of Trinity College, Dublin,
John Banim, the Irish author, Thomas Pryor, founder of the Royal
Dublin Society, William Connor Magee, Archbishop of York, and
Admiral of the Fleet Earl Beatty. Magee was involved in the tem-
perance question in the late nineteenth century, and it was he who
declared in the House of Lords: 'I would rather see England free
than England compulsorily sober.' The school is governed by the
Society for Promoting Protestant Schools in Ireland, and the

committee includes the Marquis of Ormonde, the Bishop of Ossory, and the Provost of Trinity College.

Berkhamsted School was founded in 1541 by John Incent, Dean of St. Paul's, who may well have been influenced by Colet's foundation. He was a native of Berkhamsted, and his school was intended for 144 boys. It received the estate of St. John's Hospital, of the town. An Elizabethan narrative says that 'the said Deane (not without the helpe of the Towne and Countrey) builded with all speed a faire Schoole large and great, all of brick and freestone very sumptuously with a lodging for the Schoolmaster joyning to the west end of the same. The whole building is so strong and faire that the like Grammar Schoole for that point is not to be seene in the whole Realme of England'. Despite this auspicious start, the school's fortunes were indifferent; it seldom achieved its full complement of 144 pupils. During the eighteenth century the numbers fell to as few as five. The affairs of the school were in Chancery for the remarkable period of 1741 to 1842. It was kept going by August Smith, and was finally rejuvenated by the Rev. J. M. Crawford, headmaster from 1850 to 1864. By the time of Crawford's departure Berkhamsted was relatively rich, with two boarding houses for sixty or seventy boys, as well as the 144 free scholars. Dr. Fry, headmaster 1888 to 1910, consolidated Crawford's work. Fry dipped generously into his own pocket to enlarge the school property, until today it has a prominent position in the centre of the town, on the north of the High Street; the original building, 'large and great', is still in use. Only three free places remain, awarded by the Hertfordshire County Council.*

Christ's College, Brecon, one of the leading public schools in Wales, was also founded in 1541, on the site of a dissolved monastery. It was to be a free grammar school 'for instruction of all persons willing to be taught in good literature gratis'. A school had existed at Brecon for many years previously, and Christ's College inherited buildings dating from the thirteenth century. It was reconstituted in 1853 and is now a school of just over 250 boys, only about twenty of whom are day-boys. The school is notable for its fine buildings and for the fact that it is one of the few public schools which makes arrangements for entry at eleven years, direct from the state system. Dr. Glyn Thomas, Archbishop of Wales 1968–71, was

* Old boys include Graham Greene, Hugh Carleton Greene (sons of a headmaster of the school), Claud Cockburn, Lord Fiske, Prof. Colin Buchanan, Robin Knox-Johnston, first solo non-stop circumnavigator of the world.

educated at Christ's, Brecon. Professor Alan Ross, of 'U' and 'Non-U' fame, and Lord Hall, were also at the school.

Christ's, Brecon, was a typical foundation of the Reformation, based on a former abbey school, as Berkhamsted was a typical private foundation, after the style of Colet, of the same time, and Mercers' School, London, was a typical livery company school, founded in the following year. A school had been in existence in the fifteenth century (Colet is said to have been educated there), but had been dissolved under Henry VIII in 1538. In 1542 the remaining revenues were taken over by the Mercers' Company, which established a free grammar school for twenty-five boys. The school's fortunes reflected the fluctuating fortunes of the Mercers' Company. By the end of the nineteenth century the numbers had risen to seventy free scholars, and fee-payers were also being taken. But the Mercers' School was confined by its premises in the city, off Holborn, and the Company decided to close it in the nineteenth-fifties, although the numbers were still over two hundred. Sir Thomas Gresham was educated at the school, and, on a very different plane, in the twentieth century the old boy to achieve the greatest fame was the thriller writer Peter Cheyney.

With Dauntsey's School, Devizes, we return to individual foundations. It was founded by William Dauntsey, a member of the Mercers' Company, in 1543. The Mercers' Company, represented on the board of governors, retains a close interest in it. The school did not come to prominence until near the end of the nineteenth century, being refounded in 1895, after it was discovered that the income from Dauntsey's property had not been properly and fully used. New buildings, some six miles from Devizes, were begun in 1895. The new school was opened by Joseph Chamberlain. Dauntsey's has been expanded ever since the First World War, and it now stands, with the acquisition of the imposing manor house, in grounds of 130 acres. Between the world wars it became known for its modern outlook on boarding education, under G. W. Olive, 1919–55, who turned Dauntsey's from a local into a national school. Olive had been a master at Oundle under Sanderson. The main benefactors, providing splendid modern facilities, have been S. W. Farmer and the Mercers' Company. A comparatively unusual feature of the school nowadays is that the boys wear shorts. Like Christ's, Brecon, the school facilitates entry at eleven. Old boys include A. G. Street and that fine novelist Nigel Balchin.

Other schools founded or refounded under Henry VIII are: Lewes Grammar School (1512), Colchester Royal Grammar School (1539), Northampton Grammar School (1541), Abergavenny Grammar School (1543), Henry VIII, Coventry (1545), and Archbishop Holgate's, York (1546); the last named still takes boarders. Schools founded or re-founded in the reign of Edward VI include: King's, Pontefract (1548); Maidstone Grammar School (1549); King Edward VI schools at Bury St. Edmund's (1550), Chelmsford (1551), Lichfield (attended by Samuel Johnson), Ludlow, Stourbridge (1552), Southampton and Totnes (1553);* Leeds Grammar School, now Direct Grant (1552), founded by Sir William Sheafield for the 'Education of the Youths in the Learned Languages'; Coopers' Company School, in East London, founded by Nicholas Gibbon in 1552 as a free school under that company; and Guildford Royal Grammar School, a very old school re-established in 1553; King Edward VI, Louth, 1551, was attended by Tennyson; King Edward VI Grammar School, Stratford on Avon, was re-established in 1553, but a grammar school had been founded in 1482. William Shakespeare was a pupil about 1577. Also re-founded in 1553 was King's, Grantham. It has originally been founded by Richard Fox, Bishop of Winchester, in 1528. This was the same Richard Fox who had founded King's, Taunton, and these are therefore sister schools. King's, Grantham, produced two of the greatest of Englishmen: William Cecil and Isaac Newton. The philosopher Henry More was also there. Newton is said to have been head boy at the age of fourteen. During the seventeenth and eighteenth centuries Grantham continued to send out many eminent men. Two original school buildings are still in use. Typically for a post-Reformation school, it had the Aldermen and Mayor specifically named as trustees, with the power to appoint the headmaste. And for making statutes relating to the school they were required only to seek the 'advice' of the Bishop of the diocese. Today more than one in every ten boys is a boarder.

Truro Cathedral School traces its descent from a chantry school attached to St. Mary's Church. After the suppression of the chantries it became known as Truro Grammar School, having been refounded in 1549. Originally a free school, by 1870 there were no free scholars at all. The see of Truro was founded in 1876 and the school came to

* King Edward's, Totnes, had been previously founded in 1533, and King Edward's, Southampton, in 1534.

provide the choir for the cathdral, which it still does. The Dean and Chapter assumed responsibility for the school in 1906, and the Bishop is president of the governing body. The school is now situated in spacious grounds outside the city and includes the former palace of the Bishops of Truro. The old school, in the cathedral close, has been retained as the science block; this is in keeping, for the most famous old boy is Sir Humphry Davy, the chemist and inventor of the Davy lamp (who showed, however, little aptitude for science at school). Two other old boys were closely connected with India: Henry Martyn, perhaps the greatest of missionaries to that country, and Admiral Viscount Exmouth, who scoured the seas for Anglo-Indian commerce in the Napoleonic wars.

One of the most famous foundations of Edward VI's reign is Sherborne. Latin schooling had been available at the small Dorset town of Sherborne, possibly since 705, associated with the monastery and abbey. But practically nothing is known of this except that under the Chantries Act the school was allowed to be 'carried on for the time being'. In 1550, however, it seems that a completely new school was contemplated, for the following instruction was issued: 'The kinges maiestie, by thadvice of his prevy Counsaill, is pleased and contented that a free grammer Schole shalbe erected and established in Shirborne in the Countie of Dorset and Landes to the yerely value of £20 to be geven and assured by his highnes to the maynetenaunce thereof.' Until 1871 it was known as the King's School, with more right to that title than some. The statutes of the school were taken from those of St. Paul's. It was housed in a room of the disused monastery, where it remained for fifty years, with a quadrangle and a School House for the headmaster. Apart from an addition in 1670, this site was little changed for nearly three hundred years. Under Benjamin Wilding, headmaster in the early eighteenth century (previously headmaster of King Edward's, Bath), the school began to take paying boarders, the first being from Exeter; this break with the tradition of educating only local boys caused a furore, but the principle was established and from then on boys from all over the West Country stayed with the headmaster and the usher, and eventually, when the school expanded, in the houses of other masters. Wilding was dismissed, but appealed to the Lord Chancellor and won his case. This was not the only controversy at Sherborne; from about 1650 to 1800 there seems to have seldom been a period when the headmasters were not bitterly engaged with the governors, mostly local men and old boys of the school. Naturally Sherborne did not thrive under such circumstances; boarders varied between about a hundred and under half a dozen.

Over the centuries the routine at Sherborne remained much the same. The boys were summoned to roll-call and prayers by the bell at 6.0 a.m. in the summer and 7.0 a.m. in the winter. After this there was grammar till 8.0 a.m., after which the boys went 'forth two by two and passe the streats in quiett and decent order to their breakfast'. From 9.0 to 11.0 there were more lessons, dinner being from 11.0 to 12.30. There was more work from 1.0 to 3.0 p.m. and 4.0 to 5.0, 'at which hour, thaie all having said the appoynted praier and sung a psalme shall depart for all night'. In the evening the gates were locked and boarders prevented from going into the town without permission. Holidays were restricted by statute to no more than thirty days a year; the master was allowed another thirty on top of this, which he must have been well able to use, and the usher another twenty. There were six forms, the headmaster having the top three, the usher the remainder, all in the same room. The curriculum included Latin, Greek and arithmetic, but little time was spent on the last two.

Dr. Ralph Lyon, headmaster 1823–45, introduced a system of school examinations; this was considered so unnecessary at the time that he was obliged to pay for the printing himself. Sherborne first became a school with a reputation known throughout the country under H. D. Harper, headmaster 1850–77. He had previously been head of Cowbridge School in Glamorgan, which he had raised to a high standard. On his arrival there were forty boys at Sherborne, two of them boarders, the remainder local boys receiving a free education; he was the only master. When he left, to become Principal of Jesus College, Oxford, there were 278 boys, only thirty of whom were day-boys; there were eighteen masters. One of the boys Harper brought with him from Cowbridge was to become Sir Lewis Morris, poet and instigator of a University of Wales. Harper played an important part in the founding of the Headmasters' Conference. There was a brief decline after Harper's departure, brought on partly by the bad publicity following a celebrated law case in which a master sued Harper's successor for libel; a great deal of petty rivalry and school politics was aired in the press, and numbers fell so low that one housemaster sold his house (which he was entitled to do). The headmaster resigned in 1892, publishing as he did so all the relevant correspondence in *The Times*. After that the school revived, particularly under the fruitful headships of Nowell Smith and A. R. Wallace (formerly headmaster of Blundell's). However, Sherborne seemed fated to be the centre of controversy. In 1917 a boy who had recently left, Alec Waugh, still only seventeen, wrote a novel called *The Loom of Youth*. It was the first of the realist public school novels, depicting boarding life in the raw, and it was something of a sensation; many Shirburnians were horrified. In 1946 *The Guinea Pig*, by W. Chetham-Strode, who had also been at Sherborne, appeared as a play and later a film: a good account of the attempts of a public school to come to terms with a new society.*

Perhaps the two most famous schools named after Edward VI are at Bath and Birmingham. King Edward's, Bath, was founded in 1552 for the free education of ten poor boys of the city. Funds were to be provided from 102 properties, including the famous hot springs, which had formerly belonged to the priory. For nearly two hundred years the school occupied the nave of St. Mary's Church. By 1870 the number of free foundations had increased to fifty, the property of the school being not invaluable. In 1762 the school moved to new buildings, and again in 1961. It is now a Direct Grant day school. Old boys of King Edward's, Bath, include William Prynne, the Puritan, Admiral Sir Sydney Smith, Sir W. E. Parry, Arctic explorer, Sir H. Bartle Frere, S. A. Pears, the first great headmaster of Repton, and Major-General J. G. le Marchant, founder of the R.M.C. Sandhurst. According to his headmaster, le Marchant was 'the greatest dunce I have ever met'. King Edward's, Birmingham, was founded in the same year, after a petition from certain of the townspeople, as a free school 'for the educacion instrucion and institucion of children and younge men in Grammer forever'. It was endowed with the possessions of the Guild of the Holy Cross. The governors were to be 'twentie honeste and discrete men Inhabitants of the towne and parishe of Birmingham'. The

---

* Other distinguished old boys of Sherborne: A. N. Whitehead, the great mathematician, General Sir Charles Munro, who was in charge of the evacuation at Gallipoli, John Cowper Powys, author and poet, Viscount Boyd, a government minister between 1938 and 1959, Admiral Sir H. R. Moore, Commander-in-Chief Home Fleet 1944–45, Gerald Sparrow, Lord Milligan, M. W. McCrum, headmaster of Tonbridge and Eton, C. Day-Lewis, the Rev. David Sheppard, actor Robert Harris, historian Hugh Thomas, Christopher Chataway and John le Carré.

grammar school prospered, and when the town grew to a great metropolis it gave birth to an educational complex of five more grammar schools and a High School for girls—now about four thousand pupils. King Edward's began its great reputation for scholarship in Victorian days under James Prince Lee, 1838–69, who had been a master at Rugby under Arnold. King Edward's itself is now a Direct Grant day school of some seven hundred boys, many of them receiving free education, in pleasing accordance with the ancient foundation.*

Bedford School was almost certainly the direct successor to an earlier foundation that may have gone back to before the Conquest. At the dissolution of the monasteries it was handed over to the Mayor and corporation, receiving its licence in 1552 from Edward VI, with the customary command to instruct 'in grammatical learning and good manners'. However, it was not well provided for, and in 1566 Sir William Harper (or Harpur), a Lord Mayor of London, endowed the grammar school in his home town, granting it lands in Bedford and in London, South Bloomsbury. By 1868 there were about 225 boys in the school, sixty of them boarders. Harper's fine School House remained the school's centre until 1892, when the school moved to its present buildings nearer the open country. Harper's estate became extremely valuable; it is still one of the most important landholders in central London. In 1866 it brought in £3,914, worth perhaps ten times that figure today. Bedford, still called Bedford Grammar School until shortly before the First World War, changed from a rich local grammar school to an important national school. This was achieved under the head-masterships of Phillpotts and Carter. By 1913 there were eight hundred boys, two hundred of them boarders. The school developed into one of the four main services schools, with Cheltenham, Haileybury and Wellington, supplying officers for the overseas and military services. A prospectus of 1913 said of the O.T.C.: 'It is most desirable that all boys over fourteen should join. Uniform supplied. Boys not in corps required to attend such drill when

* E. W. Benson, Archbishop of Canterbury, Sir Nathan Bodington, founder of Leeds University, Sir Francis Galton, discoverer of anticyclones, Edward Burne-Jones, artist, Sir Napier Shaw, the first modern meteorologist, H. V. Morton, Field-Marshal Viscount Slim, Air Marshal Sir Robert Saundby, Enoch Powell, J. R. R. Tolkien, Kenneth Tynan, Leonard Cottrell and Godfrey Winn figure among the old boys.

ordered.' At this time the boarding and tuition fees were £83 per annum.*

Bedford had the educational schism of most large towns from the end of the eighteenth century, centred round the classics versus modern controversy. Unlike most old grammar schools, but like Birmingham, it was rich enough to provide a modern school itself, thus safeguarding its position; the Harper trust was quite able to provide for another school, the Commercial School as it was first called, later known as Bedford Modern. For a time its entrance and fees were the same as that of the grammar school: free day-boys to be sons of inhabitant householders, others paying a £10 entrance fee and a guinea annually. Competition between the two schools was furious in the nineteenth century; on at least one occasion the police had to be called to separate the boys. But in this century the schools have gone much their own way, Bedford taking on the role of a national public school with some day-boys, while Bedford Modern has taken over the role of the good local day school with some boarders. Bedford Modern's most famous old boy this century is Christopher Fry.

The foundation of Shrewsbury School was typical of the mid-sixteenth century. The townspeople were worried about the lack of educational facilities owing to the religious changes, and they petitioned the king for the foundation of a grammar school. Edward VI and his advisers agreed, and a charter was signed on 10 February 1552. The school, it seems, was 'free' only in the sense that it was free of church control; although most schools of this time provided for a few scholars without fees, the ambiguity of the word 'free' seems to have caused some confusion. Nine years later Thomas Ashton became headmaster and made the school into one of the best in England. Although the charter only provided for one usher, Ashton engaged two. A year after he arrived there were 266 boys in the school, many of them boarding at houses in the town. This may well have made Shrewsbury the largest school in the country at that

---

* Bedford, not surprisingly, has produced two Chiefs of the Air Staff, Marshals of the R.A.F. Sir C. Newall and Sir Thomas Pike, a Chief of the Imperial General Staff, Field-Marshal Sir C. J. Deverall, and a Vice-C.I.G.S., Lieut.-General Sir W. Pike. Others: Vice-Admiral Sir J. Hughes-Hallett, M.P., naval commander on the Dieppe raid, Jack Beresford, one of Britain's greatest rowers, H. H. Munro ('Saki'), Hesketh Pearson, Sir Eric Drummond, the first Secretary-General of the League of Nations, 1919–33, Sir Frank Nelson, head of S.O.E. in the Second World War, Sir Pierson Dixon, Joseph Godber.

time; the headmaster of Westminster described it in 1586 as 'the largest school in all England'. New ordinances were issued under Ashton, the most important being that masters were to be appointed by St. John's College, Cambridge (already serving Sedbergh in much the same way), and were preferably to have been educated at the school. Shrewsbury continued successfully until about 1700, producing three Speakers of the House of Commons. But between 1700 and 1800 it was in deep decline, the result not only of the worsening in education generally but of disputes with the town and a succession of headmasters from St. John's as incompetent as those that college was sending to Sedbergh. In 1797 the headmaster of Rugby wrote wryly of Shrewsbury: 'There is a school there . . . [which] was once the Eton or Westminster of Wales and of all Shropshire.'

In 1798 a Bill was passed repealing Ashton's ordinances, taking the school out of the control of the town and headmaster, and placing it in the hands of trustees, men of local standing in Shropshire; St. John's retained the appointment of headmaster, but a better choice was now encouraged. The first headmaster under the new order was a Fellow of the college, the Rev. Samuel Butler. The renewed prominence of Shrewsbury was due entirely to this appointment, and to the fact that in the nineteenth century the school had only three headmasters (they cover, indeed, 110 years), all of them of the highest quality. Few schools, if any, had such an advantage at that most important time in the history of the public schools. Butler virtually restarted the school. Arriving at the age of twenty-four, he remained for thirty-eight years. He found the school in poor shape, not least in discipline. He was a martinet, and made frequent use of the birch, although he tried to deny it. Of one boy he wrote: 'I flogged him by main force.' To a parent he wrote: 'With regard to the punishment itself, it is one which I hold to be the best for little boys and the worst for big ones, and which I administer accordingly.' He inflicted it, on average, three times a week. As he said, 'it became a question whether I or the boys were to govern'. In 1818 some boys rebelled, and Butler was obliged to seek police protection; similar revolts occurred at Eton, Winchester and Charterhouse at about the same time.

Butler instituted the custom of Speech Day as early as 1821. He did not believe in widening the curriculum of the old schools, and he told Lord Brougham that the old grammar schools were founded to teach 'learned languages' and not 'English reading, writing and accounts'; he believed that separate 'commercial' schools should be founded for such purposes, and this in fact was what happened at many places, including Bedford, as has been seen. Butler resigned in 1836, having been granted the bishopric he had long desired. At one time he had written: 'I slaved and toiled under every difficulty and disadvantage. . . . I felt myself under-estimated and underpaid.' He had found less than twenty boys at the school: he left it with well over two hundred. In his closing words to the school Butler prayed that 'my successors may labour faithfully, zealously and happily in their calling, training those who are confided to their care in the principles of true religion and sound learning, and endeavouring to make them good Christians, good scholars and honourable and use- ful members of society. Amen.' His successor was yet another St. John's man, B. H. Kennedy, who had been educated at the school under Butler. He was a considerable classicist, being author of the famous Latin primer, and a brilliant teacher. His regime lasted from 1836 to 1866, and under it Shrewsbury gained a high academic reputation. Kennedy was followed by the Rev. W. H. Moss, it goes almost without saying a Fellow of St. John's and a boy at the school under Kennedy. Under Moss there were two great events: the in- clusion of the school in the seven schools of the Public Schools Act, which abolished the right of St. John's to appoint the headmaster (although this system had certainly justified itself in the end), and a move to a site of twenty-seven acres outside the town. On this basis Shrewsbury expanded in the twentieth century from about 300 to 539 boys in 1936, and 580 today.

The duties of a praeposter, or prefect at Shrewsbury, were pro- pounded between the wars: 'The duty of a praeposter is to promote the welfare of the School, both by his example and by his authority. He is therefore responsible for maintaining a tone worthy of Shrewsbury, and for discouraging all such things as would in any way lower that tone. It is further his duty to see that the Rules of the School are observed, and he is especially charged with the protection of the younger members of the School.' Old Salopians include Sir Philip Sidney, soldier, statesman, diplomat and poet. In a famous letter, Sidney's father wrote to him at Shrewsbury: 'Let your first action be the lifting up of your mind to almighty God by hearty prayer, and feelingly digest the words you speak in prayer with continual meditation. . . . Apply your study such hours as your discreet

Master doth assign you earnestly, and the time I know he will so limit as shall be both sufficient for your learning, yea, and safe for your health; and mark the sense and matter of that you do read as well as the words, so shall you enrich your tongue with words, and your wit with matter, and judgement will grow, as years groweth in you. Be humble and obedient to your master, for unless you frame yourself to obey others, yea, and feel in yourself what obedience is, you shall never be able to teach others how to obey you. Be courteous of gesture, and affable unto all men, with diversity of reverence according to the dignity of the person; there is nothing that winneth so much with so little cost.' Other Salopians are the first Marquess of Halifax ('the Trimmer'), Charles Darwin, Gathorne Hardy (first Earl of Cranbrook), Sir Charles Newton, archaeologist, Graham Wallas, political economist, Sir Frederick Jackson, explorer of Africa, Lord Croft, and General Sir Bernard Paget, Commander-in-Chief Home Forces in the Second World War. Writers this century who were at Shrewsbury include Sir Owen Seaman, H. W. Nevinson, Paul Dehn, Nevil Shute, Francis King and Richard Hillary. Of the latter, his biographer says: 'This bright mind and quick imagination were just at the point to be caught and directed by a really good teacher. Such a one, with all the necessary tact and understanding, there was at Shrewsbury in the person of Mr. McEachran. Richard confided to this master, who had lent him various books, that he wanted to become a writer. . . . McEachran's genius was not to think this presumptuous in a fifteen-year-old boy, and instead to lead him by way of worthwhile books to an appreciation of good writing, and to encourage in him an ambition which is so often the subject of ridicule if anyone professes before attempting it. Richard was never to forget McEachran's influence. His name came up often in his talk, and once, broadcasting in America, he named him as the greatest influence in his life. Shrewsbury set its stamp upon him.' Brian Inglis is another writer from Shrewsbury: 'That first term was spent doing little else but absorbing the school code of what was done. I was soon aware that it bore little resemblance to the school rules. . . . At Shrewsbury everything was rigidly prescribed, according to seniority as measured by year-group. Like race-horses, the boys—though we always referred to each other as "men"—were known after the scrum age as two-year-olds, three-year-olds and four-year-olds, each having its distinctions and privileges. New boys wore that ultimate degradation, the Eton collar. . . . Masters were not trusted to beat boys; monitors were. How extensively they availed themselves of the privilege depended less on the state of indiscipline in the house than on how much they enjoyed beating as a pastime.'*

Bromsgrove School was also re-founded by Edward VI, in 1553, and was given a charter by Mary and Philip. A school had existed at Bromsgrove previously, the first mention being 1548, and it may have been in existence before 1476. The school was re-endowed by Sir Thomas Cooke in 1693 for the free education of twelve poor scholars of the town or neighbourhood in Latin, English, writing and arithmetic, and with exhibitions to Worcester College, Oxford. There were many fee-paying boarders, however, and Cooke's endowment caused Bromsgrove to become one of the leading schools in the eighteenth century, when so many others were on the decline. The school fell on hard times in the early nineteenth century, and from then on was slow to grow. One headmaster was dismissed for staying nine days in a public-house, another was 'guilty of frequent inebriation in public as well as private, in the pothouse and elsewhere'. The school revived later in the century, opening a 'Modern Department' about 1860. By 1919 there were 190 boys, and Bromsgrove came to the fore under R. G. Routh, 1913–31. Amazingly enough, after so many years, the Cooke family retain their association with the school, providing an hereditary governor, and so does Worcester College.† Edward VI was also responsible for the establishment of Bridewell penitentiary, in 1553, in what had previously been a royal palace built for Henry VIII. It was mainly for vagabonds and loose women, and lasted for over three hundred years, being closed in 1855. The school associated with Bridewell in its later years, lives on as King Edward's School, Witley, in Surrey.

*

We now come to the last two great schools founded in the reign of Edward VI: Christ's Hospital and Tonbridge. Christ's Hospital is one of the most noble achievements in English education, founded, and continued over the centuries, out of goodwill and charity. It is

* Old Salopians in other fields: A Chenevix-Trench, headmaster of Bradfield, Eton and Fettes, Sir F. Catherwood, Richard Todd, actor, Richard Ingrams, editor of *Private Eye*.

† A. E. Housman, Lord Thomas of Remenham, Air Chief Marshal Sir Basil Embry, Sir Noel Hall, Principal of Brasenose College, Oxford are old boys.

said to owe its existence to a sermon preached before the boy king by Nicholas Ridley, Bishop of London, in 1552. Ridley's subject was charity, and Edward was so impressed that he asked the bishop for suggestions as to how he could best comply. Ridley impressed upon him the special needs of London, and suggested he should speak to the Lord Mayor. The result of this was the establishment of St. Thomas's Hospital, the re-endowment of St. Bartholomew's Hospital, the establishment of Bridewell prison and the establishment of a school and home for 'fatherless children and other poor men's children' in the premises of the old Grey Friars monastery near Newgate, which had been put to little use since its dissolution in 1538. The school was, for the time, lavishly provided: a master (at £15 per annum), clerk and writing master, a doctor, various educational and domestic assistants, and a matron with twenty-five sisters. The school, or Hospital as it was known opened on 23 November 1552, with 380 children, boys and girls. Education began the following year.

From soon after the start, the boys were wearing the uniform of blue habits and yellow stockings, much the same as they wear today. They were immediately a familiar sight in London, as they remained for centuries, known to the citizens of the place as 'Blues'. Before long the school began to develop as a grammar school for boys rather than as a home for foundlings; the girls were gradually removed elsewhere, ending up at Hertford. This development took place slowly and over a long period; very small children were still at the Hospital in the seventeenth century. Of actual schoolchildren in 1581, 115 were day-children from the city, and only forty-two from the Hospital itself. Most children left the school early to enter commercial life as writers and clerks in the City, or in the East India Company's service. Compared to Winchester and Eton, few went on to Oxford or Cambridge. The school became so popular among trading houses, who looked to it for recruits, that a special wing, the Royal Mathematical School, was set up in 1673 to provide an education in arithmetic and navigation. The Royal Navy also took an interest in Blues thus educated. At this time Latin was still the main subject at schools, at the expense of all others, and Christ's Hospital was the only large school in England providing what was later known as a 'modern' education. 'Blue Coat schools', based on Christ's Hospital, so named because of the traditional dress, were set up in towns and cities all over the country (the last one appears to have been at Wigan in 1773). Few of these survive: among those that do are Bristol (Queen Elizabeth's Hospital), Reading Blue Coat, Chetham's (Manchester), King's Hospital (Dublin) and Liverpool Blue Coat.

Christ's Hospital also provided the traditional education, reaching its peak in that dead period educationally, the late eighteenth century. The Rev. James Boyer, himself an Old Blue, was a grammar master from 1769 to 1799; he produced the three most famous Old Blues: Charles Lamb, Samuel Taylor Coleridge and Leigh Hunt. Lamb was always concerned about his old school, and looked back with a mixture of horror and affection on his days there. 'I remember those bathing excursions to the New River. . . . How merrily we would sally forth into the fields; and strip under the first warmth of the sun; and wanton like young dace in the streams; getting up appetites for noon, which those of us pennyless (our scanty morning crust long since exhausted) had not the means of allaying. . . . How faint and languid, finally, we would return, towards night fall, to our desired morsel, half-rejoicing, half-reluctant, that the hours of our uneasy liberty had expired! It was worse in the days of winter, to go prowling about the streets objectless—shivering at cold windows of print-shops, to extract a little amusement.'

All this passing about in London made the boys one of the characteristic sights of the city. Lamb wrote of 'the respect, and even kindness, which [their] well-known garb never fails to procure [them] in the streets of the metropolis'. And Coleridge, usually more critical of his old school than Lamb, wrote: 'The tradesmen and householders of London look with an eye of peculiar affection on the Blue-coat boy as he passes along the streets on one of his leave days; the boys seem to meet with friends and relations everywhere, and are in consequence distinguished by their civility, good manners, and modest pride.' The boys evidently spent as much time as they could out of the school, for life in it was harsh. Not only was the diet hardly above subsistence level, floggings seem to have been an everyday occurrence, and bullying was rampant. At length one boy committed suicide, hanging himself from a window. This brought a public outcry, and a Royal Commission was set up to report on the school, containing such eminent names as W. E. Forster, the Very Rev. Henry Liddell and John Walter, of *The Times*. Their report had two main recommendations: more power to the headmaster and a removal of the school to open surroundings. 'It has been pressed upon us by the eminent authorities to whom we specially refer that this removal is absolutely necessary in order to enable the Head Master, with his staff of assistant masters, to exercise the control over the boys which is so advantageously exercised in all other large schools.' In 1892, after much protest from Old Blues, it was announced that Christ's Hospital would move to a site of over a thousand acres at Horsham in Sussex. The move was made in 1902. The old premises were sold for well over a quarter of a million pounds; they became part of St. Bartholomew's Hospital and of a new General Post Office.

Although some traditional links with London remained, the character of the school, in its somewhat forbidding new buildings, dominating the countryside for miles around, was inevitably changed. And London, too, had lost part of its history. However, Christ's Hospital still provides a charitable education, with numerous ways of entry, divided between Presentation (of governors, corporate bodies, etc.) and Competition from ten to thirteen years. The school attained high academic distinction, maintained and improved by C. M. E. Seaman, headmaster from 1955 to 1970, an Old Blue like many before him, who was awarded the C.B.E. on his retirement.*

With Tonbridge we come to the last of the great schools of the reign of Edward VI. Like Bedford, it owed its existence to one man. Tonbridge was a small place, with only a few hundred people, and the setting-up of a school there does not seem to have been as the consequence of the dissolution of a chantry or other church school. Sir Andrew Judd had been born at Tonbridge, had made a fortune as a skinner in the Muscovy trade, and in 1553 he applied for and received a charter to found a school at his birthplace. He entrusted the government of the school to the Company of Skinners. To provide for the school he bought some houses in the City and thirty acres in the then rural area of St. Pancras. When London later expanded over this area, it brought some wealth to the school. Judd

---

* Celebrated Old Blues of recent times: Sir Barnes Wallis, Lord Brock, surgeon, Keith Vaughan, artist, Michael Stewart, former Foreign Secretary, Sir William Glock, Graham Hutton, economist, Air Commodore E. M. Donaldson, one-time world air speed record holder, Jack Morpurgo, Michael Wilding, actor, and John Snow, 'as fast a bowler as the school had ever known' according to his father; two important poets, Edmund Blunden and Keith Douglas, Colin Davis, conductor, Constant Lambert, composer, and three notable journalists, Bernard Levin, Robert Pitman and Ian Trethowan.

seems to have had a school primarily for fee-paying boarders in mind, inevitable perhaps in respect of the smallness of Tonbridge town or village, but most unusual for a benefactor at that time and for two hundred years. He said in his statutes: 'I desiring the benefit of the inhabitants of the said town of Tonbridge in boarding of scholars and otherwise do will that the master of the said grammar school shall not take to board diet or lodge in his house or rooms or otherwise above the number of twelve scholars and the usher not to take above the number of eight scholars.' During its first two-and-a-half centuries there were, in fact, usually about forty boarders and ten day-boys at the school; all admitted had to be able to read 'perfectly' both English and Latin, which made it difficult for local boys, for whom good primary education was not easy to obtain. The school, it seems, was intended for the sons of gentry, both local and from London. According to its historian, D. C. Somervell (a master from 1919 to 1950), Tonbridge 'was but a small and perhaps insignificant institution in the sixteenth, seventeenth and eighteenth centuries'. An interesting letter from the headmaster of the seventeen-sixties to an inquirer gives a good idea of the school: 'My plan of education [is] entirely a classical one and to qualify youth for the university, where we have several exhibitions. I find it indeed necessary to have a French master in the house, and a dancing master attends the school from London once a week to teach those whose parents wish them to learn. Boys in general who are intended for trade go from me to some academy about thirteen or fourteen years of age. There is a very good writing master in the town greatly under my own direction who attends my school every day after classical hours (which are eight every day except holy days) are over.' The fees for board and tuition were £20 per annum.

From 1772 to 1843, over seventy years, a hereditary succession of Knoxes, grandfather, father and son, were headmasters, a unique occurrence in the public schools. In 1825 Judd's statutes were at last revised, allowing for a much larger number of boarders in the school houses. Thus the foundations were laid for a larger scale; but little was done in this direction until the headmastership of Dr. J. I. Welldon, 1843–75. Welldon started with forty-three boys: when he left there were 235. Welldon was a strict disciplinarian, a good teacher and firm administrator. 'It was Dr. Welldon's custom to take every form in the school once a month. The cane was always within reach on these occasions. . . . His habits of exercise and hydropathic treatment (he was a worshipper of cold water in every form) allowed him little time for reading.' Under Welldon day boys were increased as well as boarders, families coming to live at Tonbridge in order to take advantage of the school and its very advantageous terms for local boys. At about the same time the school, through its London property, was becoming rich. When Tonbridge was examined under the Endowed Schools Act, the need for reform became clear. The upshot was that the Skinners' Company provided two new schools for local boys, at Tunbridge Wells, Skinners' School (1887), and in Tonbridge, Judd School (1883), known until the nineteen-thirties as Judd's Commercial School. In this way they contrived to keep control over Tonbridge School and to continue it as a school for fee-payers, both day and boarding. The school grew under C. Lowry, 1907–22, who was the first lay headmaster Tonbridge had ever had. But there was a serious decline in the nineteen-thirties, during which decade numbers dropped by over a quarter. The headmaster was H. N. P. Sloman, son of A. Sloman, a headmaster of Birkenhead School. The reputation of Tonbridge was restored by E. E. A. Whitworth, 1939–49, previously headmaster of Bradfield, the Rev. L. H. Waddy, 1949–62, and M. W. McCrum, 1962–70, by which time its reputation had never been higher. Tonbridge now has over five hundred boys, of whom about one hundred are day-boys.* Tonbridge is one of the leading rackets schools, an expensive sport played at only twelve schools in England, and little anywhere else in the world. The first school to introduce it was Harrow, in the eighteen-twenties. The others are: Charterhouse, Clifton, Eton, Haileybury, Malvern, Marlborough, Radley, Rugby, Wellington and Winchester.

*

The founding of schools continued under Philip and Mary, although not with the same activity as under the previous Protestant reign. Queen Mary's, Walsall (1554), Hampton Grammar School (1557), Bangor Grammar School (1557) date from this reign. Sir John Gresham founded his school at Holt in 1555, having bought the Manor House, the Gresham family home, from his brother for

---

* Old boys include Dr. Owen Chadwick, Field-Marshal Lord Ironside, Marshal of the R.A.F. Lord Douglas, C.-in-C. Fighter Command, 1940–42, E. M. Forster, Sir Herbert Baker, the architect, Sidney Keyes, Sir Leslie Rowan, civil servant, and the cricketers J. G. W. Davies and Colin Cowdrey.

this purpose. The property with which he endowed the school was put in the control of the Fishmongers' Company. The Company had great responsibility from the start, because Gresham died before the school was completed. The foundation was for fifty boys. Gresham's was for long closely associated with Caius College, Cambridge, to which this small school sent over eighty boys in two hundred years. Gresham's began to expand in this century under the headmastership of G. W. S. Howson, 1900–19, who had been a master at Uppingham under Thring. Howson was associated with liberal or forward-looking ideas in education. Greek was taken off the curriculum. The school has produced Lord Reith, Sir Owen Wansbrough-Jones, scientific adviser to the army, General Sir Robert Bray, Sir Christopher Cockerell, inventor of the hovercraft, and H. A. Hetherington, editor. It has a remarkable record in the arts, having produced W. H. Auden, Benjamin Britten, Lennox Berkeley, composer, J. M. Richards, architectural writer, John Pudney and Peter Brook. Auden recalled: 'Fagging, during one's first year or so, was extremely light, hot water was plentiful, and the cooking, if undistinguished—no one seems ever to have solved the problem of school maids who are almost invariable slatternly and inefficient—was quite adequate. . . . On the academic side I can't say much because I remember so little.'

Most major schools of old foundations owe their prominence today to great headmasters of the nineteenth century; one of the last to do so was Oundle, which was still a minor grammar school at the turn of the century. It was founded by William Laxton, a leading London trader, eight times Master of the Worshipful Company of Grocers, and a Lord Mayor. Born at Oundle, in Northamptonshire, he left in a codicil to his Will, of 22 July 1556, property in London to found a school at his home town. He died five days later. The Grocers' Company, who had been named as trustees, founded Laxton's school on the basis of an old grammar school that had existed since 1485. The first master, John Sadler, received a salary of £18, with a house, and the usher received £6 13s. 4d., of which he 'thinketh the stipend very small'. The Wardens of the Grocers' Company ordained in the statutes that the master be 'whole of body, of good report, and in degree a master of arts, mete for his learning and dexterity in teaching, and of right understanding of good and true religion set forth by public authority, whereunto he shall move and stir his scholars'. Forty-eight scholars, who had to be 'able to write competentlie and to read both English and Latin', were enrolled. The school did well till the Great Fire of London, which impoverished the Company to such an extent that it was unable to pay the salaries of master and usher. Oundle remained almost dormant during the eighteenth century, but by the beginning of the nineteenth there was an improvement, and new buildings were erected from time to time. In 1875 the demand locally for a school providing a modern education was met by the Grocers' Company opening the 'Laxton Grammar School' in the town, 'Oundle School' becoming primarily for boarders (which it had nearly always taken). The same headmaster was to be appointed for both schools. Neither school flourished, but in 1892 the scene at Oundle was transformed by the appointment of a science master at Dulwich, F. W. Sanderson, to the headmastership. Sanderson, who had not been to a public school himself, remained at Oundle till his death in 1922. In thirty years he made Oundle one of the most famous schools in the country, and he was certainly the most notable educationist of his day. He was not satisfied with the public-school education laid down by Arnold and Thring, and he planned an education which had a greater contact with everyday life, while not neglecting academic study. He believed in the study of science, but in the wide sense of the word. In 1913 he insisted, 'General education is the chief aim' of the school. With this in mind he introduced engineering and metallurgical laboratories, workshops, a foundry, an observatory, a farm and botanical gardens. Every boy was expected to have some experience of this side of the school's activities. Every boy found something which he could do well. It was typical of Sanderson that when he arrived singing was confined to the choir, the other boys listening. He insisted on the whole school taking part in choral activity. Sanderson's approach was incorporated in many of the new public schools of this century, and his importance can hardly be over-estimated: the public school of to-day is as much a product of Sanderson as of Arnold.

Oundle expanded beyond recognition under Sanderson, with the acquisition of new houses and land; the town came almost to serve the school, rather than the reverse. By Sanderson's death there were 583 boys. The last plea of Captain Robert Falcon Scott was, 'For God's sake look after our people,' and his son, the naturalist Peter Scott, was sent to Oundle. H. G. Wells, a socialist and one of Sanderson's greatest admirers, sent his son to Oundle under Sanderson.

Oundle has become one of the greatest of all public schools. It is still based on the independent house system, placed about in the town, although three of these are joined for catering and dining (this is a trend which will inevitably continue in those schools which still have separate eating arrangements for each house; Eton is planning a communal dining complex). The projected increase in the size of Peterborough, only thirteen miles away, which the planners intend to more than double in size by 1985, does pose some threat to the setting of Oundle. It has kept in the van educationally, with computer training, practical teaching of history (at 'O' levels, the syllabus is to the school's own design), and the maintaining of a house for entry at eleven years. Oundle continued to add to its reputation under G. H. Stainsforth, 1945–56, who went on to Wellington, R. J. Knight, 1956–68, who went on to Monkton Combe, and B. M. W. Trapnell, previously headmaster of Denstone. The school is still governed by the Grocers' Company.

Although Sanderson was not an athlete, Oundle was to become one of the leading of all sports schools; its rugby football fixture list is reputed to be the strongest of any school in the country. One of the glories of Oundle, as of Tonbridge, are the stained-glass windows in the chapel; the windows at Oundle are by John Piper. Old boys include E. B. Strauss, the psychologist, R. J. Harrison, Professor of Anatomy at Cambridge, W. B. Reddaway, Professor of Economics at the same university, Clough Williams-Ellis, the architect, Lord Crowther, the economist, Rt. Hon. Kenneth Robinson, Sir Hugh Wontner, Sir Geoffrey Vickers, V.C., Colonel Harry Llewellyn, show-jumper, and Arthur Marshall, author.

Brentwood School, in Essex, also dating from 1557, was founded not by a city merchant but by a leading jurist, Antony Browne, who became Chief Justice of Common Pleas just before the death of Queen Mary. As at Oundle, it was several years before the school got under way, and the foundation-stone of the new building (still in regular use) was not laid till 1568, when Browne's step-daughter and her husband performed the ceremony. Statutes were drawn up by Sir Antony Browne, a kinsman of the founder, and others, in 1622. They required the instruction of boys in 'virtue, learning and manners', which is still the motto of the school. Brentwood School was to provide a free education for all boys between eight and eighteen of the parish of Southweald, within three miles of the school house, or of the founder's kin. It gained a good reputation. In 1787 the headmaster advertised that he 'has a large commodious House for the reception of Young Gentlemen who will be boarded, washing included, and taught the English, Latin and Greek Languages, at twenty-three guineas per annum. Entrance Three Guineas. Writing and Arithmetic, Dancing and French, by proper Masters.' Browne's scheme remained much the same until 1851, when a new arrangement was sanctioned by the Court of Chancery and Act of Parliament; under this, Brentwood remained a free school for Greek and Latin, but for other subjects an annual fee of £6 was to be exacted. Accommodation for forty-five boarders was provided at the School House. By 1877 the annual fees for boarders were £66. By this date, also, the school boasted of a gymnasium and swimming bath; older boys had 'separate apartments' for sleeping and study, and conditions at Brentwood were evidently well in advance of those at other schools. Ten almsfolk continued to be supported by the same foundation. These arrangements were added to or altered in 1870, 1893, 1910 and 1958. During the present century the school grew rapidly, and there are now over a thousand boys, with five boarding houses.*

Repton is another school founded under a Will, that of Sir John Port, a wealthy landowner. He provided for a school to be established in either Etwall or Repton, by his Will of 1557. There are still four hereditary governors, connected with the foundation. Port's chief executor, his nephew Richard Harpur, bought, in 1559, the surviving premises of the old priory of Repton, dating from the twelfth century, for £37 10s. od. The priory is still the central feature of the school. The priory had belonged to the Thacker family, who still lived in the neighbouring Hall. The early days of the school were marked by long and bitter arguments between the Thackers and the school, which eventually came to a head in the High Court of Chancery in 1664; the background to this was the nuisance caused by the boys, for early on Repton seems to have been a fairly large school. By 1622 there were two hundred pupils, about sixty of them boarding in the town. But the school experienced the familiar decline later, and in 1704 it was reported that, 'The Master it seems of late years had received his salary without ever appearing in the Schole'; there were 'only a few ragged children' in attendance. Fees were charged for nearly twenty years in the late eighteenth century, but to little effect, and the school became a free one again

---

* Sir Frank Lee, Hardy Amies and David Irving are old boys.

in 1787, except for a charge of one guinea when the numbers exceeded sixty (to pay for a third master). In 1803 the master was ordered to concentrate on 'Grammar Boys' and to teach 'Town Boys' only when he had the time. In 1832 the free tuition was limited to boys of Etwall and Repton, at least ten years old, who could already read and write. This process was continued under the head-mastership of Dr. Peile, whose fees were as high as sixty guineas in the eighteen-forties, and who went so far as to pay a local man to teach the town boys free in order to encourage them not to seek education under Port's legacy. This brought about a legal case in 1852, when it was suggested Peile was acting illegally. Peile, sur-prisingly, won. The ground was thus prepared for Dr. S. A. Pears, 1854–74, who turned Repton into a major school.

Pears made Repton well known, and during his time many awards were won at the universities. He was a convinced classicist. At the Tercentenary Dinner, he said: 'Even if we shall one day light upon a language more full, more exact and more comprehen-sive than the Greek and the Latin, and if authors should arise equal and even superior to the greatest of antiquity . . . we should yet choose the originals for our guide and study, and leave to others those which would be after all but imitations or developments.' He followed this up in his evidence to the Endowed Schools Inquiry Commission in 1865:

Question: 'It has been stated that, looking at the occupation of a large number of the middle class, any benefit to be derived from teaching Latin would be greater if the period of commencing Latin were postponed; if the boy's mind were opened early in life by those branches of science which tend to cultivate habits of observation; have you any experience on the subject?'

Pears: 'No. I have no experience on that subject, but I have a very strong opinion that the opening of the mind by simply putting knowledge into it is a delusion. I think you should from the earliest days endeavour to make the style of your system that class of sub-jects on which a boy can work and can be made to work. It is extremely difficult, I think, in teaching physical science to insist on work.'

It is indicative of the wide variety of backgrounds to the public-school system that two schools similarly founded at the same time, such as Oundle and Repton, should owe their prominence in society to two men so utterly opposed as Sanderson and Pears. The classical tradition continued at Repton long after Pears. C. B. Fry, one of Repton's greatest sons, described his schooldays as 'six years of solid and undiluted Latin and Greek'; Fry went on to become one of the leading classicists of his generation, in addition to captaining Oxford at cricket, football and athletics, playing cricket and football for England, and holding the world record for the long jump. Another author, Edmund Candler, wrote: 'The dead languages were our portion at Repton and the tradition of pedagogy saw to it that they remained dead.'

In 1910 the governors appointed the Rev. William Temple to be headmaster. The son of Frederick Temple, who had been headmaster of Rugby, before becoming Archbishop of Canterbury, he went on to become Archbishop of Canterbury himself. He was followed in 1914 by the Rev. Geoffrey Fisher, who remained until 1932, and also became Archbishop of Canterbury.* Michael Ramsey, who followed him as Archbishop of Canterbury, was a boy under Fisher. Repton therefore has a quite remarkable connection with Canterbury this century.

An innovation which would not have pleased Pears was the Civics Class, begun by two assistant masters in 1917—D. C. Somervell and Victor Gollancz; the latter, a socialist, had been directed to the school instead of military service, and his pacifist views brought considerable controversy inside the school. Gollancz made 'a speedy and enforced departure from Repton', but he considered his time there one of the most interesting experiences of his life. The Civics Class, however, remains; visiting lecturers take part in discussions on contemporary economic and political problems.

C. B. Fry wrote of Repton, in his autobiography: 'When the cinema people searched for a school with the most typical English surroundings in order to glorify Mr. Chips, they chose Repton, and they also, curiously enough, chose me to come and help produce the old-time cricket and football scenes, but I could not do this because I had to go and watch a Test Match. In truth, I do not think that any of the great schools is more typically English than Repton. For one thing, it is situated in the middle of England and under its ancient name of Repandunum was the capital of the Saxon kingdom of Mercia. Before that it was an important Roman station, and the foundations of the school buildings are upon Roman remains. Part of the ruins of a very early Priory lie along the bank that bounds the

* His son F. W. Fisher, a Reptonian, became Warden of St. Edward's, Oxford.

cricket field. . . . The view of the old Priory through the school arch as one walks towards it along the ancient wall which bounds the playing-fields from the village is one of the fairest instances I know of historic England exhibited in shapely grey stone.'*

* Apart from those mentioned, Reptonians include: General Sir A. Wauchope, High Commissioner in Palestine during most of the nineteen-thirties, C. G. Bruce, mountaineer, Sir Harry Brittain, founder of the Pilgrims' Club, Sir E. Bullard, geophysicist, C. W. Guillebaud, economist, Basil Rathbone, actor, N. C. Hunter, dramatist, Anthony Devas, artist, Sir Vincent de Ferranti, Sir Desmond Lee, Headmaster of Clifton and Winchester, and the authors Christopher Isherwood and Denton Welch, neither of whom cared for Repton at all. Repton has always been a sports school, and is particularly strong in cricket. It has supplied more Test Match cricketers than any school except Eton and Winchester. Apart from Fry, old boys in the sporting world include Harold Abrahams, winner of the gold medal in the 1924 Olympics 100 metres, H. W. 'Bunny' Austin, hero of many Wimbledon dramas before the war (and winner of the public schools' singles in 1923, 1924 and 1925), L. C. H. Palairet, who was, according to Sir Pelham Warner, 'possibly the most beautiful batsman, so far as pure style goes, that ever lived', H. S. Altham, of Hampshire, F. S. G. Calthorpe, England and Captain of Warwickshire, D. B. Carr, England and Captain of Derbyshire, A. J. Holmes, Captain of Sussex, B. H. Valentine, England and Captain of Kent, and Richard Hutton, Yorkshire and England.

4.

ELIZABETHAN SCHOOLS

THE reign of Elizabeth renewed the activity in education that had lapsed since the death of Edward VI. The most famous Elizabethan foundation is that of Westminster—'The Royal College of St. Peter in Westminster'. A school had existed for some centuries before, in connection with the Benedictine monastery. A school house had been built in 1461, on the side of what is now Dean's Yard. After the dissolution of the monastery, the school remained on the same premises, but whether or not there was a break is not certain. Henry VIII took an interest in refounding the school, in which there were forty scholars—King's Scholars—and two masters. Before long more boys were being taken, town boys; these were privately boarded or lived at home. The school survived the restoration of the monastery under Mary, and was re-founded by Elizabeth after the second dissolution of the monastery. It is from this foundation that the modern school dates, although the re-foundation differed little from that of Henry VIII—a Head Master, usher and forty scholars; scholarships were provided at Christ Church, Oxford, and at Trinity College, Cambridge. (From 1598 to 1764 every headmaster was from Christ Church.) William Camden, antiquary, was a master from 1575 to 1589. Of him, Ben Jonson, who was at Westminster, wrote:

> Camden most revered head to whom I owe
> All that I am in arts, all that I know.

The Dean of Westminster was to have authority (the Dean is still the chairman of the governors). From the start, Westminster benefited from its position, only a few hundred yards from the Palace of Westminster, and the seat of government and justice. In an age during which influence was all, the boys of Westminster were well situated, as the latest historian of the school has shown, with revealing examples.

Richard Busby became headmaster in 1639. He remained at the

post till 1695, by which time he was, not surprisingly, the most famous schoolmaster in the land. High claims have been made for Busby; he was, in fact, a character and a man devoted to one aim in life—the continuation of the school in difficult political times. Being so near the seat of political power, Westminster has been more exposed to the winds and gales of politics than most schools. Busby, with some aplomb, steered the school through Civil War, Commonwealth and Restoration, under three dynasties and through three changes of religion. His explanation was modest: 'The fathers govern the nation; the mothers govern the fathers; but the boys govern the mothers, and I govern the boys.' John Locke, Sir Christopher Wren and John Dryden were all at Westminster under Busby. At the time of Busby the school was superior even to Eton, and it was perhaps inevitable that a decline should set in afterwards; Westminster, for one thing, has never been a very rich school. By the nineteenth century the school enjoyed a mere shadow of its former glory. The growth of London, which brought slums almost to the precincts of the Abbey, and the lack of interest of the Dean and Chapter in everything but the revenue, which after the expenses of the college had been allowed they shared out amongst themselves, brought the school into some disrepute. Numbers fluctuated throughout the century, but were seldom satisfactory. Conditions were notorious. James Anthony Froude, the historian, wrote: 'Order was kept, or was supposed to be kept, by the seniors. We were flung in together to fight our own way and sink or swim, the strong to rule and the weak to go to the wall. . . . When I had crawled to bed and to sleep, I have been woke many times by the hot points of cigars burning holes in my face.' Queen's Scholars were no longer accepted free, and by 1860 their fees came to nearly £100, a high fee at that time. Conditions in the boarding houses were almost as bad as in college. Food was meagre in the extreme, furnishings less than sparse (some boys slept in chairs or under the stage), lessons for small boys were conducted standing, and discipline was harsh, to say the least. Some improvements, albeit inadequate, were made by H. G. Liddell, 1846–55, the first headmaster not to have been a boy at the school for over 250 years. Queen Victoria contributed £800 towards better accommodation. In 1860 a move to the country was suggested by Dean and Chapter, but this was turned down after an uproar of dissent from old boys. Of the twenty-three old Westminsters up at Oxford or Cambridge in 1868 (as compared to 161 from

Eton), none of them had won open awards, as compared to thirteen open awards from Manchester Grammar School out of its twenty-one students at the two universities. More buildings were acquired from the Chapter in the eighteen-eighties, for the school had begun a modest recovery. However, it was not till the twentieth century that Westminster regained its former importance.

Revival may be said to have started under Dr. James Gow, 1901–19, who had already brought Nottingham High School to such renown. Gow was followed by Dr. H. Costley-White (who had been headmaster of Liverpool and Bradfield), under whom a new boarding house, Busby's, was opened. He was followed by J. T. Christie, 1937–50, headmaster of Repton, the first lay headmaster of Westminster since 1598. The venerable school hall and college, built by Christopher Wren, were burnt to empty shells as the result of enemy action on 10 May 1941. At the end of the war, after evacuation, there were only 135 boys in the school. The fortunes and reputation of Westminster were restored under three headmasters, all outstanding in different ways: J. T. Christie, a great teacher, Dr. Walter Hamilton, an able administrator, under whom a new boarding house, Liddell's, was opened, and Dr. John Carleton, an old Westminster, who spent his entire career at the school, thirty-eight years apart from war service, headmaster 1957–70. Today the school is still closely connected with the Abbey; there are still forty Queen's Scholars (receiving nearly half the fees), and the connection with Christ Church and Trinity is maintained.*

The Merchant Taylors Company founded their school in 1561 at the insistence of one Richard Hilles. Members of the Company had already founded King's, Macclesfield, Wolverhampton Grammar

---

* Westminsters not mentioned include: William Cowper, Richard Hakluyt, Edward Gibbon (whose health broke under the strain), Warren Hastings, his successor in India, William Cavendish-Bentinck, Jeremy Bentham, Robert Southey, Lord Raglan, of the Crimea, Edward Gibbon Wakefield, of colonial reform, G. A. Henty, that creator of so many public-school heroes, Sir E. H. 'Eddie' Marsh, Stephen McKenna, novelist, Lord Adrian, Viscount Davidson, politician, Sir Roy Harrod, Sir Adrian Boult, Sir Henry Tizard, A. A. Milne (who wrote in his autobiography 'there are no baths in College. College was built by Sir Christopher Wren. One cannot have everything. Probably there are no baths in St. Paul's Cathedral'), Stephen Potter, Sir Max Aitken, John Freeman, Hugh Massingham, Jack Hulbert, Peter Ustinov, Sir John Gielgud, Angus Wilson, Lord Byers, Michael Flanders, A. Wedgwood Benn, Sir Philip Magnus, Reginald Prentice and Robert Carr, both M.P.s, Anthony Sampson, and David Holloway. Kim Philby was a scholar.

School and Bedford. Buildings, the Manor of the Rose, were purchased in Suffolk Lane, between London Bridge and the present
Cannon Street Station, for £566 13s. 4d., of which Hilles contributed
£500. It was to be an extremely large school: 250 boys, of whom one
hundred were to be educated free. No less that forty-three scholarships were provided for the new school at St. John's College,
Oxford, founded by the Merchant Taylor Sir Thomas White in
1555. The statutes were closely based on those of St. Paul's, written
nearly half a century before; some of them were copied word for
word.

The first headmaster of Merchant Taylors' was one of the most
notable masters of the sixteenth century, Richard Mulcaster. He
had been educated at Eton and King's, and he had advanced ideas
on education. He believed, for instance, that the lowest forms should
be taught by the best man, that there should be training colleges for
university teachers, and that there should be close co-operation
between parents and masters: 'Parentes and maisters should be
familarly lynked in amitie, and continual conference, for their
common care.' He was in favour of day schools as opposed to
boarding schools, but Merchant Taylors' took boarders in the
houses of the masters, and other boys boarded in the City. 'The end
of education and train,' he said, 'is to help nature unto her perfec-
tion.' He was not a co-educationist. 'I do not advocate sending
young maidens to Public Grammar Schools or to Universities as has
never been the custom in this country.' Mulcaster wrote two important books, *Positions* and *Elementarie*, but few took much notice
of the ideas of this thoughtful and interesting man, a far greater
educationist than, say, Busby of the next century. He was frequently
rowing with the Company, and eventually resigned in 1586; he
he later became High Master of St. Paul's. During his day Merchant
Taylors' produced Edmund Spenser and six of the translators of the
Authorised Version of the Bible. The school continued steadily for
many generations without achieving eminence, surviving the plague
and having to be rebuilt after the Great Fire.

By the nineteenth century Merchant Taylors' was, like so many
great schools, struggling on in the decayed shell of former respectability. Conditions were almost as bad as those at Westminster.
Charles Matthews, the actor, remembered his masters thus: 'Two
more cruel masters than Bishop and Rose never existed. . . . Lord,
the fourth master, was rather an invalid, and, I believe, had been

prescribed gentle exercise; he therefore put up for, and was the successful candidate for, the flogging department. Rose was so great an adept at the cane that I once saw a boy strip, after a thrashing from him, that he might expose his barbarous cruelty, when the back was actually striped with dark streaks like a zebra.' It is pleasant to record that 'Gardner, the lowest in grade, was the only mild person amongst them'. Despite his experiences, Matthews sent his son, Charles James, also to be an actor, to Merchant Taylors'. The son, in his turn, recorded his impressions: 'I became a fag—cleaned three or four pairs of boots every morning, washed the tea-things, and did duty as warming-pan to my young master by lying in his bed on cold nights till he required it. . . . Latin, Greek and Hebrew were daily administered in large doses, while my native English was left to be picked up as best it might in the cloisters, which formed our playground, and in the streets of the City, where, between school hours, I might have been seen wandering, without my hat, like the little ragamuffin I was, or running up Suffolk Lane on a dark night in my bed-gown, in my capacity of fag, after having been lowered from the bedroom window in a sheet. . . . It is true I boarded in the house of Mr. Cherry, the headmaster, but I scarcely ever saw him out of school, and I never remember to have heard his voice, except when in anger.' The area was becoming more and more dingy. One inmate recalled: 'It looked gloomy enough. On the one side were large offices several storeys high, and the old School, with headmaster's house adjoining; on the other, extensive warehouses equally lofty; and the narrowness of the lane made it doubly dark and dreary—the summit of the buildings seeming almost to touch one another.' Teaching was done in the Great Schoolroom, about 85 ft. by 30 ft. There were no desks, only a table for the monitors, the remainder having to work on their knees. There were no lights, every boy having to provide his own candle. Up till nearly 1850 there was no fire. 'It was lighted very imperfectly by windows on either side, large enough, indeed, but obscured by the heavy leading of the small diamond panes and by long-standing accumulation of dirt.' The scene was much the same as at Christ's Hospital, Mercers' and St. Paul's, with which schools, as well as later with the City of London School, there were frequent fights. No provision was made for feeding boys at midday, even up to about 1870. One old boy recalled: 'Some went to the chophouses which still existed in the neighbourhood, others to the restaurants in Cheapside. I myself went to the Chelsea bun house opposite Fishmongers' Hall, and at a later period to the bar at Cannon Street Station, where I had a glass of stout and an Abernethy biscuit.'

Under J. A. Hersey, 1845–70, an old boy and Fellow of St. John's, which college 'advised' on the appointment of headmasters, there was some improvement. Merchant Taylors' was one of the nine schools selected for report by special Commission in 1861. The Commission recommended the withdrawal from London of Westminster and Charterhouse, primarily boarding schools, while St. Paul's and Merchant Taylors', primarily day schools, should remain. What happened in the end was that St. Paul's and Charterhouse moved out, Merchant Taylors' moved into the Charterhouse premises, and Westminster stayed where it was. The governors of Charterhouse declared they would consider no less than £120,000, but accepted £90,000.

The school moved to its new site under William Baker, headmaster 1870–1900, another old boy of the school (the fourteenth out of the twenty-two appointed till that time). Most of the old Charterhouse was demolished, and what was virtually a new school was opened in 1875. Merchant Taylors' became almost entirely for day-boys. By the nineteen-twenties it was necessary to accept boys travelling from as far as Hertford, Rickmansworth and Leigh-on-Sea; 25 per cent lived north of the Thames. There were the problems of space, of playing-fields and of expecting parents to send their boys into the heart of the metropolis daily. A new headmaster, Spencer Leeson, declared: 'We can carry on where we are for a few years to come, the tide running rather against us, and continue to do good work; but the tide will increase in strength as the years go on, our handicaps will grow and we are likely eventually to find ourselves outstripped and left. At Charterhouse Square we can never rejoin the number of the great schools of England.' This was a bold challenge; it was accepted, and the school moved to spacious new grounds on the edge of London at Sandy Lodge, the new buildings being designed by Sir Giles Scott. St. Bartholomew's bought the old buildings, as it had done those of Christ's Hospital. A service of farewell to the City of London, after 372 years, was held at St. Paul's Cathedral and was attended by a congregation of three thousand.

Since 1933, therefore, Merchant Taylors' has been a school for the north-west suburbs, with one boarding house for sixty boys. It has to be admitted that such moves of the great London schools have completely changed their character, something which the retention of old panels, obelisks and other souvenirs of the past can do little or nothing to halt. But what happens when schools remained in the City too long was shown by the fate of Mercers' School, and certainly Merchant Taylors' retains its place among the great schools. Spencer Leeson went on to become headmaster of Winchester. He was followed by N. P. Birley, 1935–46, previously headmaster of King's, Canterbury, and Hugh Elder, 1946–61, previously headmaster of Dean Close. A feature of the school has been the remarkable record of its old boys' Rugby club, which joined the senior clubs about 1890, by which time it was already playing Oxford Cambridge, Gloucester, Cardiff, Rosslyn Park and Blackheath (in that year it won nineteen and lost six of its matches).*

Other Elizabethan schools founded at about this time are St. Olave's and St. Saviour's (1561 and 1559, amalgamated 1899), now at Orpington; Kingston Grammar School (1561), the successor to a chantry school; Royal Grammar School, High Wycombe (1562), a re-foundation of a much older school; Darlington Grammar School (1563); Wyggeston Grammar School, Leicester (1564); Presteigne Grammar School, founded by John Beddoes in 1565; Queen Elizabeth's, Wakefield (1567), the successor to a chantry school founded in 1509; Hardye's School, Dorchester, founded by Thomas Hardye in 1569 for boys of Dorchester, Fordington and Frome, to provide free education 'for children of all degrees'; Cheltenham Grammar School (1572); Queen Elizabeth's, Barnet (1573); Ruthin School, Denbighshire, re-founded in 1574 by Gabriel Goodman, Dean of Westminster; Lord Williams' Grammar School, Thame, founded by the Will of the peer of that name, dated 1558, and established as a free school in 1575 for relatives of the founder, sons of his tenants and the inhabitants of the town and nearby villages, others paying a fee; and Carmarthen Grammar

* As well as those already mentioned, Old Merchant Taylors' include: Lord Clive, founder of the Indian Empire, Alfred Marshall, the great economist, Admiral Lord Mountevans, Robert Falcon, Scott's second-in-command, W. Joynson-Hicks (Viscount Brentford), and Reginald Maudling, both Home Secretaries, E. H. Carr, journalist and scholar, author Edward Shanks, Sir Cyril Norwood, Lord Greenwood, Lynn Chadwick, sculptor, Sir Richard Fairey, aviation engineer, H. R. F. Keating, novelist, Michael Edwardes, historian, Anthony Lejeune and Nigel Calder, editor. Three Old Merchant Taylors' have held the Order of Merit: Gilbert Murray, Lord Hailey and Sir James Jeans.

9. A political cartoon by Gillray depicting Dr. Busby
settling his accounts

10a.   Westminster.   Little Dean's Yard, 1840

10b.   School, Westminster, 1843

11a. Rugby, 1808

11b. The Headmaster's
House, Rugby, 1950

12. Thomas Arnold, by T. Phillips, 1839

School (1576), associated with Queens' College, Cambridge, the school of Beau Nash. Elizabeth College, Guernsey, was founded in 1563 by charter of the Queen. Solihull School may date from the late fourteenth century, but before 1560 all is conjecture. It was re-founded in 1602 by Thomas Waringe and others. By 1868 there were between forty and fifty boys in the school, which did not begin to expand along public-school lines until the end of the century. The School House was built between 1880 and 1910; there have been many additions since then, and there are now nearly a thousand boys, a few of them boarders.

Sir Roger Manwood's, at Sandwich, in Kent, is an interesting case of an old grammar school becoming a leading school only in very recent years, and *as a result of state aid*. Manwood was a lawyer holding various offices of the Cinque Ports, and M.P. first for Hastings and then for Sandwich, where he had attended the chantry school, which had been closed in 1547. He founded his school in 1563, the governors to be the mayor and jurats. A school house was built, and the school opened in 1565. The school had a good start, but during the long period between 1610 and 1858 it was generally in decline. The decision of the Charity Commissioners in 1890 was that the school had either to be re-established, with additional endowments if necessary, for there had been periods in the second half of the nineteenth century when it had been no more than an empty building, or that Manwood's endowments would have to become part of general educational expenditure for the district. This threat to the school's identity brought about some local activity, and Sir Roger Manwood's slowly began its rebirth and has grown right up to today. New buildings were erected just outside the town in 1895. The fees of what was a new school in all but name and part-endowment were £8 tuition and £52 boarding, though, 'mindful of the founder's statutes', some scholarships for free places were offered to local boys. A science block was added in 1897, and gradually the school expanded beside its pleasant playing-fields. Three head-masters, the Rev. W. Burton, 1914–35, E. P. Oakes, 1935–60, and J. F. Spalding, brought the school to the fore in Kent. After the 1944 Education Act, Sir Roger Manwood's became a Voluntary Controlled School, the upkeep of the school and the provision of educational essentials becoming the responsibility of the Local Education Authority, but the school's endowments gaining it some slight autonomy; six governors were of the foundation, twelve were to be

appointed by the L.E.A. Tuition fees were abolished, entry being at
eleven. This state interest was as successful as it was at Cranbrook,
which became, as we have seen, a Voluntary Aided School, as distinct to a Voluntary Controlled School, giving it two-thirds of the
governors instead of one-third. The boarding fees still had to be
paid, and because these were low as compared to the usual boarding-
plus-tuition fees of other schools, the governors were able to expand
the boarding side after the Kent Education Committee had been
convinced of the soundness of the idea. By an almost miraculous
coincidence, two large residences adjoining the school grounds came
on the market almost simultaneously, and Sir Roger Manwood's, a
minor grammar school when independent, became a public school
under state control. Whether or not this was the intention of the
planners of the 1944 Education Act, is of course, another matter. All
this was achieved under Oakes, a great, if little-known, headmaster.
Oakes was also responsible for reviving the school's closed scholarships to Lincoln College and Gonville and Caius, these having been
dormant for many years. Old boys include W. J. Brown, that very
Independent M.P.

Felsted School, in Essex, is a good example of a chantry becoming
a grammar school. The founder, Lord Riche, a prominent Tudor
statesman, Lord Chancellor and local landowner, had this to say in
his Deed of 21 May 1564: 'Whereas I did ordeyne amongst other
thinges certayn ordinaunces rules prayers and other ceremonyes
which now be by the lawes and statutes of this realme of Inglande
taken awaye abrogated and admichillate that ys to says certeyne
marres dyiges placebo and ringing of belles. Now knowe you that
for a more purpose and entente of goddes glory and for the commen
welthe to be had and made I the said Lord Riche do ordeyne and
constitute that the Chapleyne of the said ffoundacion and hys
successours shalbe an able person and sufficient in lernyng and
qualities to teache and instructe such male childerne borne or hereafter shalbe borne in Essex to the number of foure score in the lernyng of Grammer and other Vertues and godly lernyng according
to Christes religion.' Thus was founded Felsted School. The appointment of headmasters was to remain with the Riche family,
later to become the Earls of Warwick (eventually passing to the
Earls of Winchilsea). Boarders must have been contemplated from
the beginning, for, like Tonbridge, the school was too large for such
a small village. Under Martin Holbeach, 1627–49, it achieved some

fame in the surrounding counties. John Wallis, the mathematician, was at the school at this time: 'I was sent to School to Mr. Martin Holbeach, at Felsted, in Essex; who was reputed (as indeed he was) a very good School Master. He there taught a Free School of the Foundation of the Earl of Warwick. At this School, though in a country village, he had at that time above an hundred or sixscore Scholars; most of them strangers, sent thither from other places upon reputation of the school; from whence many good Scholars were sent yearly to the University.' The 'strangers' boarded at houses in the town, including the Vicarage. Christopher Glascock, 1650–90, maintained the reputation of the school. Simon Lydiatt, 1690–1712, was the last great master of Felsted of this period; he initiated an annual gathering of old boys, at the school, for a service and feast, in 1707, and this is perhaps the longest surviving old boys' day in the country. Felsted then went into a period of decline and for a time was a preparatory school for other schools. By the early eighteen-thirties Felsted was without any pupils at all.

In 1851 an act was passed (on the same day as the Brentwood School Act) putting the school under eleven trustees, all of them resident in Essex, and making arrangements for new premises. Thus ended the system of patronage after nearly three hundred years. Under W. S. Grignon, 1856–75, the first headmaster appointed by the trustees, the school revived; but Felsted became plagued with bitter disputes between headmasters and trustees; the dismissal of Grignon was a *cause célèbre* of its day, receiving considerable notice in the press, and was the subject of a letter from the newly formed Headmasters' Conference: all to no avail. One of the complaints of the trustees was that Grignon treated his staff with disdain, giving their salaries to the matron to hand out. The next headmaster, D. S. Ingram, 1875–1900, who came from Blundell's, worked hard to put the school on its feet. Ingram came from one of those families which produce headmasters; he was related to Rowland Ingram, headmaster of Ipswich and Giggleswick, and J. E. C. Welldon, Master of Dulwich and headmaster of Harrow. It was H. A. Dalton who finally revived the school; he doubled the number of boys in his first three years; in 1893 there were 241. Frank Stephenson, 1906–33, continued the process, and Felsted became again one of the leading schools, despite financial difficulties brought about by the ambitious programme of expansion under Dalton and Stephenson. Julian

Bickersteth, who had been head of St. Peter's, Adelaide, was the first lay headmaster in the school's history.*

Another school was founded in the following year by a lawyer colleague of Chancellor Riche, Sir Roger Cholmeley, Lord Chief Justice. Riche, who had been associated with Edward's Will, in which an attempt was made to keep the Catholic Mary from the throne, had survived Mary's reign without trouble, for he seems to have been a true Catholic, but Cholmeley, who became Lord Chief Justice in the year after Riche resigned his Chancellorship, was also associated with the Will and spent some months in the Tower as a result. In founding his school, he may well have been emulating the former Lord Chancellor. He established Highgate School as a free grammar school for forty boys living in Highgate and neighbouring parishes; by the nineteenth century these scholarships were for Highgate, Holloway, Hornsey, Finchley and Kentish Town. Foundation Scholarships, for partial payment of the fees, survive. The constitution of the school was changed by the Charity Commissioners; of the twelve governors, one is still appointed by the Lord Chief Justice. The school was rebuilt in 1868, on the original site. Since the beginning of this century the number of boys has risen from under four hundred to over 650, and the boarders from a quarter to a third of the total (in 1913 the annual fee for boarders was £85). The boarding houses and fields are a short distance from the main buildings, and boys thus pass to and fro in this historic part of London.†

Cholmeley died only two months after Highgate School was incorporated by Elizabeth. In his Will he left a house, in Newgate Market, London, to Lincoln's Inn. This house was then in the tenure and occupation of one Lawrence Shyriff, grocer. This same Shyriff,

---

* Old Felstedians: J. W. H. T. Douglas, captain of Essex and England, Olympic boxing gold-medallist, and England amateur footballer, a sportsman equalled only by C. B. Fry; Colonel S. F. Newcombe, the greatest of all Arabian Desert heroes of the First World War; F. B. Halford, who held the world motorcycle speed record in the nineteen-twenties, and later designed the De Havilland Comet jet engine; J. R. H. Weaver, President of Trinity College, Oxford, 1938–54; Air Chief Marshal Sir Leslie Hollinghurst, responsible for British airborne operations during the Normandy landings; and Kenneth Cross, architect.

† Old boys of recent times include R. W. V. Robins, Paul Rotha, Alex Comfort and C. A. R. Crosland, Secretary of State for Education 1965–67, one of the most able politicians to hold that post.

or Sheriff, was by a most remarkable coincidence the founder of the next public school to be started, Rugby School.

*

Sheriff was a member of the Grocers' Company who had served Elizabeth when she had been a princess, and he had acquired property near London and Rugby, his native place. In his Will of 1567 he instructed his executors to 'cause to be builded neare to the messuage or mansion house of the said Lawrence in Rugby aforesaid, a fayre and convenyent schoole house . . . [and] should cause an honest, discreete, and learned man, being a Master of Arts, to bee retayned to teach a free grammar schoole in the said schoole house, to serve chiefly for the children of Rugby and Brownesover aforesaid. . . . And further, the will and intent of the said Lawrence was and is, the same schoole shall bee for ever called the Free Schoole of Lawrence Sheriffe, of London, grocer. . . . And further, that the said schoolmaster of the said schoole for ever should have yearly for his sallary or wages the sum of twelve poundes.' In a codicil to his Will, Sheriff added some property in Middlesex, eight acres of open pasture called Conduit Close, at that time let for £8 per annum. It was to this codicil that Rugby School was later to owe so much, and which more than anything else turned it into a great foundation. For, with the expansion of London, the pasture was to become Lamb's Conduit Street, Great Ormond Street and other streets neighbouring the Harpur estate of Bedford School.

The school did not get off to a good start, for the income from Sheriff's estate was not substantive at first and there were legal troubles. By 1750 the school house was said to be so dilapidated that it was beyond repair. The trustees, 'twelve gentlemen of Warwickshire', moved the school to a new site in the seventeen-fifties, where it still stands; the estate taken over was the old manor of Rugby, with four fields, which gave ample space for further expansion if necessary. This well-judged move set Rugby School on its successful course. The school was already the leading school in the county, but it achieved national reputation under the headmastership of Dr. Thomas James, 1778–94, under whom the number of pupils rose to nearly three hundred. Under his successor, Dr. Henry Ingles, 1794–1807, there was a rebellion, in 1797, from which the school took some time to recover; desks and other furniture were burned in the Close, the headmaster's door was blown off its hinges, and troops (in the guise of a recruiting party) were brought to the scene. Dr. Ingles's reaction was to flog even more boys, which had been the cause of the trouble in the first place. He was followed by Dr. John Wooll, 1807–28, under whom Rugby's reputation was fully restored, the numbers reaching 381, a very high figure indeed for the time. In the nineteenth century the provisions of Sheriff's Will were honoured by the establishment of the Lawrence Sheriff Grammar School, in much the same fashion as the Laxton Grammar School at Oundle. When Wooll resigned, therefore, his successor took over one of the major schools in England. And his successor was Dr. Thomas Arnold, a crammer for university entrance, in his thirty-second year, whose claims for the post rested on a brilliant undergraduate career as a classicist. Soon after his appointment Arnold wrote: 'With regard to reforms at Rugby, give me credit, I must beg of you, for a most sincere desire to make it a place of Christian education. At the same time my object will be, if possible, to form Christian men, for Christian boys I can scarcely hope to make. . . . Both [my wife] and myself, I think, are well inclined to commence our work, and if my health and strength be spared me, I certainly feel that in no situation could I have the prospect of employment so congenial to my taste and qualifications.'

Arnold's three main qualities were the seriousness with which he took himself, his muscular view of Anglicanism and his very forceful personality. What he did at Rugby was not to change, let alone found, the public school system, but to turn out the first of the 'public-school type', a phenomenon quite unknown before Victorian times. He was the originator of public schools being 'character builders'. As Lytton Strachey well put it in *Eminent Victorians*: 'So far as the actual machinery of education was concerned, Dr. Arnold not only failed to effect a change, but deliberately adhered to the old system. The monastic and literary conceptions of education which had their roots in the Middle Ages, and had been accepted and strengthened at the revival of Learning, he adopted almost without hesitation. Under him the public school remained, in essentials, a conventional establishment devoted to the teaching of Greek and Latin grammar. Had he set on foot reforms in these directions, it seems probable that he might have succeeded in carrying the parents of England with him. The moment was ripe; there was a general desire for educational changes; and Dr. Arnold's great reputation could hardly have been resisted. As it was, he threw the whole weight of his influence into the opposite scale, and the ancient system became more firmly established than ever. The changes which he did effect were of a very different nature. By introducing morals and religion into his scheme of education, he altered the whole atmosphere of public school life. Henceforward the old rough and tumble . . . became impossible. After Dr. Arnold no public school could venture to ignore the virtues of respectability.'

Arnold also stressed the importance of the 'house system'. Dean Stanley says of Arnold: 'Every house was thus to be as it were an epitome of the whole school. On the one hand every master was to have, as he used to say, "each a horse of his own to ride". On the other hand, the boys would thus have someone at hand to consult in difficulties, to explain their case if they got into trouble with the headmaster, or the other masters, to send a report of their characters home, to prepare them for confirmation, and in general to stand to them in the relation of a pastor to his flock. "No parochial ministry" he would say to them, "can be more properly a care of souls than yours." '

It was typical of Arnold—and quite unlike the ordinary picture of him—that he never took a decision on an important matter of policy if the vote of his staff went against him.

Strachey does give Arnold the credit for introducing the prefect system, but this is certainly incorrect, as it was in force at many schools long before Arnold's time. Arnold himself had been at Winchester under Goddard, and based his regime partly on that of Winchester. He may also have been influenced to some extent by Rowland Hill (originator of the uniform postal charge), who ran an experimental school near Birmingham; although Hill was far in advance of anything that would have appealed to Arnold, for instance he believed in the boys governing themselves as much as possible, he did believe that moral influence should be the predominant force in discipline. Arnold's most genuine innovation was expulsion for offences other than rioting, almost unknown before his time. Since then some distinguished men have been asked to leave Rugby, including Walter Savage Landor and Philip Toynbee. His reputation owes much to the magnetic personality which so impressed his former pupils, in later life if not so much at the time, and to the fame bestowed on him by his aulogistic biographer, A. P. Stanley, and by Thomas Hughes, whose *Tom Brown's Schooldays* ('by an Old Boy') first appeared in 1857. This book, an extraordinary best-seller, did much to shape the idea of what a public school should be in the minds of several generations. Hughes was one of the many successful men who came from Rugby in Arnold's time—an unanswerable tribute to him—becoming a judge and M.P.; he wrote his book, at Wimbledon, sixteen years after leaving Rugby, which may account for some at least of its gentle glow. Hughes's explanation for his hero's late appreciation of the Doctor, however, is quite convincing. A master reminds him:

‘ "Do you remember when the Doctor lectured you and East at the end of one half-year, when you were in the shell, and had been getting into all sorts of scrapes?"

‘ "Yes, well enough," said Tom, "it was the half-year before Arthur came."

‘ "Exactly so," answered the master. "Now, I was with him a few minutes afterwards, and he was in great distress about you two. And, after some talk, we both agreed that you in particular wanted some object in the school beyond games and mischief; for it was quite clear that you never would make the regular school work your first object. And so the Doctor, at the beginning of the next half-year, looked out the best of the new boys and separated you and East, and put the young boy into your study, in the hope that when you had somebody to lean on you, you would begin to stand a little steadier yourself, and get manliness and thoughtfulness . . . not one of you boys will ever know the anxiety you have given him, or the care with which he has watched over every step in your school lives." Up to this time Tom had never wholly given in to, or understood, the Doctor. At first he had thoroughly feared him. . . . It was a new light to him to find that, besides teaching the sixth, and governing and guiding the whole School, editing classics and writing histories, the great Headmaster had found time in those busy years to watch over the career even of him, Tom Brown, and his particular friends —and, no doubt, of fifty other boys at the same time . . . the Doctor's victory was complete from that moment over Tom. . . . It had taken eight long years to do it, but now it was done thoroughly and there wasn't a corner of him left which didn't believe in the Doctor.' Unfortunately, however, this conversion was made on Tom's last day at the school.

One of the most impressive tributes to Arnold came from Dr. Moberley, the headmaster of Winchester. He wrote, shortly after Arnold's death in 1842: 'A most singular and striking change has come upon our public schools—a change too great for any person to appreciate adequately who has not known them in both these times. This change is undoubtedly part of a general improvement in our generation in respect of piety and reverence, but I am sure that to Dr. Arnold's personal earnest simplicity, strength of character, power of influence and piety, which none who ever came near him could mistake or question, the carrying of this improvement into our schools is mainly attributable. He was the first. It soon began to be a matter of observation to us in the University that his pupils brought quite a different character with them to Oxford than that which we knew elsewhere. I do not speak of opinions; but his pupils were thoughtful, manly-minded, conscious of duty and obligation when they first came to college; we . . . looked on Dr. Arnold as exercising an influence for good, which (for how many years I know not) had been absolutely unknown to our public schools. I knew personally but little of him . . . but I have always felt and acknowledged that I owe more to a few casual remarks of his in respect of the government of a public school than to any advice or example of any other person.' Many headmasters of the second half of the nineteenth century had been at Rugby, and thus Arnold's ideals of 'manliness' and piety were spread. Assistant masters of Arnold who went on to great careers as headmasters included J. Prince Lee of King Edward's, Birmingham, Vaughan of Harrow, and Cotton of Marlborough. Boys under Arnold at Rugby became headmasters of Harrow, Marlborough, Lancing, Haileybury, Sherborne, Cheltenham, Felsted, Bury St. Edmunds, Leamington, Berkhamsted, Bromsgrove, Monkton Combe, Berwick and Carlisle Cathedral School.

Samuel Butler, grandson of the Samuel Butler who was headmaster of Shrewsbury, wrote a more critical account (under the thin veil of 'Dr. Skinner') in his autobiographical novel *The Way of All Flesh*. 'Like all houses, Dr. Skinner's had its own smell. In this case the prevailing odour was one of Russia leather, but along with it there was a subordinate savour as of a chemist's shop. This came from a small laboratory in one corner of the room—the possession of which, together with the free chattery and smattery use of such words as "carbonate", "hyposulphite", "phosphate", and "affinity", was enough to convince even the most sceptical that Dr. Skinner had a profound knowledge of chemistry. I may say in passing that Dr. Skinner had dabbled in a great many other things as well as chemistry. He was a man of many small knowledges, and each of them dangerous. . . . The table of the library [in the headmaster's house] was loaded with books many deep; MSS of all kinds were confusedly mixed up with them—boys' exercises, probably, and examination papers—but all littering untidily about. The room, in fact, was as depressing from its slatternliness as from its atmosphere of erudition. Theobald and Ernest, as they entered it, stumbled over a large hole in the Turkey carpet, and the dust that rose showed how long it was since it had been taken up and beaten. This, I should say, was no fault of Mrs. Skinner's but was due to the Doctor himself, who declared that if his papers were once disturbed it would be the death of him.' Butler continued,'. . . he was always there; there was no knowing at what moment he might not put in an appearance, and whenever he did show, it was to storm about something. . . . He called Ernest "an audacious reptile" and said he wondered the earth did not open and swallow him up because he pronounced Thalia with a short i. "And this to me," he thundered, "who never made a false quantity in my life." Surely he would have been a much nicer person if he had made false quantities in his youth like other people. . . . Only once in the whole course of his school life did he get praise from Dr. Skinner for any exercise, and this he has treasured as the best example of guarded approval which he has ever seen. He had to write a copy of Alcaics on "The Days of the Monks of St. Bernard", and when the exercise was returned to him he found the Doctor had written on it: "In this copy of Alcaics —which is still excessively bad—I fancy that I can discern some faint symptoms of improvement". . . . On the day of his leaving [when] he was sent for into the library to be shaken hands with, he was surprised to feel that, though assuredly glad to leave, he did not do so with any special grudge against the Doctor rankling in his breast. He had come to the end of it all, and was still alive, nor, take it all round, more seriously amiss than other people. Dr. Skinner received him graciously, and was even frolicsome after his own heavy fashion. Young people are almost always placable, and Ernest felt as he went away that another such interview would not only have wiped off old scores, but would have brought him round into the ranks of the Doctor's admirers.' Butler got his own back on Arnold and, with evident satisfaction, he urged all schoolmasters to 'bear in mind when any particularly timid drivelling urchin is brought by his papa into your study, and you treat him with the contempt which he deserves, and afterwards make his life a burden to him for years —bear in mind that it is exactly in the disguise of such a boy as this that your future chronicler will appear. Never see a wretched little heavy-eyed mite sitting on the edge of a chair against your study wall without saying to yourselves, "Perhaps this boy is he who, if I am not careful, will one day tell the world what manner of man I was." '

Whatever manner of man Arnold was, and there seems to have been some disagreement, he certainly made a lasting impression, one way or the other, on his former pupils. And ever since his time Rugby has remained undisputably one of the greatest schools.

Rugby has given its name to the handling game in football, which was traditionally first played at the school. In Arnold's day there were no compulsory games. As Lytton Strachey said: 'The modern reader of *Tom Brown's Schooldays* searches in vain for any reference to compulsory games, house colours, or cricket averages. In those days, when boys played games they played them for pleasure.' Indeed, it was this lack of organisation that is said to have been responsible for the first picking up of a football and running with it.*

Harrow School has much the same history as Rugby. It owes its foundation to the Will of another middle-class property-owner of Middlesex, John Lyon. Lyon inherited land from his father and he became the largest landowner in Harrow. (As well as land in Harrow, the school owns Shepherd Market in Mayfair.) Lyon provided for the education of thirty local boys, in the church school, but in his Will of 1471, and the royal charter which he obtained at the same time, Lyon made provision for his own school at Harrow. He survived another twenty years, and his wife twenty years after that,

---

* Rugbeians include F. W. Walker, the great High Master of St. Paul's, Charles Dodgson (Lewis Carroll), William Temple, archbishop, Arthur Waley, the orientalist, R. H. Tawney, Rupert Brooke, the lexicographers G. W. Fowler (for many years a master at Sedbergh) and Sir Ernest Gowers, Neville and Austen Chamberlain, Major-General Sir Ernest Swinton, the originator of tanks, Philip Guedalla, biographer, Sir Pelham Warner, Sir Arthur Bliss (who found music treated 'with condescension, if not worse'), Wyndham Lewis, Viscount Goschen, Sir Richard Acland, Lord Elton, P. H. B. Lyon, headmaster of Edinburgh Academy and Rugby, Sir Robert Birley, headmaster of Charterhouse and Eton, Sir Denis Truscott, Lord Mayor, Robert Henriques, Angus Maude M.P., Field-Marshal Sir James Cassels, Anthony Quayle, actor, Sir Anthony Milward, Sir Edmund Compton, the first ombudsman, Collie Knox, journalist, Maurice Green, editor, and William Deedes, M.P.

so it was forty years before the provisions could be put into effect, and the school house was not built until 1615. The school was to provide free education for local scholars, and the governors were to be leading men of that parish. Lyon ordered that the governors 'shall not receive any girl into the said school'.

William Hide was headmaster from 1628 to 1661, but Harrow did not become a major school until Thomas Bryan, 1691–1730, under whom the school became predominantly a boarding school, with over a hundred boarders. There was the typical eighteenth-century slump after Bryan, but the fortunes of Harrow School were really restored by Dr. Robert Sumner, headmaster 1760–71, under whom numbers rose from eighty to 250. Three future Governor-Generals of India were at Harrow under Sumner. On his death there were the first of three famous riots, the boys preferring the usher to the new headmaster, Benjamin Heath, an Eton under-master, appointed by the governors. The boys petitioned the governors in terms which revealed not only their precocity, but how the rivalry with Eton was already well under way: 'As most of us are independent of the foundation [i.e. fee-payers], we presume our inclinations ought to have some weight in the determination of your choice. . . . A school of such reputation as our late master has rendered this ought not to be considered as an appendix of Eton. . . . A school cannot be supported when every individual is disaffected towards the master; neither will the disregarded wishes of the members want opportunities in showing their resentment.' Promin-ent in the riots was Richard Wellesley, future Governor-General, who was expelled and continued his education at Eton. Heath was succeeded by his brother-in-law and assistant master, Dr. Joseph Drury, under whom the numbers reached 345. Drury was an ad-vanced educationist. He abolished the birch for all but the younger boys, and associated with his pupils socially after work was over. He was far in advance of his time, and the remarkable number of men he produced who made notable contributions to society is the measure of his success; among them were four prime ministers, Lord Goderich, Sir Robert Peel, Lord Aberdeen and Lord Palmer-ston (Harrow had already produced one prime minister, Spencer Percival). A contemporary considered Palmerston 'the best-tempered and most plucky boy in the school'. There was another rebellion on Drury's retirement, in 1805. Byron, who considered Drury the 'best and worthiest friend he ever possessed', was a ringleader; a plan to dynamite the walls was only stopped when some boys appealed for the preservation of walls on which the names of so many of their fathers' were carved. There was another revolt in 1808, this time about the powers of monitors, whose traditional rights had been threatened by the new headmaster, the Rev. George Butler;* the boys barricaded the London Road and seized the keys of the birch cupboard.

Harrow was now established as the leading rival to Eton and many of the great families of England preferred it for their boys. By 1816 there were only three free scholars at the school. One of the few day-boys was Anthony Trollope, who walked three miles to school through muddy lanes. He recalled: 'I might have been known among all the boys at a hundred yards distance by my boots and trousers. The indignities which I endured are not to be described. As I look back, it seems to me that all hands were turned against me —those of masters as well as boys. I was allowed to join in no plays. Nor did I learn anything, for I was taught nothing.' The decline under Butler was arrested by C. J. Vaughan, who had been a master at Rugby under Arnold. Under him the school numbers rose from eighty boys to 470, making Harrow one of the largest schools in Britain. Vaughan remodelled Harrow on Rugby. He was succeeded by H. M. Butler, who had been head boy of the school under Vaughan. Butler remained from 1859 to 1885 and under him the school as it is today finally took shape. During Butler's time the great tradition of Harrow songs was begun, with the appointment of John Farmer as organist. Among Butler's pupils were one arch-bishop (Lord Davidson), seventeen judges, four Viceroys of India and no less than sixty-four generals, including two of the better generals of the First World War, Sir Horace Smith-Dorrien and Lord Horne. But his two most famous old boys were John Galsworthy and Stanley Baldwin, well described in one of the school's histories as 'a man who somewhat uniquely played the game of politics as though it were cricket.' On becoming prime minister, Baldwin said: 'When the call came to me to form a government, one of my first thoughts was that it should be a government of which Harrow should not be ashamed. I remembered how in previous governments there had been four or, perhaps, five Harrovians, and I determined to have six.' Harold Macmillan, as has been seen, said

* Father of three sons who became headmasters of Harrow, Liverpool and Haileybury.

much the same thing, in the context of Eton, when he became prime minister. Baldwin told the Harrow Association, on 19 July 1923: 'You mean by your greeting to assure me that you wish me well, as I know you do, and that whether I succeed or fail you have the belief in me that as a son of the Hill I will run straight; that I will bear my share of the burden; that if I fail I will not whine; and that if success is mine I will not be puffed up . . . and that I will, with God's help, do nothing . . . which shall cause any Harrovian to say of me that I have failed to do my best to live up to the highest ideals of the school.'

Harrow was reconstituted under the Public Schools Act of 1868, the governing body from then on being nominated by the two universities, by the Lord Chancellor, the Royal Society and the headmaster and staff. Something of Lyon's wishes was preserved by the establishment in 1876 of the Lower School of John Lyon, at Harrow, which provided a modern education, in accordance with the Act of 1868; this school received half the Lyon endowment, but even there the tuition was not entirely free. The governors at John Lyon School are the same as those of Harrow.

Butler was followed by Dr. J. E. C. Welldon, who had been Master of Dulwich. Under Welldon was a not very promising boy who was destined to become the greatest politician and statesman in British history, then known as Winston Spencer-Churchill. One newly appointed master in Churchill's time asked despairingly of his class: 'What am I to do with boys who know nothing?' The young Churchill replied: 'Please, sir, teach us.' Churchill later recalled: 'Mr. Welldon took a friendly interest in me and, knowing that I was weak in the Classics, determined to help me himself. His daily routine was heavy; but he added three times a week a quarter of an hour before evening prayers in which to give me personal tuition. This was a great condescension for the Head-master, who of course never taught anyone but the monitors and the highest scholars. I was proud of the honour: I shrank from the ordeal. If the reader has ever learned any Latin prose he will know that at quite an early stage one comes across the Ablative Absolute. . . . I was often uncertain whether the Ablative Absolute should end in "e" or "i" or "o" or "ibus", to the correct selection of which great importance was attached. Mr. Welldon seemed to be physically pained by a mistake being made in any of these letters. I remember that later on Mr. Asquith used to have just the same sort of look on his face when

I sometimes adorned a Cabinet discussion by bringing out one of my few but faithful Latin quotations. It was more than an annoyance; it was a pang. Moreover, Head-masters have powers at their disposal with which Prime Ministers have never yet been invested. So these evening quarters of an hour with Mr. Welldon added considerably to the anxieties of my life.' Churchill remained a life-long critic of the classics 'for the prime structure of our education.'*

*

Sutton Valence School, built into the side of a steep hill with remarkable views across Kent, was also founded by a merchant, William Lambe, of the Company of Clothworkers, after whom Lamb's Conduit Street in London is named (he had constructed the water-works there on Lawrence Sheriff's property). Lambe founded the school at his native village in 1576, four years before he died; 'a Grammar Schoole for the education of youth in the feare of God, in good manners, in knowledge and understanding'. He provided thirty pounds a year, together with a house and garden. Lambe also gave gifts to Christ's Hospital and Maidstone Grammar School. Sutton Valence achieved a good reputation during the seventeenth century, but in the eighteenth and during parts of the nineteenth it sunk low indeed. In 1786 the *Gentleman's Magazine* reported that 'through the inactivity and neglect of some of its late masters [it] has been rendered almost useless, and the mastership become nearly a sinecure'. The income from Lambe's endowment had become quite inadequate, and the headmaster had to hold at least one curacy in the neighbourhood. During the eighteen-thirties the school closed down altogether. At this time the Clothworkers, who were the

* Harrovians not mentioned already: Admiral Codrington, Sidney Herbert, Richard Brinsley Sheridan, William Southey, poet, Earl of Shaftesbury, Marquess of Dalhousie, Cardinal Manning, Gerald du Maurier, Sir John Fortescue, historian of the British Army, Lord Lytton, G. M. Trevelyan, L. S. Amery, Jawaharlal Nehru, Lord Templewood, Lord Brabazon, artists Edward Le Bas and Victor Passmore, Sir Cecil Beaton, Field-Marshal Earl Alexander of Tunis, Field-Marshal Viscount Gort, Air Chief Marshal Sir Philip Joubert, C.-inC. Coastal Command 1941–42, Sir Arthur Bryant, Sir John Summerson, Lord Rothschild, first-class cricketer and adviser to the Cabinet, Tom Harrison, of mass-observation (who wrote the standard work on the birds in the district), Aidan Crawley, Lord Orr-Ewing, Sir Peter Studd, Eric Lubbock (now Lord Avebury), King Hussein of Jordan, L. P. Hartley, Sandy Wilson, John Mortimer, and Sir Terence Rattigan, whose *The Browning Version* is one of the best of all portrayals of public-school life.

trustees, appear to have been shamed into refounding the school. Sutton Valence re-opened under the Rev. C. W. Goodchild in 1839. The numbers were to be limited to sixty, up to the age of sixteen: twelve sons of the Clothmakers, twenty-four local scholars, twelve boarders and twelve fee-paying day-boys. These numbers were seldom achieved.

Sutton Valence was no more confortable than other schools of the early nineteenth century. Forty years later one of the first boys of the new foundation recalled: 'The large cold school-room, barely warmed by a huge stove, and traversed by all who must needs pass to the higher ground behind; they will certainly not forget the chilly, white-washed dormitories, with the bare passage where the washing apparatus was placed. . . . I suppose my contemporaries must have become so accustomed to rats and their vagaries in that old house that any succeeding experience of them has been tame in the extreme; when one has gone to bed slipper in hand, ready to strike the wall near one's bed to scare away these pests, one may fairly be considered rat-proof for the remainder of life.' Conditions were greatly improved by the opening of a new building in 1864, and the arrival of Dr. J. D. Kingdon in the same year, under the regime of whom, and of his successor, G. L. Bennett, 1883–1910, Sutton Valence became a leading school in Kent. Four years after Kingdon arrived, there were thirty-two boarders and eight day-scholars. In 1910 the Clothworkers relinquished their care of the school and passed it on to the United Westminster Schools, of the City of Westminster.*

Seven years later Edmund Grindal founded St. Bees, near the Cumberland coast. Grindal, who was successively Bishop of London, Archbishop of York and Archbishop of Canterbury, was the son of a farmer of Hensingham, Cumberland. He had been precentor at St. Paul's, and was probably influenced by Colet's foundation. He did not please Elizabeth as Archbishop, claiming too much independence for the Church, and he was making arrangements for his resignation when he died, in 1583. Grindal left considerable benefactions to Queen's College, Oxford, and Pembroke, Cambridge, and these colleges still provide representatives on the board of governors. The endowment came from lands at Croydon, then bringing in £50 per annum. Grindal was buried at Croydon, and by a strange coincidence was succeeded as Archbishop of Canterbury

* Sir R. S. Champion, Governor of Aden, and Dr. A. R. Vidler are old boys.

by that Croydon man John Whitgift. Grindal required the master to 'carefully seek to bring up all his scholars equally in learning and good manners', and 'chiefly labour to make his scholars profit in the Latin and Greek grammar'. The school-house of St. Bees was built in 1587, and it is still in daily use. The school was further endowed by James I. For years the school was plagued with legal wrangles. The most notorious of these was probably that which concerned the letting of land in 1742 by the governors to the Lowther family; the lands were used for coal-mining. The rent was exceedingly low; when a headmaster drew attention to this sixty years later, he was obliged to resign. The Charity Commissioners investigated, a long suit in Chancery took place; eventually the Lowthers made a payment and St. Bees was able to develop, although its isolated position made expansion difficult. The nineteen-thirties, a difficult time for nearly all public schools, nearly finished St. Bees. Numbers fell to such an extent that in 1938 it was summarily announced that the school would close. It was saved by a meeting of old boys in June, which promised the school an annual grant, and by a new head-master, J. S. Boulter. The school re-opened as usual in September with seventy-one boys. Despite these low numbers, it honoured its Rugby fixtures, including matches against Rossall, Sedbergh and Stonyhurst, winning the first. There is no doubt that St. Bees was saved by the determined and generous action of its old boys, who were necessarily not as numerous as those of a large school.

With Oakham School, in Rutland, we return to a school founded by a clergyman, Robert Johnson. Johnson, Archdeacon of Leicester, had been chaplain to Sir Nicholas Bacon, who had benefited St. Alban's School. A Puritan, he had travelled abroad for three years, and founded a grammar school at Oakham and at nearby Upping-ham, in 1854. At Oakham he instructed the master to 'teach all those grammar scholars that are born and bred up in the town of Oakham, freely without pay, if their parents be poor and not able to pay, and keep then constantly at school'. Oakham is now a Direct Grant school, with more than half the pupils boarders, but stays close to the wishes of its founder. Johnson's other school, at Uppingham, remained as a local grammar school, if somewhat less reputable than that at Oakham, until the late nineteenth century. Its fame is due entirely to the headmastership of Edward Thring, 1853 to 1887, for whom great claims are justly made.

Thring was a clergyman from Somerset, educated at Eton and at

King's College, Cambridge. When he was accepted at Uppingham, in his early thirties, he had experience only of being a curate. He was determined to make this little-known country grammar school one of the major schools of England by improving the standards both educationally and socially. He spent money lavishly and debts accumulated, but by the time of his death, still at his post, Thring had achieved his object. Although he wrote much on the subject, Thring was not a great innovator, educationally, like Sanderson of Oundle. He continued the work of Arnold. He believed in paying more attention to the individual boy, and for this reason he insisted on keeping the school to around three hundred boys (there had been only twenty-five on his arrival). Life under Thring was more pleasant than it had ever been at a public school before. He said of contemporary schooling: 'The human being has been left out.' The gymnasium he had especially built, in 1859, was possibly the first at any school in the country. He had beds partitioned off in the dormitories, and each boy was given his own study (his 'castle'). Thring was against routine, and he provided new activities and interests in the school in the form of games, handicrafts and the arts, especially music. All this, he believed, would help to shape a boy's character more satisfactorily than the bear-garden conditions he remembered from his own days at Eton. Many fathers who had suffered at school as he had were inclined to agree with him. Uppingham became famous in Britain and abroad as a civilised place of education, a reputation which it has retained. As far as schoolboys are concerned, Edward Thring, at Uppingham, was the best thing that ever happened to the public schools. Thring, however, did not include in his reforms the stranglehold that the classics had in Victorian schools. One who arrived at the school a year after his death recorded: 'Our education in school was more limited, more in keeping perhaps with the world immediately around us than with the busy world outside; it seems strange to think now that in 1888 every man jack of us was compelled to learn, or more strictly to be taught, the language of the cultivated Athenian; that the bulk of us know nothing of the secrets of science, and that the study of French was quite adequately described by the harassed student of the classics, which he did not savour, who dumped his books in his French instructor's class-room with the heartfelt ejaculation: "Thank Heaven! at last a slack hour." Even "lines" written in Detention were always either Greek or Latin.'

Thring not only set a new standard for conditions at boarding schools, he also founded the Headmasters' Conference, in 1869, which enabled headmasters for the first time to speak with one voice in matters which concerned them, and in due course brought many matters to public attention which might otherwise have rankled for years in solitary breasts. From Thring's time Uppingham expanded until town and school have become virtually inseparable. Another well-known headmaster at the school was Sir John Wolfenden, 1934–44, who made the unusual sideways move to Shrewsbury. Uppinghamians since Thring's day have been renowned for their easy manners and style. The archetypal Uppinghamian was the debonair bemonocled Viscount Soulbury, who, as President of the Board of Education in 1940, pioneered the use of film in schools.*

Uppingham has long been a great cricketing school, and it has produced C. S. Hearst (Kent), A. P. F. Chapman (Kent and England), F. G. H. Chalk (Kent), and A. F. T. White (Worcestershire).

Queen Elizabeth's Hospital, Bristol, now Direct Grant, was founded by the Will of John Carr, a Bristol merchant, in 1586, along the lines of Christ's Hospital. It was specifically charged with 'the education of poor children and orphans', and has kept to this until the present day. It was entirely a boarding school until 1920, having moved to its present site from the city centre eighty years before. Boarders still wear the traditional Blue Coat uniform. W. Friese-Greene, pioneer of the cinema, was educated there. Queen Elizabeth's Grammar School, Wakefield, was founded, in 1591, at the bequest 'made unto us by the inhabitants of the town and parish', and it was endowed by the Savile family. Wallasey Grammar School (1595) and Wellingborough School also date from the late sixteenth century. Wellingborough owed its existence to an endowment of property made for charitable purposes in 1478 which had been added to from time to time. In 1595 it was decided that this was to be used for educational purposes and the school was established. Wellingborough was early to provide an education in English and 'accounts'. In 1687 a Jesuit managed to get the headmastership; his true identity was not discovered until after he had mysteriously

---

* Others: Sir Frederick Macmillan, the publisher, Sir Malcolm Campbell and his son Donald Campbell, both holders of world speed records, Sir Patrick Abercrombie, the town planner, Lieutenant-General Sir Brian Horrocks, and authors A. A. Willis and William Sansom.

disappeared. The school moved to a new site on the outskirts of the town in 1881.

Trinity School, Croydon, and Whitgift School were founded by John Whitgift, who followed Edmund Grindal, founder of St. Bees, as Archbishop of Canterbury. Whitgift had risen to prominence via Cambridge University; he became Master of Pembroke Hall, Trinity College, and vice-chancellor. As archbishop he usually pleased Elizabeth, and he became a member of her council in 1586. Macaulay's description of him as 'a narrow, mean, tyrannical priest, who gained power by servility and adulation' is most unjust. He founded his school and almshouses (or Hospital) in 1596. The building, a handsome quadrangle, was completed in 1599, at a cost of £2,716 11s. 1d. The pupils were to be taught free of charge, in Greek and Latin, but the master was allowed to accept payment from the more well-to-do parents of the parish. By the end of the eighteenth century Whitgift School had declined to such an extent that the headmaster was receiving the endowment, with no pupils at all. When it got going again, it was still hampered by its statutes. At length the school was split in two, by order of the Court of Chancery, in 1852. One part, for poor children, was to be able to take 250 students. This became Whitgift Middle School, the name of which was changed to Trinity School in 1954. This school moved to spacious, modern premises in Shirley Park, about a mile from Croydon, in 1965. It gained a high reputation under the headmastership of O. Berthoud, 1952–72, who transformed the school. The other school of the foundation, named Whitgift School, opened in new premises in 1871, catering for middle-class day-boys. Both schools benefited from the rapid urban growth of Croydon as a dormitory suburb. Whitgift School moved to its present site in Holing Park, South Croydon, from its former premises, in 1931. Both schools have the same governing body, seven of them appointed by the Archbishop of Canterbury.*

Aldenham School was founded in 1596 by Richard Platt, 'Cytyzen and Brewer of London', endowing it with three fields at St. Pancras, which eventually came to be of great value. The Brewers' Company have always been the trustees of the school, which was intended for

---

* Old Whitgiftians: Sir Newman Flower, Churchill's publisher, Marshal of the R.A.F. Lord Tedder, Deputy Supreme Commander, 1943–45, Lord Diplock, judge, Sir Burke Trend, Group-Captain John 'Cats-eyes' Cunningham, Colonel Colin Mitchell, M.P., and Raman Subba Row, the Test cricketer.

'children of poore people inhabitinge in the Parishe of Aldenham and the children of the Freemen of the Companye of Brewers'. The early history of the school is mostly a story of a long struggle to survive; at one time the numbers fell to two, and the headmaster closed the school. It seems the standard of education was not high enough to encourage the brewers to send their sons to Aldenham, on the coach from the White Swan in Holborn, and there was but little local demand for its facilities. At times headmasters were obliged to drop the classics, the teaching of which Platt had stipulated, and on those occasions the numbers picked up. From 1802 the land at St. Pancras began to be built on, and Aldenham revived somewhat under J. C. Cantrell and Alfred Leeman; it advertised for boarders in the late nineteenth century, as it had in the eighteenth century. The statutes were observed by the father buying himself into the Brewers' Company. 'In order to render a pupil, not otherwise qualified, eligible for admission into the School, his Father, or surviving Parent, must attend at a Court of the Brewers' Company, to be admitted to the Freedom; this to persons of respectability, on supplying satisfactory references, is attended with no difficulty, and only involves the outlay of £20 for the Freedom, and the deposit of a further sum of £20.' These 'Private Pupils' were limited to the number of forty, and their fees were fifty guineas per annum. By this time the fees for Foundationers were £35 per annum, Foundationers being nominated from the private pupils or by the Company. These somewhat dubious practices, approved by the Endowed Schools Commissioners in 1875, had the merit of putting Aldenham on its feet. The Brewers' Company was able to benefit the school much more freely in the twentieth century than hitherto, and by the outbreak of the First World War Aldenham was in a flourishing state. Today it is still on its original site, with over three hundred boarders and a few day-boys, admitted irrespective of the Company (which still, however, retains representation in the governing body).*

Emanuel School was founded in 1594 under the Will of Lady Ann Dacre. She left £300 for a hospital and school in Tothill Fields, Westminster, for twenty poor people and twenty poor children. The institution came under the control of the Lord Mayor and Aldermen of London in 1623. In 1794 the number of children was increased to twenty-eight, and there were further extensions in 1822 and 1843.

* Old boys include General Sir Richard Gale, England cricketer J. G. Reeves, broadcaster Jack de Manio.

In 1873 the school was severed from the almshouses and brought, together with other schools in Westminster, under the United Westminster Schools. Emanuel benefited from rents in Yorkshire. In 1892 the site and buildings were sold for £37,500 and the school moved to Wandsworth. According to Besant, the old school was 'the most beautiful of the venerable places' of London.

One of the last schools to be established in Elizabeth's reign was the grammar school at Kimbolton, Huntingdonshire, founded in 1600 by H. Balye and W. Dawson for the instruction of town children in grammar. Boarders stayed in private houses in the town. In the last third of the nineteenth century town inhabitants were still paying only thirty shillings a year for the education of their sons at the school. For a time it became an 'Agricultural School', but reverted to a grammar school before the end of the century. Thus it continued until the late-nineteenth century, when it declined into near oblivion. The original buildings were demolished in 1875 and a new school built just outside the grounds of Kimbolton Castle. The school was resumed by William Ingram, headmaster 1913–47. He found nine boarders and twenty day-boys in the school. The present boarding houses, in the High Street of what has been described as one of the fifteen most beautiful villages in England, were acquired during his administration, and a new science block built. Since 1913 Kimbolton has only had two headmasters, and one need look no further for reasons for its flourishing state in the splendid and historic castle (which the school purchased from the Duke of Manchester in 1950) and in the High Street, as a Direct Grant school. Kimbolton is the best example in the country of a school flourishing as never before under the Direct Grant system. From a minor and insignificant grammar school that took boarders, it has become a fine boarding school. After Eton and Dulwich, it has perhaps the finest collection of paintings owned by any school.

The last Elizabethan school was Newcastle under Lyme High School, founded in 1602, by Richard Clayton, for the free education of thirty poor children. Queen Elizabeth, last of the Tudors, died on 24 March 1603. Archbishop Whitgift was at her death-bed, and it was he who crowned James VI of Scotland, James I of England.

5

SEVENTEENTH-CENTURY SCHOOLS

THE seventeenth century saw a gradual decline in all education in Britain, and indeed in Europe, but this did not become dramatic until the end of the century; the first forty years were the zenith for the grammar schools; after that few indeed were founded. One of the reasons for the decline was that Latin was ceasing to be the sole medium of learning, and the schools taught little else. Richard Mulcaster had already written on the advantages of English as compared to Latin, but nearly all schools stuck rigidly to the traditional ideas.

The first post-Elizabethan great school was founded in one of the ways that had so marked the previous century: by endowment of a prosperous merchant, Peter Blundell, a Mercer who made a fortune selling Devon kerseys in London. Blundell succeeded in getting the services of the Lord Chief Justice as executor, and his Will was faithfully carried out, the school opening at his home town of Tiverton in 1604. The numbers were to be no more than 150 boys. An impressive school house was built, and 'foreigners' were accepted as well as local boys receiving free education. The first master was Samuel Butler, who gave the school a good start. Samuel Wesley, brother of the evangelist, was a later headmaster. The school had a local reputation, and generations of West Country families attended it, notably Coves and Seymours. It first received wider prominence under Henry Sanders, headmaster 1834–47, who produced several public figures. Unfortunately Blundell's had also achieved a less enviable reputation; bullying, hardship and ill-discipline had reached such a state by Sanders' reign that even the early Victorians, accustomed to the horror stories from Eton, Winchester and elsewhere, were shocked. One boy, undergoing some traditional ritual, was said to have been burned to death in front of an open fire. There was constant warfare between boarders and day-boys, and the latter so customarily got the worst of this that the townspeople formed a committee in December 1838, to take up the matter with the school's trustees. The dispute was put before the Court of Chancery, who decided strongly in favour of the townspeople. Blundell's school was to be a free grammar school for the town. The Vice-Chancellor declared, 'Neither the Master nor the Usher of the said School ought to receive any payments from or in respect of any of the boys educated in the said School, or ought to take any boarder.'

For a time Blundell's remained the grammar school for Tiverton. This period is described in the school history by Snell as 'the dreary interval caused by the fatuous decree in Chancery'. But, having made their point, the townspeople did little to prevent the school reverting to its old position, as part boarding school. Nothing had been said about assistant masters not taking boarders, and this they began to do. Latin and Greek had to be taught free, but there was nothing to prevent charges for other subjects. In 1874 A. L. Francis, an assistant master at Dulwich, became headmaster, the first layman to do so, and he established Blundell's as an important school, after its long and unhappy history, especially in regard to its bad conditions for boarders and its conflict with the town, this latter in marked contrast to the experience of so many other country-town schools. Francis moved Blundell's to its present site outside the town in 1882. The most famous old boy is R. D. Blackmore, author of *Lorna Doone*, which contains an interesting account of the school. 'My father being of good substance, at least as we reckon in Exmoor, and . . . well able to write his name, sent me his only son to be schooled at Tiverton, in the county of Devon. For the chief boast of that ancient town (next to its woollen-staple) is a worthy grammar school, the largest in the West of England. . . . Here, by the time I was twelve years old, I had risen into the upper school, and could make bold with Eutropius and Caesar—by aid of an English version —and as much as six lines of Ovid . . . if you doubt my having been there, because now I know so little, go and see my name, "John Ridd", graven on that very form. Forsooth, from the time I was strong enough to open a knife and to spell my name, I began to grave it in the oak, first of the block whereon I sate, and then of the desk in front of it, according as I was promoted from one to other of them: and there my grandson reads it now.'*

* Others: Frederick Temple, Archbishop of Canterbury, A. V. Hill, Nobel Prize winner, writers J. C. Squire, Edward Hutton and Anthony Smith, Professor C. E. M. Joad, General Sir Walter Walker, who prevented another Vietnam in Borneo, Lord Stokes, and the rugger international Richard Sharp.

Other early schools of this period are Peter Symonds', Winchester (1607), and Hulme Grammar School, Oldham, founded in 1611 by James Assheton for boys to learn the 'English, Latin and Greek tongues, and in good manners withal'. The grammar school at Oldham later received the further endowment of William Hulme, the eventeenth-century philanthropist, who founded four exhibitions at Brasenose College, Oxford, in memory of his son.

One of the great schools of Ireland also dates from this era. Portora, the Royal School for Fermanagh, is one of the three famous Royal Schools of Ulster, founded under charter of James I, for Protestant children of the plantation of Ulster, the others being at Armagh (1608) and Dungannon (1614). Portora was established as a Protestant grammar school at the village of Lismaskea in 1608, but moved to the county town of Enniskillen in 1641. New buildings were put up in 1777, on Portora hill, overlooking Lough Erne and the town. For most of its history the school came under the crown, in the person of the Viceroy in Dublin, but since the Irish Educational Endowment Act of 1885, which revised the constitutions of several Irish public schools, Portora has been governed by an independent governing body, of which the Bishop of Clogher is chairman. Portora gained a national reputation under the headmastership of Dr. William Steele in the nineteenth century, boarders coming from all over Britain. Steele built the assembly hall at his own expense in 1861. In recent years there has been considerable new building, and the modern aim is 'to retain the English public-school pattern while offering entry to all day-boys who can benefit by the schooling'. Portora is the leading rowing school of Ireland. Its greatest sons are Oscar Wilde and Samuel Beckett, awarded the Nobel Prize for literature. Wilde had a curious career at Portora. Although it was very much a games school, he was excused cricket and football, as he detested both. He had refused to play cricket, 'because the attitudes assumed were so indecent'. The staff seemed to forgive his rebellious attitude because he was so brilliant at his work (he won a scholarship and an exhibition to Trinity, Dublin). It was Wilde who declared: 'Education is an admirable thing, but it is well to remember from time to time that nothing that is worth knowing can be taught.'

*

The two greatest schools of the seventeenth century are Charterhouse and Dulwich. Charterhouse was founded in 1611, by Thomas

Sutton, on the site of the old monastery of that name, which had been closed in 1537. Since the dissolution, the buildings, on the environs of London, had passed through several hands, eventually being purchased by Sutton from the Howard family for £13,000. Sutton, as this figure indicates, was an extremely wealthy man, probably one of the richest in the country. While serving in various official posts, he had made a fortune through what had best be described as high finance. Following the example set in the previous century, he made provision for an impressive charity: a hospital, or home, for men of good character who had fallen on evil days, and a free grammar school. In the early days of the foundation, the hospital played a larger part than the school. It was not until the second half of the eighteenth century that Charterhouse became comparable with the other great London schools, Merchant Taylors', St. Paul's and Westminster (although Lovelace, Addison, Steele and John Wesley had all been pupils there). Matthew Raine, headmaster 1791–1811, did much to improve the school's academic reputation. His pupils included Henry Havelock, of Lucknow fame, and George Grote, the historian of Greece. By Raine's last year, and for a further four years, a Carthusian was prime minister (Lord Liverpool), Archbishop of Canterbury (Manners Sutton) and Lord Chief Justice (Lord Ellenborough), an achievement probably never equalled by any other school.

By this time a boarding house, Verites, had joined the foundation scholars, known as Gownboys. The school experienced mixed fortunes under the controversial headmastership of John Russell, 1811–32, at one time having nearly five hundred boys on the roll. Russell abolished corporal punishment as early as 1818, only ten years after a mutiny by the boys. Russell was followed by Dr. Saunders, 1832–53, who founded another boarding house. Saunders felt restricted by the school's location, London having grown all round it many years previously. This problem was tackled by Dr. William Haig Brown, who might well be considered the founder of the modern Charterhouse. He was only the third non-Carthusian to hold the office (having been educated, like Francis of Blundell's, at Christ's Hospital).

Support for a move to the country was given in the Public School Commissioners' report of 1864, which declared that 'the school would thrive much better if removed to some eligible site in the country'. Accordingly, the premises, as has already been seen above, were sold to Merchant Taylors' and a site of seventy acres chosen at Godalming, a few miles from Mrs. Haig Brown's home. The school moved there in 1872. Old Charterhouse, in the nineteenth century, was well described by one of its most famous former pupils, W. M. Thackeray, in his novel *The Newcomers*. 'He dismissed his cab at Ludgate Hill, and walked thence by the dismal precincts of New-gate, and across the muddy pavement of Smithfield, on his way which he had trodden many a time in his own early days. There was Cistercian Street, and the Red Cow of his youth; there was the quaint old Grey Friars Square, with its blackened trees and garden, surrounded by ancient houses of the build of the last century, now slumbering like pensioners in the sunshine. Under the great arch-way of the hospital he could look at the old Gothic building, and a black-gowned pensioner or two crawling over the quiet square, or passing from one dark arch to another. The boarding houses of the school were situated in the square, hard by the more ancient buildings of the hospital. A great noise of shouting, crying, clapping forms and cupboards, treble voices, bass voices, poured out of the schoolboys' windows. Their life, bustle and gaiety contrasted strangely with the quiet of those old men, creeping along in their black gowns under the ancient arches yonder, whose struggle of life was over.'

Nothing could have been more different to these somewhat un-prepossessing surroundings than the romantic edifice which the architect produced in Surrey. The names of the three old houses were retained, the hostel system having been considered but re-jected. But Haig Brown decided to spread the scholars through the school, and thus Gownboys became an ordinary house. The move had been made by 120 boys: within a year the number had doubled. As predicted by the Charity Commissioners, the school thrived. New houses were founded by various assistant masters, eventually coming under control of the school (the last to do so, in 1921). Haig Brown retired in 1897. Charterhouse has been fortunate in its head-masters this century: Sir Frank Fletcher, previously Master of Marlborough, Sir Robert Birley, later headmaster of Eton, Brian Young and A. O. Van Oss. A new building scheme of £1,000,000 is planned, to cater 'for a hundred years ahead'. The headmaster was quoted as saying: 'Naturally, we don't know what things will be like then. Maybe we shall be all sixth form. Maybe co-ed. . . . Study bedrooms were the answer because they are flexible.' Charterhouse shares with Westminster in being one of the founders of modern Association Football; the first rules, drawn up in 1863, were drawn by a committee consisting mainly of the old boys of these two schools. In his *Goodbye to All That*, Robert Graves gave a highly critical account of Charterhouse. 'From my first moment at Charterhouse I suffered an oppression of spirit that I hesitate to recall in its full intensity. . . . The school consisted of about six hundred boys whose chief interests were games and romantic friendships. Everyone despised school-work . . . the apathy of the classrooms surprised and disappointed me.' Nevertheless, he won a classical exhibition to St. John's College, Oxford.*

Haverfordwest Grammar School was re-founded by Thomas Lloyd in 1613. It was a free school, as was Owen's School, in East London, founded in the same year by Dame Alice Owen. 'Lady Owen's' School, as it was known until this century, was governed by the Brewers' Company; the foundation was originally for twenty-four poor children of Islington and six of Clerkenwell. The connection with the Brewers' Company remains; they are still the trustees and are responsible for the management of the school's estate as well as for the appointment of the Foundation governors, who form two-thirds of the total board.

West Monmouth School, at Pontypool, was founded in the following year. It should not be confused with Monmouth School, also founded in 1614, by William Jones, a member of the Haberdashers' Company in London, who had been born near by. James bequeathed a large sum to found the school, which is still associated with the Haberdashers' Company. The original foundation was for a hundred boys, of the town and county, but Monmouth has long since drawn its pupils from all over the country. By the eighteen-seventies there were no longer any free places, but the fees at Monmouth have always remained comparatively low. Monmouth School

---

* Carthusians not already mentioned include: Sir Charles Trevelyan, the administrator in India, H. G. Liddell, Greek scholar and headmaster of Westminster, T. L. Beddoes, poet, Max Beerbohm, Lord Baden-Powell, Ralph Vaughan Williams, Sir J. Forbes Robertson, actor, Lord Beveridge, Lord Pearce, Sir Patrick Hastings, lawyer, Ben Travers, dramatist, Robert Graves, R. C. Robertson-Glasgow, cricketer and writer, Orde Wingate, Richard Hughes, novelist of Wales, Field-Marshal Sir Richard Hull, Professor Hugh Trevor-Roper, William Rees-Mogg, editor of *The Times*, Peter May, captain of M.C.C., novelist Brian Glanville, and politicians Geoffrey Johnson-Smith, James Prior and Dick Taverne.

was the scene of a curious incident during the reign of James II, when two headmasters, one for the king and one against him, claimed the post. One master commandeered the schoolroom: the other the master's house. This situation continued for some years, until finally settled by arbitration.

Wilson's Grammar School, Camberwell, was founded in 1615 by the Rev. Edward Wilson, the vicar. Twelve poor scholars were to be provided for. For a time in the nineteenth century the school was closed, as it was not as well endowed as some. In 1958 Wilson's took over the nearby Greencoat School, which had been founded in 1706. (The Red Coat School is across the river at Stepney; the Grey-Coat School, Westminster, was founded in 1698—now girls only.) Hertford Grammar School was founded in 1617 by Richard Hale. Foyle School, Londonderry, was founded also in 1617; here George Farquhar and Sir George Lawrence received their early education. Hastings Grammar School was founded in 1619 by the rector, William Parker; between 1791 and 1813 it was amalgamated with Rye Grammar School.

One of the most remarkable facts in post-Reformation English education was that Cambridge had no secondary school. The only schools appear to have been two college choir schools. Well aware of this deficiency, and perhaps conscious of the happier state in Oxford, the corporation, in 1576, appointed a committee 'to devise and put in wrytinge some good devise for the creating of a grammar schoole within the said towne, and how ye charges of the same maie be borne and raysed'. The possibility of levying a rate soon put an end to the discussion, and it was not until an endowment provided by Stephen Perse, Fellow of Caius College, that Cambridge got its school. Perse was a wealthy physician, well known in Cambridge. In his Will, made out three days before his death in 1615, Perse provided for the construction of 'a convenient house to be used for a Grammar Free Schoole, with one lodging chamber for the Master and another for the Usher'. The master was to receive £40 a year and the usher £20; both were to be graduates of Cambridge. The hundred free scholars were to come from Cambridge, Barnwell, Chesterton ot Trumpington, 'and no more, nor any other'. The school, with specially built premises, was opened in 1618.

It was Perse's wish that his school should be a unifying influence on Town and Gown. Unfortunately, for many generations the opposite was the case. The Master and Fellows of Caius were the trustees, and it cannot be said that they always honoured the trust placed in them. Private schools rose in competition, and all too often the townspeople preferred these to the Perse School. During the eighteenth century the Junior Fellows of Caius passed the posts of master and usher to each other. The number of free places was whittled away to fifteen, while the salary of master and usher increased. The school was left deserted, and the fellows did the teaching in their college rooms. The trustees made an effort to better this situation in 1787, and the Perse School was re-opened. In the seventeen-nineties the first scholarship at Caius for over a hundred years was obtained. In 1816 part of the premises was taken over for the Fitzwilliam collection, but as the numbers of the school had not reached the intended hundred boys for at least a century and a half, if ever, this was little hardship. There was some revival under James Bailey in the eighteen-twenties, who took in a few boarders. By the time Bailey left there were fifty pupils. By 1830, however, Master and Fellows of Caius were drawing £840 instead of the £9 ordained by the founder. It was this scandalous abuse of the foundation's funds that eventually led to a public meeting of protest in Cambridge. This led to legal proceedings, the trial occupying three days in the Rolls Court. Although Caius College admitted irregularities, the judge did not remove the trusteeship from it. The matter was referred to the Chancery Court, where a revised scheme for the school was eventually announced in 1841. The school was to be rebuilt and the salaries of master and usher substantially increased; paying pupils were to be admitted as well as the hundred scholars, provided the teaching staff was increased accordingly. The 'free' scholars were to pay £1 per annum.

The Perse School improved under these regulations, the Master and Fellows of Caius no doubt having been embarrassed by the court proceedings and publicity. New regulations were drawn up under the Endowed Schools Act of 1869, when for the first time the City of Cambridge was allowed a say in the school's affairs. This has remained the basis of the school's government, town and county now being in a majority on the governing body. The Perse School soon began to thrive as it had never done before; at last the citizens of Cambridge, now that they could control it, were prepared to use the school in the numbers that Perse had expected nearly three hundred years before. It was able to survive the establishment of the Cambridgeshire High School in 1900, which might otherwise have proved fatal, as this took a few boarders and became a member of the Headmasters' Conference. The Perse School's two boarding houses date from 1909. Under Dr. W. H. D. Rouse, 1902–28, the Perse School achieved a national reputation for the first time. Rouse had made a study of Rugby under Arnold, and had written the history of that school. Under him the Perse was considered the most advanced public school in Britain, Rouse was famed for the 'direct method' of teaching, in languages, classics and English. Rouse, a brilliant linguist and classical scholar, taught Sanskrit at the university throughout his headmastership. He started the direct method by speaking only Greek or Latin. He taught English by using dramatics. Rouse claimed that under his system a boy of sixteen obtained better results in Latin after 450 school hours than he did under the traditional system after 2,160 hours. In his day, Rouse and his work were as widely discussed as was that of Sanderson, and the direct method began to spread to other progressive schools. The school history states: 'Perhaps no other master in the long history of English public school education has been surrounded by so able, so generous, and so devoted a body of workers and colleagues . . . [during] one of the most remarkable and most successful experiments ever made in the history of English education.' The success of Rouse's work may be measured by the fact that in the years 1939–59 Perseans were appointed to the masterships of four colleges and to five university chairs. Much of Rouse's 'revolutionary' work is now commonplace in the public schools, but the famous 'Mummery' stage is still a feature of teaching at the Perse. Stanley Stubbs, a former business man, who had been a housemaster at Gresham's, was headmaster 1945–69. The school moved to a completely new teaching block, in Hills Road, in 1960. This is one of the most successful modern school buildings in Britain, a pleasing contrast to some of the disgracefully drab and dull blocks built elsewhere. Between the wars, the Perse held a place now occupied perhaps by Sevenoaks. There is always a temptation for a pace-setter to strive to maintain its position, which usually proves disastrous. The Perse School wisely avoided the temptation, and it has now consolidated its position. The Perse School shares with Harrow and Westminster the distinction of being the only public schools which have produced two Nobel Prize winners; in the Perse's case G. P. Thomson (Physics) and R. Norrish (Chemistry).*

* Other old boys: Sir Robert Tabor, promoter of the use of quinine for fever,

Dulwich College is another personally-founded school. In this case it was an actor-manager, Edward Alleyn, who wanted to join the fashion of starting an educational charity. He founded his 'College of God's Gift', a school and almshouses, in 1619, at the country village of Dulwich, south-east of London. Twelve poor local scholars were to be freely taught, and others up to a total of eighty could also be admitted. Alleyn envisaged boarders from the beginning. His instructions, like Colet's, went into great detail, even advising on diet, which included 'a goode messe of pottage' and 'beere without stint'. The opening of the college was a considerable event, being attended by Francis Bacon, Lord Chancellor, and Inigo Jones, and ending with a magnificent banquet.

Alleyn laid down that the headmaster should always bear his name. This provision continued until the mid-nineteenth century, but was side-tracked to some extent from 1746, from when the name Allen was acceptable. In his Will, Alleyn left to his college six feather-beds, six feather bolsters, twelve pair of sheets . . . and six pewter chamber-pots. Unfortunately Alleyn's statutes led to protracted law-suits. In 1857 the whole foundation was re-constituted, and two schools were formed. Dulwich remained the classical school, and Alleyn's School, as the lower side was later named, provided a modern education for day-boys only.* The first master of Alleyn's, who established it as a leading day school for the rapidly expanding population of the Camberwell area, was the Rev. W. F. Greenfield. Dulwich College was itself soon famed for the breadth of its curriculum. The Master, Dr. Alfred Carver, purchased two neighbouring houses, and these became the first boarding houses of the new foundation. (There are now four boarding houses; Blew dates from 1874, Ivyholme from 1885, and the Orchard from 1895.) The value of the endowment, which had been about £800 a year in the seventeenth century, was worth £18,411 by 1870. In that year the college moved to new buildings near by; they were built in what was described as 'the northern Italian style of the 13th century'. Alleyn's used the old school until its own buildings were completed at the other side of Dulwich Village.

E. H. Palmer, explorer of the Sinai desert, Sir Keith Falkner, Director of the Royal College of Music, F. R. Leavis, English critic, Marius Goring, actor, and Peter Hall, producer.

* Not to be confused with Alleyne's Grammar School, Stevenage, founded by Thomas Alleyn in 1558, or Alleyne's Grammar School, Stone, Staffordshire, 1558.

13a. Harrow, 1862

13b. Charterhouse

14.   Edward Thring

15a. Blundell's

15b. Dulwich, 1790

16a. Ampleforth

16b. Royal Belfast Academical Institution

In 1686 the College received a bequest of pictures, and later the munificent collection of old masters of Sir Peter Francis Bourgeois. Dulwich Gallery is one of the oldest in Britain, pre-dating the National Gallery by some twenty years. It is one of the finest small galleries in Europe. In 1971 the governors sold one of the paintings in order to raise the money to improve security arrangements. The gallery includes works by Correggio, Cuyp, Gainsborough, Guido Reni, Hogarth, Huysmans, Landseer, Lawrence, Lely, Murillo, Poussin, Raphael, Rubens, Teniers, Tiepolo, Titian, van Dyck, van der Velde and Sir Joshua Reynolds, including a splendid self-portrait.

Dulwich has always been a good school, and it grew rapidly after the move. In 1868 there were 130 boys. By 1878 the figure had increased to 564; 656 in 1900 and 924 in 1926. Since the Second World War Dulwich has consistently been among the leaders, when not actually in the lead for scholarships to the universities. Among the most notable Masters this century have been A. H. Gilkes* and C. H. Gilkes, father and son, R. Groves, 1954–67, brother-in-law of Christopher Smith, Master of Haileybury, formerly headmaster of Campbell College, and C. W. Lloyd. Old Alleynians include G. E. Moore, Lord Shawcross, two brothers who became professors of literature, G. Wilson Knight and W. F. J. Knight, P. G. Wodehouse, Raymond Chandler, C. S. Forester, Air Marshal Sir Clifford Sanderson, Air C.-in-C. during the Malayan insurgency, and Michael Powell, film director. Dulwich is famed for its cricketers, including the three Gilligan brothers, S. C. Griffith, H. T. Bartlett, Trevor Bailey, A. W. H. Mallet and O. J. Wait. Between the wars there were no fewer than four Alleynian captains of Sussex. Old boys of Alleyn's School include authors V. S. Pritchett and Michael Hastings, Henry Cotton, and several Surrey cricketers.

C. S. Forester, in his autobiography, gives a valuable picture of public-school life in London before the First World War. He attended two schools, and sat for scholarships at several others. He wrote of Dulwich: 'Paper and books, and lavatories and science, and masters and money, and trousers and girls all were known by names quite new to me. There were new conventions regarding singing hymns at morning prayers, and addressing or encountering "bloods" and the tieing of one's necktie, and the mentioning of one's parents, and one's attitude towards coloured boys. Many of the school rules were enforced not by authority, but by the boys themselves, and it

* Father of A. N. Gilkes, High Master of St. Paul's.

was the boys who decided whether other rules should be observed at all. Soon after my arrival the Master (that was his title, not "Headmaster") issued a decree that, in future, boys might wear soft collars—mounting laundry costs and a shortage of starch had done their work. But in all the time I was there I never saw a soft collar worn. Public opinion decided against soft collars, and public opinion saw to it that they were not worn. It should have needed the example of a blood of the deepest dye, a man with at least cricket and football colours, before anyone there dared to make a move in the matter. . . . It was utterly taboo to discuss whether one's parents were wealthy or not, but it was quite permissible to discuss their profession or rank in society . . . the absence of social eminence could be compensated for, oddly enough, by the possession of the right kind of motor-car. . . . Everyone yearned to wear the insignias of rank. There was a different kind of tie and hatband for each of the three Elevens and the three Fifteens; for Prefects and for the Sixth [etc.]. . . . Wherever the bloods assembled were to be seen the most bewildering assortment of striped ties and banded caps—it took a year or two to learn the significance of every combination of stripes and bands. It was not done to wear one distinctive hatband with another sort of tie—the unfortunate possessor of two different "colours" had to plan out his attire on rising in the morning to ensure uniformity. . . . The ideal refreshment at eleven o'clock (but sometimes even lordly ones could not afford it) was a hot bun, fresh from the oven, into which were stuck two sticks of hot milk chocolate. The fiery interior of the bun reduced the chocolate to a desirable viscosity, and then this delectable combination of warm new bun and melting chocolate was washed down with a lemonade.'

*

Merchant Taylors', at Great Crosby, was founded by John Harrison, a member of the Company, in memory of his father, who had gone to London from that place. He knew nothing of the town, and if he had done he may well have thought better of his plan. Crosby was a small village with hardly enough potential pupils to support the ambitious grammar school Harrison had in mind. He wrote his Will in 1618, and part of his great assets were left for the school. He instructed his executors to 'erect and build in Great Crosby in the parish of Shefton in the County of Lancaster, where my father was born, within convenient time after my decease, one free grammar school for the teaching, educating and instructing of children and youth in the grammar and rules of learning for ever, which shall be called by the name of the Merchant Taylors' School'. Harrison died in 1619. At that time there were thirty-five grammar schools in Lancashire, nearly half of them established in the previous fifty years. The building at Great Crosby was as grand, or grander, as any of them. It remains, little changed, and is the oldest building in the town. Harrison's wish was that the school should be controlled by the Merchant Taylors' Company, and this the Company generously agreed to; it already, of course, controlled the school of the same name in London, and Wolverhampton Grammar School. The school did not flourish under early headmasters, less through their own failings than through the disinterest of the local populace in a classical education. Edward Mollineux, 1652–60, achieved more success, and during the general decline of the late seventeenth century Merchant Taylors', Crosby, did rather better. This was because the school was more fortunate than most in its headmasters and because of the growth of Liverpool, only a short distance away. John Waring and Gerard Waring, father and son, were headmasters 1677–1730. During this time the school began a connection with Trinity College, Dublin. This was due to the comparative ease of the short sea journey from Liverpool as compared to the exhausting and long journey to Oxford or Cambridge.

As other schools, especially in the south, grew in reputation, so Merchant Taylors' went into decline. The wealthy traders of Liverpool began to withdraw their support from the school at Crosby. One pupil at the start of the century, the author James Gregor Grant, wrote of going to Crosby as a boarder: 'We were sent to an endowed school, of good old standing (I think from Elizabeth's time) in the village of Great Crosby, on the coast, about five-and-a-half miles from Liverpool. How vividly I remember the little journey! in a post-chaise, with closed windows, for the morning was one of bitter winter, and the snow drifted against them, and plastered the poor driver, and clogged the roads, and loaded the hedges—till the hedges ceased to enclose us and only the sea-shore and bleak common remained ... at last, with mixed feeling of novelty, curiosity and perhaps fear, we entered the dull, dead, silent, solitary village ... we saw nothing but snow-clad moor and desert sandhills. We heard nothing but the roar of the sea-waves and the melancholy cries of the sea-birds . . . we were boarded and lodged; not in the school-house, the residence of the Headmaster, but with a worthy couple.'

During this period the number of boys never rose much above fifty. This was better than the experience of many schools, but by about 1840 Merchant Taylors' was at a low state; the school was hardly active. At last the Company took action, and in 1849 the headmaster's salary was raised (to £120), the number of free scholars limited to forty, and the curriculum was expanded to include some modern subjects. Unfortunately, the first headmaster under the new arrangements was not a success, and it was not until the Rev. S. C. Armour, 1863–1903, an admirer of Arnold, that Merchant Taylors' developed into a leading school. A move was made to new buildings in 1878. In 1909 the Merchant Taylors' Company handed over control of the school to a board of local governors.

Sebright School, Worcestershire, which closed in 1971, was founded under the Will of William Sebright, Town Clerk of the City of London. Sebright died in 1620. His school had a chequered existence. By 1877 it was 'in abeyance', but was re-opened by the Endowed Schools Commissioners. By 1904 it had thirty boys, four of them boarders. By the nineteenth-sixties the numbers were 250, but it was still found impossible to continue.

The idea of founding combined almshouses and schools had spread from England to Scotland. Several were founded between 1623 and 1700, the first by George Heriot, jeweller and goldsmith to the king. Known as 'Jingling Geordie', Heriot left £23,625 for his school for 'poor fatherless boys, freemen's sons of the town of Edinburgh . . . in imitation of the public, pious and religious work founded within the city of London called Christ's Hospital'. The money was invested wisely in land, and the school prospered. The curriculum was purely classical at first, but modern subjects were added in the nineteenth century. By 1872 there were 180 boys, between the ages of seven and fourteen. English, French and mathematics were taught as well as the classics.*

The foundation of Latymer Upper, Hammersmith, dates from 1624. Edward Latymer made provision for the clothing and education of eight poor boys of Edmonton and eight from Hammersmith.

* Former pupils include Sir Henry Raeburn, painter, Sir James Miller, Lord Mayor of London, Sir Alexander Johnston, chairman of the Board of Inland Revenue, and Arthur Marwick, historian.

A school house was not erected until 1756. By 1816 the numbers were thirty, all of primary age. Owing to an increase in the value of the property, a senior school was opened in 1894. Old boys include Harold Craxton, musician, Peter Walker, M.P., and John Prebble, author. (The Edmonton part of the foundation survives as Latymer School, Edmonton.)

Chigwell School, in Essex, was founded in 1629 by the Archbishop of York, Samuel Harsnett. He intended it for *all* the children of Chigwell, and two each from the parishes of Loughton, Woodford and Lamborne, in primary education, and for twelve free scholars from Chigwell, and two each from the other parishes, in the classics. Harsnett's statutes were unusual in other respects. He thought more of the physical and moral well-being of the boys than of learning. To strike a boy on the head or face was punishable by a fine of forty shillings. The master had to be 'neither Papist nor Puritan, of a grave Behaviour, of a sober and honest Conversation, no Tyler nor Haunter of Alehouses, no Puffer of Tobacco'. Particular attention was to be paid to scripture. This, Harsnett said, 'I more desire than the seasoning them with learning.' The original buildings at Chigwell are still in use. The school, in which over one-third of the boys are boarders, is sited in forty-five acres between Epping and Hainault forests. The greatest old boy is William Penn, the Quaker and founder of Pennsylvania.

There had been a grammar school at Exeter since at least the fourteenth century. It had produced the great political philosopher Richard Hooker. After the Reformation, the next grammar school was founded in 1627, but the present Exeter School dates its foundation from 1633. The new foundation was controversial because it had been laid down in previous statutes that only one school should exist for seven miles around the town. Since then the city had expanded considerably, and the existing school was not free. The citizens got their way and a free school was established, which became Exeter School. By the late nineteenth century it was advertising for boys from British families in India and the West Indies. 'Situation healthy, and suited to West and East Indian boys and delicate constitutions.' In 1880 it was moved from its old site in the city centre to new buildings designed by W. Butterfield, architect of Keble College, Oxford. Boarding arrangements at Exeter are advanced. 'Boarders are treated as day boys whose home is School House and are given, in accordance with their age and sense of responsibility, the controlled freedom and guidance that their parents would give them.' There are no prefects.

Bury School was endowed by the Rev. Henry Bury in 1634, although a parish school evidently already existed. Unlike some founders, Bury provided for parents and pupils tipping the staff. 'My intent and meaning is not to debar the Master and Usher from that common privilege in all free Scholes of receiving Presents, Benevolences, Gratuities, etc., from their Scholars, their Parents and Friends. I am so far from putting so hard a thing upon the Master and Usher, that I do require the Parents of all such youths as have the benefit of Education at my free Schole to be kind to the Master.' In 1725 Bury was re-endowed by Roger Kay. It moved to its present site in 1966.

The first case of a major school being founded by two brothers occurred in 1641. George Hutcheson was a writer and notary who made a great deal of money. He died in 1640, leaving part of his fortune for the founding of a hospital for elderly men. Thomas Hutcheson died in the following year, also without children, and the combined fortunes were left to the hospital, and for a school for twelve poor orphans of Glasgow, mentioned by Thomas in his Will. The first boy was admitted in 1643, in the premises on Hutcheson's Street. The school expanded, but the original building was still in use well into the nineteenth century. A new building was put up in Crown Street in 1841. By the mid-nineteenth century Hutcheson's had over 150 pupils. The headmaster received a salary of £120, as well as a house. The Endowed Institutions Act of 1869 enabled the school to extend its facilities and to make itself available for all. Hutcheson's is now in receipt of a Direct Grant from the Scottish Education Department. In 1960 it moved from Crown Street to Crossmyloof, on the outskirts of the city, where it provides for over eight hundred boys. The most famous former pupil is John Buchan, Lord Tweedsmuir.

Rye Grammar School, Sussex, was founded in 1638 by Thomas Peacock; it is now comprehensive. Tiffin School, Kingston, was founded in 1638 by Thomas and John Tiffin for four boys. Originally it was elementary, but the endowment greatly increased in value, and in 1874 it became a modern secondary school. Rivalry with the Kingston Grammar School was keen; in 1904 there were 376 boys as compared to sixty at the grammar school.* Reading

* John Bratby was educated at Tiffin.

Blue Coat (formerly known as Aldworth's Hospital) was founded in 1646 by Richard Aldworth, an East India Company merchant, and opened in 1660. It was based on Christ's Hospital, of which Aldworth was a governor. It moved to Sonning in 1947. Colfe's Grammar School, Lewisham, was founded by the Rev. Abraham Colfe in 1656. Palmer's School, Gray's, Essex, previously at Westminster, was founded by the Rev. James Palmer in 1650, together with an almshouse, for the education of twenty poor boys; it still takes boarders. It came under the United Westminster Schools. Bradford Grammar School existed during the fifteen-forties, but was not incorporated until 1662 as the free grammar school of the town. Woodbridge School was founded by a number of inhabitants of the town, in 1662, as a free grammar school for the instruction of ten boys, already proficient in English, and to prepare them for the universities, trades or navigation. Chard School, Somerset, was founded in 1671 by William Symes for the purpose of 'vertue and learning for a thousand years'. It was greatly improved during the nineteen-sixties, but following the failure of an appeal fund its closure was announced in 1971, after three hundred years of existence. Midhurst Grammar School was founded in 1672, by Gilbert Hannam, for twelve poor men's sons, preference to be given to those who would stay till fit for the university. Reigate Grammar School was founded in 1675 by the parishioners themselves. Swansea Grammar School was founded in 1682 by Hugh Gore, Bishop of Waterford. It was destroyed in an air-raid in 1941.

Also in 1675, we cross the Irish Sea again for the oldest Dublin public school, the Royal Hospital, which came to be known as the Blue Coat School. A free school had existed in Dublin before, but in 1671 'the Mayor, Sheriffs, Commons and Citizens' of Dublin petitioned Charles II for a hospital and Protestant school, modelled on Christ's Hospital, London. A charter was granted for the founding of an institution to be 'named, Incorporated, and called the Hospital and Free-school of King Charles the Second, Dublin'. The hospital and school was granted ground rents from Oxmantown Green and St. Stephen's Green, and later it also gained the fee simple of over eight hundred acres, mostly in County Tipperary. After a number of disputes, the first pupils arrived on 5 May 1675, nearly six years after building had begun; there were sixty of them, three being girls. The salary of the assistant master was £5 a year, teaching writing and arithmetic from 7 to 11 a.m. and 1 to 5 p.m.;

the first of these, after two years, ended in debtors' prison, not surprisingly. By 1680 the salary of the headmaster, who was also the chaplain, was £40 a year. In 1723 the school benefited from the bequest of Erasmus Smith, who left valuable rents for charitable purposes. By 1731 there were 160 boys in the school. By this time the original building was in a dangerous condition. While the school played a useful part, the hospital seems to have done little for Dublin. According to one authority (Craig), 'The only aged person who seems to have benefited by it was one of its founders, William Smith himself, who, having been Mayor of Dublin for six terms and Lord Mayor for one, came in 1679 to live in the Hospital himself.' At length the governors (basically the city aldermen under the chairmanship of the chief magistrate) accepted an ambitious plan by the leading Dublin architect of the day, Thomas Ivory. Although lack of resources led to Ivory's original plan being scaled down, he nevertheless produced one of the masterpieces of Georgian Dublin (the cupola, however, dates from 1894). In 1840 an act was passed which in effect ended King's Hospital as the Dublin royal, or grammar, school, and which began its later history as an independent public school, governed by the Archbishop of Dublin and other dignitaries (as Charles II had indeed intended). There were by now many other schools in the city, and within twelve years of the act the number of boys had halved, but the school recovered at the turn of the century and by 1906 there were 130 pupils. King's Hospital, no longer a free school, continues to play an important part in Irish Protestant education.

The two last public schools to be founded in the seventeenth century were both the result of what had become the traditional method, personal endowment. Haberdashers' Aske's was founded, in 1690, by Robert Aske at Hoxton. Aske was a member of the Haberdashers' Company, and half the governors are still appointed by that Company. An account of 1770 states that there were then 'twenty poor citizens, who have each their lodgings and firing, and diet at a common table together, and every two years a gown and three pounds a year in money, which hereafter may be increased. Likewise as many boys enjoy the same benefit, and are also taught to write and cypher to fit them for callings'. In the late nineteenth century the premises at Hoxton, by then swamped by the growth of London, were quite unsuitable. The school was split in two, opening at Hatcham and Hampstead in 1903. The Hampstead school, which is partly boarding, moved to new buildings at Elstree in 1961. This school is unusual in that boys are educated from the age of seven. Old boys of the foundation include Lord Soper, Professor W. N. Medlicott, historian, and journalist Alan Whicker. Another London school of this period was Archbishop Tenison's, 1697, originally at St. Martin-in-the-Fields, now at Kennington. Coatham School, or Sir William Turner's, was founded by Turner for thirty poor scholars in 1692. By 1869, when it was re-opened, it had hardly existed for a hundred years. Originally it was at Kirkleatham, but moved to Coatham, near Redcar, in the late nineteenth century. By 1905 there were still only twelve boys, although the figures have risen by 1972 to the startling 895.

6

EIGHTEENTH-CENTURY SCHOOLS

BY the start of the eighteenth century the decline in British education, that had begun in the previous century, was well under way. As has been seen, many schools during this period had less than half a dozen pupils. The determination to retain the classical languages as the main part of secondary education was causing an increasing disillusion with the grammar schools. The only great schools to be founded in the eighteenth century were due to a more liberal attitude towards freedom of worship and religion, notably Kingswood, founded by the Methodists, and Stonyhurst and Downside, founded by the Roman Catholics. In Scotland the situation was somewhat better, and schools continued to be comparatively well attended, and there was always an interest in education. The Scottish Act of Settling Schools, 1696, had required every parish to have a school of its own, the parish being responsible for the schoolhouse and the teacher's salary.

The first school to be founded in the new century was Battersea Grammar, in 1700. Rochester Mathematical School was founded by Sir Joseph Williamson, in 1701, to provide a non-classical education for the merchant service and other occupations. Then came Dame Allan's, the second important grammar school to be founded at Newcastle upon Tyne. The school was founded by Dame Eleanor Allan, who gave property at Wallsend, the income from which was to be used by the establishment of a school. Over the years further bequests were made. Dame Allan's moved in 1786, and was refounded in 1821. The new school was run by the clergy. Fee-payers were admitted after further changes to the statutes in 1877, and the school, still closely linked to the diocese, finally moved to modern premises in 1935.

Lord Weymouth School, at Warminster, in Wiltshire, was founded in 1707 by Viscount Weymouth for the free instruction of the youth of Warminster, Deverill, Longbridge and Monckton Deverill. During the nineteenth century the school became entirely fee-paying. By about 1870 there were fifty pupils, thirty-five of them boarders. Today Lord Weymouth School has over two hundred pupils, more than half of them boarders. The Viscounts Weymouth remain patrons of the school. The Liverpool Blue Coat school, the oldest school in that city, was founded in 1708 by Bryan Blundell, master mariner, for orphans and fatherless children. The school opened in a new building in 1718. The Blue Coat is now a voluntary aided day and boarding school, in fine Victorian premises to which it moved in 1906. Colston's School, Bristol, originally known as Colston's Hospital, was founded in 1710 by Edward Colston. It is governed by the Society of Merchant Venturers, and today well over half the boys are boarders. Prices School, Fareham, was founded in 1721, and Parmiter's School, Bethnal Green, was founded in 1722.

Churcher's College, Petersfield, was founded by Richard Churcher, a merchant of the East India Company, who retired to Petersfield. The school, founded by his will of 1723, was to provide free tuition for certain boys of the town provided they entered the mercantile service of the East India Company. After 1745 all pretence at honouring the East India Company provision was abandoned, although the coat of arms of the school remains to this day an East Indiaman. Churcher's gained in reputation during the nineteen-thirties; in 1935 there were 231 boys, of whom ninety-one were boarders. The boarding element had long been a feature of this small country-town school. In 1906 the Inspectors had noted: 'It is most satisfactory to note—in marked contrast to the majority of country Grammar Schools—the continued increase in the number of boarders.' Other schools which take boarders founded at about the same time are Rishworth School (1724) and Bentham Grammar School (1726), both in Yorkshire and both co-educational.

The next two schools, chronologically, are Scottish. George Watson's College, Edinburgh, was founded by a gentleman of that name who had been the senior accountant of the Bank of Scotland, and had done remarkably well financially. He required that overseeing the children should be 'an unmarried person, of good respect, and free of the burden of children. . . . His principal care shall be to see that the children and servants be brought up and instructed in the fear of Almighty God'. By the early nineteenth century pupils were being taught English and French, as well as the classics, 'so as to be ready for the University', but the main aim was still religious:

'to prepare orphans for the business of life and the purposes of eternity'. In 1845 there were eighty boys between seven and fifteen; when they left school they were given £50 and another £50 at the age of twenty-five. In 1852 a special bill was passed in Parliament to enable George Watson's to take day-boys. From 1870 it has been entirely a day school. Watson's has produced many eminent former pupils.* Robert Gordon's College, Aberdeen, was founded by a Danzig merchant of that name, who returned to Aberdeen and died in 1732, having set up a trust for his school three years earlier. It was for the sons and grandsons of hard-up burgesses and merchants of the town. By the end of the century it had sixty boys from nine to sixteen, with three resident masters. The school was the first in Scotland to apply for a grant to teach science, which it won in 1859. In 1881 Robert Gordon's became a day school, but a boarding house was re-established in 1937.

Portsmouth Grammar School was founded in 1732 by William Smith, doctor to the Portsmouth Garrison. The nearby Taunton's School, of Southampton, was founded, by an alderman of that name in 1752, as a trade school, due to King Edward's of that city remaining strictly classical. Chatham House Grammar school, Ramsgate, traces its descent from a private school founded in 1797; the county grammar school established in that town in 1909 took over the Chatham House buildings in 1921. Bancroft's School, at Woodford Green in Essex, is one of the last of the many public schools to have been founded by a City merchant's Will. Francis Bancroft, who died in 1727, left all his personal estate on trust to the Company of Drapers, to found and build almshouses and a school for a hundred poor boys. It was originally at Mile End in East London, but moved to its present site in 1884. The school is still under the control of the Drapers' Company, although on the Direct Grant list.†

*

* James Pryde, the artist, Viscount Waverley, Chancellor of the Exchequer in the Second World War, Lord Kilmuir, Home Secretary, Lord Dunrossil, Speaker of the House, Lord Cooper of Culross, Lord President, David Daiches, David Steel, M.P., Sir Basil Spence, and many medical men.

† Victor Purcell, orientalist, Sir Henry Self, Sir Graham Cunningham, Controller-General Munitions and Production, 1941–46, and Lieut.-Colonel Charles Newman, V.C., who led the St. Nazaire raid, 1942 are among the names of former pupils.

The remaining public schools founded in the eighteenth century came almost entirely from a new and different origin: the establishment of greater religious freedom in British society. The first of these was Kingswood School, Bath. This was founded in 1748 by John Wesley. Wesley was highly critical of the schools of his day, both on religious and educational grounds. Many of the schoolmasters, he declared, were ill-versed in religion: 'men who are either uninstructed in the very principles of Christianity, or quite indifferent as to the practice of it, caring for none of these things. Consequently, they are nothing concerned whether their scholars are Papists or Protestants, Turks or Christians'. Wesley thought also that too much attention was paid to the classics and not enough to arithmetic, geography and English. He wrote his own curriculum and regulations for Kingswood in detail. He had no time for tenderness, it seems, and he poured scorn on 'tender parents'. His regime was harsh in the extreme. Until they left school, the children were not to have one day away from it. 'They will not take him from school, no, not a day, till they take him for good and all,' Wesley declared. 'The children rise at four winter and summer, and spend the time till five in private, partly in reading, partly in singing, partly in self-examination or meditation (if capable of it), and partly in prayer.' It is not surprising to learn that Wesley encountered several outbreaks of mass weeping among his unfortunate boys. No games or recreations were allowed, and the boys were never out of sight of one of the masters. Wesley himself edited or wrote most of the textbooks.

From 1794 entrance was limited to the sons of Methodist preachers, and most of the pupils were expected to become ministers themselves. In 1831 we read of a dismayed parent writing to one of the governors: 'I was not aware by sending my boy a few presents that it would have been such a misery to him, in making him think more "about his belly than his mind".' The system of communal clothing lasted until 1843. In 1850 a new building was begun on a site overlooking Bath, and conditions, including the introduction of more school holidays, became better (holidays had begun in 1803). From 1923 Kingswood was opened to laymen (of about 520 boys at present, some 160 are ministers' sons). Since the Second World War, Kingswood has been considerably enlarged, and it now stands in 218 acres. It is a noted games school, having fixtures with Blundell's, Bristol Grammar, Cardiff High School, Cheltenham, Clifton and Marlborough.

St. Edmund's, Canterbury, was founded the year after Kingswood, in 1749, to give free education to the fatherless sons of Anglican clergy. It moved from St. John's Wood to Canterbury in 1855. Here, also, conditions were extremely grim. Breakfast was bread, butter, milk and water. Up till the late nineteenth century St. Edmund's was known as the Clergy Orphan School, and it still caters for fatherless sons of the clergy as Foundationers. Another school which had strong Anglican leanings was the Royal Masonic, founded in 1789, for the sons of Masons. Originally at Wood Green, in Middlesex, where it entered new buildings in 1865, it moved to Bushey, near Watford, in 1903. Admission is still made through the Lodge to which the father belongs, but the school is now non-denominational.

*

Compared to the regimes at Kingswood and St. Edmund's, the life of boys at the five great Roman Catholic schools founded in England in the second half of the eighteenth century was a little less severe. Here all was comparative calm. These schools, in order of foundation in England (some had originated on the Continent) are Cotton College, St. Edmund's, Ware, Stonyhurst, Ampleforth and Downside.

Apart from a few scattered and secret primary schools up and down the country, a Catholic education could only be sought outside the United Kingdom; in the case of English boys this had usually meant Douai, in France. So when Richard Challoner founded a secondary boarding school for Catholic boys, at Sedgley Park, near Wolverhampton, in 1763, he was taking a grave risk, as were his staff. The Roman Catholic Relief Act of 1778 gave some relief, but the school at Sedgley Park was still an illegal institution, although tolerated. An act of 1791 tolerated Catholic places of worship provided they had no steeple or bells, and Sedgley Park was recognised as a Catholic school. By the early nineteenth century the school was so popular that a waiting-list existed and there were usually over a hundred boys. According to the school history, 'Sedgley Park was known for the sturdy type of man it produced; and her sons were remarkable for their attachment to their Alma Mater: "the dear old Park" became a well-known term of endearment.' John Kemble, the great actor, was a student at this time. In 1873 the need for expansion was such that the school moved to

Cotton Hall, near Stoke on Trent, an estate of three hundred acres bought from the Earl of Shrewsbury, a Roman Catholic. The present aim of the school is 'to send out Catholic gentlemen'.

The unsettled state of Europe, and the new ideas, caused by the French Revolution, made the English teachers of Douai look longingly to England and its new toleration of the Catholic Church. The first group to cross the Channel, in 1793, became St. Edmund's College, Ware, which took over the Old Hall Green Academy, a primary school which through a complicated ancestry traced its descent from a secret Catholic school at Twyford in Hampshire that had existed in the sixteen-sixties. It had started at Ware in 1769 with less than twenty boys.

The next school to arrive from France was the Jesuit one of Stonyhurst. It had been founded in 1593, at St. Omer, where it had first taken English boys (who were liable to arrest if caught leaving England for the school). Pressure on the Society of Jesus in France eventually forced the school to move to Bruges, a few years later moving on to Liège. After the outbreak of the French Revolution the English priests and pupils of Liège were offered Stonyhurst Hall, a mansion built in 1592; the owner was a former pupil, Thomas Weld. Weld's son (who later became a cardinal) led them to Stonyhurst, twelve miles from Preston, in Lancashire, by way of Hull, Selby and Skipton, the last eighteen miles of the journey being done on foot. By this time the sixteen boys were so exhausted that they fell into every doorstep passed, 'perfectly indifferent to the stare and surprise of the inhabitants that surrounded them'. They arrived at Stonyhurst on 29 August 1794. The Hall had been virtually disused for forty years, was partly roofless, and in a dilapidated condition. However, it soon became a leading Catholic school, and the setting and beautiful Hall were presented to good advantage. After a few years the early discomforts were dispelled. By 1797 an annual fee of forty guineas was being charged. History, geography and mathematics were taught in addition to the classics. The holidays were one month in the summer each year.

In 1841 Stonyhurst was in a strong enough position to help found two further schools, Mount St. Mary's, Spinkhill, in Derbyshire, and St. Francis Xavier's, Liverpool. At first these supplied pupils for the senior forms at Stonyhurst, but later completed their own courses of education. The rectorship of Father Francis Clough (1848–61) brought with it many improvements, including the establishment of a resident physician, one of the first at a public school. From 1877 the old building was gradually replaced by a vast Victorian edifice on the same site. One boy at Stonyhurst during the Victorian era was the future Sir Arthur Conan Doyle. He wrote: 'It was the usual public school routine of Euclid, algebra and the classics, taught in the usual way, which is calculated to leave a lasting abhorrence of these subjects. To give boys a little slab of Virgil or Homer with no general idea as to what it is all about, or what the classical age was like, is surely an absurd way of teaching the subject. . . . The life was Spartan, and yet we had all that was needed. Dry bread and hot watered milk was our breakfast. . . . Everything in every way was plain to the verge of austerity, save that we dwelt in a beautiful building, dined in a marble-floored hall with minstrels' gallery, prayed in a lovely church, and generally lived in very choice surroundings. . . . Corporal punishment was severe, and I can speak with feeling as I think few, if any, boys of my time endured more of it.'

Other old boys include Alfred Austin, the poet laureate, General Sir E. S. Bulfin, of the Palestine campaign, Oliver St. John Gogarty, poet, Charles Laughton, William Devlin, actor, Lord Devlin, and authors Macdonald Hastings and Paul Johnson. Stonyhurst was the home of 'Stonyhurst Cricket', a single-wicket variant of the game, which flourished throughout England for eighty years, until superseded by association football (it being a winter game). Real cricket was introduced in the eighteen-sixties, the first school match, against Rossall, taking place in 1874.

Those English pupils who had stayed at Douai after the start of the Revolution were under the care of the English Benedictines of St. Gregory. Unlike the former Douai pupils who had settled at Ware, they delayed their departure, and suffered accordingly. British subjects were in danger of their lives. An attempt to escape was unsuccessful, and for several months they were crowded into a garret where they lay on straw. At last priests and pupils were given permission to embark for England, and the party landed at Dover on 2 March 1795. They had been offered the country house of Acton Burnell, in Shropshire, by a former pupil, but his death in 1811 made a new home imperative, and the society finally settled at Downside, near Bath. The Gregorians had a considerable reputation as educationists, achieved while at Douai, where conditions and education had been in advance of many English schools of the time, and Downside flourished. One of the most interesting Gregorians was Richard Stokes, who was a critic of Churchill in the war, and later became Lord Privy Seal. He once made the following reply to a journalist: 'My most gratifying appointment? The promotion to Head of the School at Downside in 1914.'*

During the late nineteenth century these Roman Catholic schools gradually took on many of the characteristics of the Victorian public school, until by 1900, apart from religious ritual and the monastic character of the staff, they differed very little from their Arnoldian Anglican rivals. Downside, for instance, became a known Services school. In 1970, however, it was stated that, 'The principal aim of the school is to train the boys in the knowledge and practice of the Catholic religion.'

The last of these schools to be established in England was that of St. Laurence, which had settled at Dieulouard, in Lorraine. It was expelled during the Revolution, and priests and boys actually arrived in England before those of St. Gregory. They had been installed at Acton Burnell, through the generosity of the owner, until the monks from Douai had been able to get to England. For a time the two communities shared facilities at Acton Burnell, until that of St. Laurence eventually settled at Ampleforth in 1802. Ampleforth became one of the great schools of the north.† The academic reputation became very high, particularly so after the Second World War, under the headship of the Rt. Rev. Dudley Price (1954–64), who had been at Ampleforth since 1933. Like some of the heads of Downside, Price had been brought up and educated at Radley as an Anglican. During the twentieth century no bodies have made more enthusiastic application of the public school system than the various Roman Catholic orders, opening new schools and in particular making very full use of the Direct Grant system.

* Other old boys: Maurice Turnbull, the England cricketer, Sir Francis Meynell, Sir Ivone Kirkpatrick and Sir George Rendel, both prominent in diplomacy at the end of the war, Sir Oliver Crosthwaite-Eyre, Sir Peter Rawlinson, Sir John Pope-Hennessy, Christopher Sykes, Patrick Wall, M.P., Auberon Waugh, and playwright Barry England.

† Old boys include Major-General Sir Francis de Guingand, Hugh Fraser, Lord Windlesham, and the novelist Piers Paul Read.

7

EARLY
NINETEENTH-CENTURY SCHOOLS

WITH few exceptions, among them the Catholic schools, secondary education in England had reached such depths at the end of the eighteenth century that Lord Chief Justice Kenyon said, in 1795: 'Whoever will examine the state of the grammar schools in different parts of the kingdom will see to what a lamentable condition most of them have been reduced . . . empty walls without scholars, and everything neglected, but the receipt of the salaries and emoluments. In some instances that have lately come within my knowledge, there was not a single scholar in the schools though there were very large endowments to them.' Soon afterwards, to widespread public disgust, Lord Eldon, in two legal decisions, showed that it was actually illegal to teach modern subjects in the old foundations set up for the teaching of the classics only. The narrow curriculum,* and the financial abuse, were not the only criticisms being loudly voiced throughout the nation at about the turn of the century. There were also the conditions, in many cases cruel and inhuman, which led in the first twenty years of the century to a series of riots at the schools when the boys themselves took protest into their own hands.

At no time in the previous hundred years had a better climate existed in which to start new schools. Firstly, there was greater religious freedom, for Catholics and nonconformists alike, and a reaction against that freedom, which affected educational thinking. Secondly, already during the eighteenth century the grammar schools had been faced with the competition of new 'modern' or 'private' schools, which provided French and arithmetic. It was 1840 before the old grammar schools were legally entitled to teach modern subjects, although many had done so before that (a century-and-a-half since John Locke, the most important of the early educa-

* There were, however, ways in which to broaden the curriculum, for instance by the employment of tutors not regarded as regular members of the staff. Thomas Gray managed to learn botany, and Shelley chemistry, while at Eton.

tional thinkers to call for a modern education, had said: 'I know not why anyone should waste his time and beat his head about the Latin Grammar'). The nineteenth century is a long story of how the old grammar schools broke away from the classical confines that were killing them and how the greatest of them joined with new schools to form the modern 'Public Schools'.

The century opened with the foundation, between 1807 and 1823, of seven important schools for Protestant nonconformists, who sought freedom from the Anglican schools, as Wesley himself had done at Kingswood.

The first school to be founded in the nineteenth century was Mill Hill. In 1806 a group of nonconformists met at the New London Tavern, Cheapside, to discuss the foundation of a nonconformist school, broadly along the lines of the Church of England grammar schools. Nonconformists often found their children excluded from Anglican schools because of religious tests. Mostly business men, they described themselves as 'gentlemen anxious to promote sound learning among Dissenters'. The school was to be strictly classical, and nothing was given away to the critics of grammar-school education. 'No translation of any Greek or Latin author, nor any editions of the classics furnished with interpretations or parsing indices, or any similar assistances, shall ever be permitted in the school.' The school was to be boarding, and a house was bought at Mill Hill, north of London, in 'a situation peculiarly pleasant and salubrious'.

Mill Hill school opened on 25 January 1808, with eighteen boys. Fees were £45 per annum. Washing, French and drawing were extras. The school was successful, and a new school house to accommodate 120 boys was begun in 1825. A classical, rather than Gothic, style was, fortunately perhaps, chosen, and the result was one of the finest new school buildings constructed in England for a century past. For long periods the school was not full, however. Curiously, like the Catholic schools, Mill Hill was noted for the way in which boys were never left alone, a master always being present; this was no doubt in answer to the critics of Eton and Winchester, and the other schools where riots had taken place early in the century, and from which horrific tales of bullying came. In the eighteen-sixties Mill Hill almost ceased to exist, and it was in fact closed for a time in 1868 owing to debt. It was refounded in the following year. Mill Hill revived under the headmastership of Dr. R. F. Weymouth, 1869–86. By 1880 there were 183 pupils. The old boys' club, one of the most famous in the country, especially in football, was founded in 1878; it is one of the very few old boys' clubs to have a permanent meeting-place, and the only one to have one in central London. Mill Hill is proud of its tradition of toleration, and although the nonconformist connection continues, it has never confined itself to the sons of Free Churchmen. It is still predominantly boarding, although there are seventy-five day-boys.*

An answer to the problem of classicists and anti-classicists was found in Belfast, at this time a city of 28,000 people. A group of nonconformist Protestant business men got together, in much the same way as the founders of Mill Hill. They obtained a good site from the Marquis of Donegal, who owned most of the city, and obtained the services of the leading architect of the day, Sir John Soane (who later designed the Bank of England). Soane, who waived his fee, produced one of the few fine buildings to be seen in Belfast. The institution was to be split between classical and English schools, each with its own headmaster, with departments also for mathematics, French and writing. This was something along the same lines as the scheme already adopted at the Royal Academy, founded in 1785 as 'a Presbyterian venture'. From the start it was stated that 'The Institution is not connected with any religious persuasion. The subscribers to the Institution are composed of all religious persuasions.' Today, notably in Ireland, the Royal Belfast Academical Institution retains this great tradition: 'Its doors are open to boys of good ability without regard to race, creed or status; it is a school of the whole community and not of a section only.' The school opened in 1814, with over 250 boys. The Institution lived up to its promises of religious tolerance, and Catholic students studied for the entrance examination at Maynooth seminary. There was at this time only one university in Ireland, Trinity College, Dublin, as compared to five in Scotland (with half the population). The founders of 'Inst', as the school was popularly known, decided to attach a department for higher education, but this faded away in 1849. But after the establishment of Queen's College (later University), 'Inst' sent on nearly

---

* Old Millhillians include Henry Shaw, founder of the city of St. Louis in the U.S.A., W. H. Wills (later Lord Winterstoke), founder of the tobacco firm, Lord Chief Justice Trevithin, Lord Justice Salmon, Lord Brain, the surgeon, Liberal politicians Lord Wade and Arthur Holt, Sir William Ramsey, President of the Rugby Union, Peter Howard, the director of Moral Re-armament, Kingsley Martin, Richard Dimbleby, and writers J. G. Crowther and Antony Brett-James.

two hundred pupils to the new college in the first seven years (as compared to only twelve from the three Royal Schools combined). 'Inst' has expanded greatly in the present century. About 1,150 Instonians served in the armed forces during the Second World War, of whom 106 laid down their lives. 'Inst' is now probably the greatest school in Ireland. Academically, and stylistically, it might well be described as the Dulwich of Ireland. Its reputation increased under the Principalship of the remarkable Wykehamist Geoffrey Garrod, 1925–40, who had previously been barrister, music critic of *The Times* and headmaster of Sevenoaks. At the end of the Second World War there were seventy-five secondary schools in Ulster, only eight of which were controlled by the L.E.A. The 1947 Education Act was similar to the Butler Act in England. 'Inst' took the lead in negotiating with the government. The school history says: 'The whole history of Inst was one of independence of outside control. It had been founded to provide an education which should be unaffected by sectional interests; it had undergone great hardships in its early years rather than surrender any part of its independence; it had, for over a century, relied on its own efforts and its own success to provide the finance necessary to its existence and well-being. . . . The Inst Board of Governors, following its tradition, chose the path of maximum independence.' 'Inst' now has over a thousand pupils. The original organisation, with five separate head-masters, under a Principal, has been successfully retained. One of the best writers about childhood in the English language, Forrest Reid, was at 'Inst'. In *Apostate* he wrote: 'It was during my last year at school that I began to write, moved by some impulse that had very little to do with literary ambition. . . . I described the green beckoning branches of the elm trees, visible through the open window; the soft breeze that entered with the sunlight, stirring the loose papers on the master's table and the old time-stained maps hanging on the wall; the voices, the sounds of ball and bat, that rose from the cricket field; the hot June sunshine on the yellow desks and forms, with their ink splashes, and names. . . . I was always delighted to get back to school again after the holidays. And each year this was pleasanter than the last.' Old Instonians include a prime minister of Northern Ireland and a President of the Royal College of Surgeons, Lord Kelvin, physicist, Lord Chief Justices (of Northern Ireland) Sir James Andrews and Sir Robert Lowry, numerous judges, General Sir James Steele, James Hamilton, the atomic physicist, historians R. B. McDowell and T. W. Moody, and the British amateur golf champion S. M. McCready. 'Inst' is probably the only school that has produced two British Lions Rugby football captains, S. Walker (1938) and R. H. Thompson (1955).

Sidcot School, Somerset, was founded in 1808 for the education of Quaker children. Caterham School was yet another founded for Protestant nonconformists, in this case primarily for the sons of Congregational ministers. Founded in 1811, it was at Lewisham for nearly seventy years, when it moved to its present site. Now a Direct Grant school, with over four hundred boys, more than half of them boarders, it is open to all. Woodhouse Grove, near Bradford, was founded in the following year for the sons of Methodist ministers, as a supplement to Kingswood, which role it maintained until 1883, when it was thrown open to all. Its object now is to make 'its sons better Christians, and better members of the church to which they belong, whatever that church may be'. The school has a connection with the Brontë family. Silcoates School, also in Yorkshire, was founded in 1820 for the sons of Congregational ministers and missionaries, but has admitted laymen's sons since 1842. It still has a strong Congregational attachment, the Yorkshire Congregational Union being the trustee.

The last of the nonconformist schools of this period to be founded was Bootham School, York, the famous Quaker establishment. It was founded in 1823 for the sons of Quakers. It is now non-denominational. Bootham is beautifully placed, in the shadow of the Minster, with one of the most pleasant cricket grounds in the north of England. There are only seven day-boys, all scholars, elected by the city.*

*

Reed's School, Cobham, was founded in 1813 by Dr. Andrew Reed, for fatherless boys. Since the Second World War the school has expanded considerably and all boys are now eligible for entrance, although many Foundationers, who have lost one or both parents, are still admitted. It has been a Headmasters' Conference school since 1966.

One of the most important schools to be founded in Ireland as a result of the Catholic Relief Acts of the previous century was Clon-

---

* Old boys: Sir George Newman, responsible for the introduction of medical inspections at schools, Philip Noel-Baker, and historians Geoffrey Barraclough and A. J. P. Taylor.

gowes Wood College, founded by the Jesuits under Father Peter Kelly, in 1814. This was a provocative act in Ireland, because less liberal conditions existed there. Father Kelly was twice called to Dublin Castle to discuss the matter, but the school survived. Today it is one of the largest Catholic boarding schools in Ireland. The most famous former pupil is James Joyce, not necessarily to the Jesuits' joy, who wrote of his despair there in *Portrait of the Artist as a Young Man*. 'The evening air was pale and chilly and after every charge and thud of the footballers the greasy leather orb flew like a heavy bird through the grey light. He kept on the fringe of his line, out of sight of his prefect, out of reach of the rude feet, feigning to run now and then. . . . Soon they would be going home for the holidays. After supper in the study hall he would change the number pasted up inside his desk from seventy-seven to seventy-six. . . . He sat looking at the two prints of butter on his plate but could not eat the damp bread. The tablecloth was damp and limp. But he drank off the hot weak tea which the clumsy scullion, girt with a white apron, poured into his cup. . . . Nasty Roche and Saurin drank cocoa that their people sent them in tins. They said they could not drink the tea; that it was hogwash. Their fathers were magistrates, the fellows said. . . . Sitting in the study hall he opened the lid of his desk and changed the number pasted up inside from seventy-seven to seventy-six. But the Christmas vacation was very far away; but one time it would come because the earth moved round always.' John Redmond and Sir Thomas Bodkin were other old boys. Development of Catholic secondary education was slow to take hold in Ireland, discouraged as it was by the Dublin authorities. The next important boarding school was St. Vincent's College, Castleknock, in County Dublin. This was founded by six young priests in 1833, five of them only recently out of Maynooth. They started at Usher's Quay, in Dublin, but soon moved to a fine mansion in the country, which had in fact been used previously as a school. In 1873 Castleknock became a lay school, run by members of the Catholic congregation.*

Christ's College, Blackheath, not to be confused with Christ's College, Finchley, founded in 1857, was started in 1823. Liverpool Institute, now a County Secondary High School in the state system, followed in 1825. Founded by private subscription on the existing

---

* Air Chief Marshal Sir W. L. M. Macdonald, W. F. Casey, editor of *The Times*, and Liam Cosgrave figure among the old boys.

Mechanics' Institute, it was divided into a high school, mainly classical, and a commercial school. It was transferred to the corporation in 1903. (Liverpool Grammar School, started in 1515, was by this time extinct.) Bearwood College, Wokingham, Berkshire, was founded for the children of seafarers in 1827; standing in a five-hundred-acre park, it is housed in the former seat of John Walter, proprietor of *The Times*.

Turning to Scotland, we find the start of the 'Academy' movement. This was the foundation of secondary schools in opposition to the old grammar schools, in answer to the desire for a more modern education, now reaching a crescendo throughout Britain. Morrison's Academy, at Crieff, Perthshire, was founded by Thomas Morrison, an Edinburgh builder, in 1813. He directed that his estate should be used to found 'an institution calculated to promote the interests of mankind, having a particular regard to the education of youth and the diffusion of useful knowledge'. Of the four boarding houses at Morrison's, one is still under the private management of a member of the staff, perhaps the last survivor in Britain of what was once almost universal at the old grammar schools.

Edinburgh Academy, founded in 1824, must have been a disappointment to many in Edinburgh. It was found to be just as classical as the Royal High School, in opposition to which it had been clearly set up. Not until some years later was the school divided into classical and modern sides. It was, at first, no improvement on the High School in other respects. 'All games had to be conducted in a small playground and the refreshment arrangements consisted of a pail with two tin mugs, refilled when necessary by the janitor's wife and never washed; this pail was used by four hundred boys . . . cricket was played at a wicket chalked on the wall; football was a general mêlée.' The Rector of the Academy was always an English clergyman, usually from Oxford. The school met from nine to three, five days a week; fees were fairly high, and the pupils were thus mainly from the middle class. Edinburgh Academy soon achieved a high academic reputation, second to none in Scotland. The Royal Commission on Scottish Education, of 1864 (the Argyll Commission), considered it one of the best schools in Britain. By 1912 there were 532 boys, seventy of them boarders; sixty years later the number is about the same, although the number of boarders has more than doubled.*

* Old Academicals: Sir Walter Raleigh, historian, Sir Andrew Noble, largely

Loretto School, at Musselburgh, was founded by an Englishman, Rev. Dr. Langhorne, curate of the Episcopal Church. He moved his boys into Loretto House in 1827. For nearly forty years, up to 1862, it was a preparatory school for Edinburgh Academy, Merchiston, Glenalmond, and the English public schools. Langhorne was succeeded by his sons. They were followed by their cousin, Dr. H. H. Almond, 1862–1903, who could be described as the Arnold of Scotland. He transformed Loretto into a major public school. Like Arnold, and unlike his contemporary Walker of St. Paul's, he set enormous store by the benefits of 'character-building'. Almond was a brilliant scholar, who had attended Glasgow University at the age of thirteen. He found only twelve pupils at the school, and left it with 124. Almond was a great believer in organised games, fresh air and hygiene, and Loretto became famous for this aspect, and for the untraditional, rational clothing the boys were required to wear. Every morning 'The Head' had an informal chat with the whole school. As the school history well puts it of this important headmaster: 'Poor food and no regular exercise had been the general custom of schools, at any rate in Scotland; but when Almond once began to make the health of the boys a personal interest, and to study it scientifically, it was impossible that he should allow these old mistakes to continue. He tried to bring medical science to bear on every particular of school life, and the introduction of a more rational habit of dress was another rational result. In this way he laid the foundation of Loretto as a distinctive and individual school, and he was the first Headmaster who openly set himself to make the physical education of his boys part of the regular school system.' When Almond died in office there was some doubt about the continuation of his trend-setting school, for it was privately owned, but the old boys, setting up a fund, came to the rescue. To this day the board of governors are all Old Lorettonians.*

The distinction of being the first Scottish school founded on the lines of an English public school belongs to Merchiston Castle, as

responsible for the modern rifle, Viscount Finlay, Viscount Haldane and J. S. Haldane, Lord Reid, Lord Justice Clyde, Admiral of the Fleet Viscount Cunningham, C.-in-C. Mediterranean, 1939–43, General Sir Philip Christison of the Burma campaign, Sir John Martin, private secretary to Winston Churchill 1940–45, P. G. Tait, physicist, and writers Alan Melville and J. I. M. Stewart.

* Former pupils: Lord Balfour of Burleigh, Ronald Jeans, author of the Charlot reviews, Sir Thomas Sellors, heart surgeon, writers George Millar and John Connell, and the racing driver Jim Clark.

Loretto was at first a primary school. Almond had been second master at Merchiston before going to Loretto. The idea was to found a boarding school, outside Edinburgh, such as Harrow or Winchester had now become, but 'modern' in approach. Like Loretto, Merchiston was at first a private school. It was founded by Charles Chalmers, a partner of William Collins, the Glasgow publisher. He took a lease of Merchiston Castle, the family seat of Lord Napier. The curriculum was distinctly modern, much to the delight of the prospective parents. Teaching methods were also remarkably advanced (no English was allowed in the French class). Not surprisingly, the school prospered, and was soon well known for its mathematics and science, several former pupils gaining distinction in these fields, and in medicine. Chalmers was followed by his son, who soon sold it to John Gibson, first Inspector for Schools in Scotland. He was succeeded by Thomas Harvey, who later became Rector of Edinburgh Academy, but the school really expanded under the headship and ownership of J. J. Rogerson, 1863–98; he handed the school over to a limited company in 1896. Merchiston Castle is now governed by a body elected or nominated by the old boys, the universities and other bodies.* Melville College, Edinburgh, was founded in 1832, on the wave of protest against classical education. It began as the Edinburgh Institution for Languages and Mathematics, the name being changed in 1936. The school is entirely administered by former pupils. Madras College, at St. Andrews, founded in 1833 from a bequest by the educational theorist Dr. Andrew Bell, was quite a different foundation, not aping the English schools and taking the place of the old grammar school. It had been preceded by Dollar Academy (1818), Clackmannanshire, also from a large bequest, which served children of all classes.

*

Just prior to the start of Merchiston Castle there had been two interesting foundations in London. London University was founded in 1836, the two first colleges, King's College and University College, having been already in existence. King's College School was part of the foundation of King's College, and was founded in 1829. At first it was mainly expected to feed the senior college with

* Old Merchistonians: Viscount Craigavon, Lord Guest, Sir Eric Geddes, Brigadier John Charteris, biographer of Haig, and Denis Johnston, the playwright.

pupils, and its premises were on the same site, at Somerset House in the Strand. The first pupils were accepted in 1831. From the start the curriculum was modern as well as classical. It soon became a general school, preparing for all the universities, the services and the civil service. By the eighteen-seventies the fees were £23 per annum, there being twelve free choral places; by this time there were twenty-four masters, and K.C.S. compared very favourably with any school in London. After sixty-eight years in the Strand, it was decided to move to a more open situation, with room for expansion; an excellent site was found beside Wimbledon Common. In 1911 the school was separated from King's College, and it now has an independent board of governors. In 1932 annual fees were still as low as £39. There is one boarding house. F. Anstey, who was at K.C.S., wrote *Vice Versa*, one of the most successful of all public school novels, and certainly one of the most enjoyable, first published in 1882. Subtitled 'A Lesson to all Fathers', it was an admonishment to all those parents who claimed at the end of the holidays, 'I wish I were in your shoes; these are the happiest days of your life.' In the book, the father's wish is granted, much to his discomfort. Based on the Strand school, the story describes the father's first school meal. 'At eight o'clock the Doctor came in and announced breakfast, leading the way himself to what was known in the school as the Dining Hall. It scarcely deserved so high-sounding a name perhaps, being a long low room on the basement floor, with a big fireplace, fitted with taps and baking ovens, which provoked the suspicion that it had begun existence as a back kitchen. The Doctor took his seat alone at a cross table forming the top of one of the two rows of tables, set with white cups and saucers, and plates well heaped with the square pieces of bread and butter . . . when Mr. Bultitude, more hungry than he had felt for years, found his place at one of the tables, he was disgusted to find upon his plate—not, as he had confidently expected, a couple of plump poached eggs, with their appetising contrast of ruddy gold and silvery white, not a crisp and crackling sausage or a mottled omelette, not even the homely but luscious rasher, but a brace of chill forbidding sardines, lying grim and headless in bilious green oil.'*

* Other old boys: jurist Frederick Harrison, Charles Kingsley, Reginald McKenna, Chancellor of the Exchequer, George Saintsbury, authority on French literature, Dante Gabriel Rossetti and W. M. Rossetti, Brig.-General Sir James Edmonds, official historian of the First World War, Sir J. Martin-

University College School has a similar history to K.C.S., but it
has no boarding tradition. It was founded, 'exclusively for secular
instruction', as an adjunct of the college in 1830. It remained in
Gower Street for over seventy years, moving to new buildings in
Hampstead in 1907. U.C.S. has a list of distinguished old boys which
is unsurpassed by any modern London school.* Compared to earlier
schools, K.C.S. and U.C.S. took on a sternly lay countenance. In
1897, out of twenty-two masters at the former and thirty-two at the
latter, only two in each case were clergymen, compared to nine
clerics out of a total of twenty-four at Merchant Taylors'.

Forest School, founded in 1834, also had a connection with
King's College, London, with which it was for a time closely associated. (Stockwell Grammar School was another school affiliated to
King's College.) The school is at Snaresbrook on the edge of Epping
Forest, the original Georgian building being still in use. Forest's aim
was to provide a modern education, with the classics taking second
place. 'To provide a course of education for youth, comprising
classical learning, mathematics and such modern languages and
other branches of science and general literature as might from time
to time be introduced.'

King William's College, at Castletown, on the Isle of Man, is an
example of a public school beng founded on early endowments that
had become valuable. The original bequest was of Bishop Isaac
Barrow in 1668. Barrow was a Fellow of Eton, and Bishop of Sodor
and Man, 1663–71; he was also Governor of the island from 1664.
He was known as a great educational benefactor on the island. King
William's is part at least of the setting for the famous public school
novel *Eric, or Little by Little*, by F. W. Farrar, headmaster of Marlborough. Another old boy who was divine, author and famous
schoolmaster was T. E. Brown, of Clifton. George Robert Stephenson, the railway engineer, and Thomas Fowler, the logician, were

Harvey, actor-manager, John Barrymore, Sir Victor Negas and A. G. Cross,
leading surgeons, Alvar Liddell, Hon. Sir Ralph Cusack, General Sir Alan Jolly,
Sir Cyril Black, Victor Goodhew, M.P., and author John Pearson.

* Lord Leighton, Joseph Chamberlain, the Marquess of Reading, Viscount
Samuel, W. S. Jevons, the economist, Ford Madox Ford, David Garnett,
Sir Bernard Spilsbury, Rodrigo Moynihan, artist, Sir Frank Newson-Smith,
Lord Mayor of London in the war, Sir E. J. Salisbury, director of the Royal
Botanic Gardens, Richard Arnell, composer, Nicolas Bentley, Edward Hyams,
Dr. Roger Bannister, mountaineer Chris Bonnington, Sir Norman Kipping, and
poets Stephen Spender and Thom Gunn.

also at the school. Farrar thinly disguised King William's as 'Roslyn School' and dedicated his book to G. E. L. Cotton, the great headmaster of Marlborough. He wrote: 'Why is it that new boys are almost invariably ill-treated? I have often fancied that there must be in boyhood a pseudo-instinctive cruelty . . . which no amount of civilization can entirely suppress. Certain it is that to most boys the first term is a trying ordeal. They are being tested and weighed. Their place in the general estimation is not yet fixed, and the slightest circumstances are seized upon to settle the category under which the boy is to be classed.'

Another old endowment put to better use at this time was that of John Carpenter, Town Clerk of London, and friend and executor of Dick Whittington. Carpenter, who died in 1442, left some property for the education of four poor children born in the City of London. 'John Carpenter's Children', as they were known, were sent to various schools, including Merchant Taylors', and, especially, to Tonbridge. By the early nineteenth century there was dissatisfaction in the corporation of London about the application of the Carpenter bequest. The matter was taken up by one Warren Stormes Hole, chairman of the City lands committee in 1833. The value of Carpenter's property had become very considerable and a new school, from the bequest, was founded by the City in 1834, after debates on the subject in Parliament. Carpenter's plea for the 'poor and destitute' was hardly respected, although the City of London School has never been for the wealthy. However, consciences were partly salved by the establishment of the Freemen's Orphan School at Brixton, in 1854; also administered and maintained by the City, Freemen's is now at Ashtead Park. The City of London School opened its doors in 1837 with a curriculum as progressive as any in England, including modern history, natural history and book-keeping, as well as French and the classics. Science was introduced in 1847—with Manchester Grammar, U.C.S. and one or two others, among the first in England. The school soon became known at the universities, especially at Cambridge. By 1859 there were 603 boys on the roll. The school's academic reputation was made by an outstanding headmaster, E. A. Abbott, an old boy, 1865–89. It is apt that the last school to be founded before the Victorian age should have taken such an uncompromising attitude, like Forest School, to a modern education, heralding as it did at last a new attitude to secondary education.

In 1882 the school buildings were sold for £60,000 and the school moved to a new site on the Victoria Embankment. During the nineteen-seventies it is to be moved again, about a quarter of a mile down river. Playing-fields, naturally, have always been a problem; they are now at Grove Park. Kingsley Amis was at the school: 'It had lots of identical passages and a vast agoraphobic playground filled with self-possessed boys in black coats and striped trousers.'*

* Old Citizens include Lord Ritchie, Chancellor of the Exchequer and originator of County Councils, Sir Sydney Lee, second editor of the *Dictionary of National Biography*, P. M. Horder, collegiate architect (including Somerville), Arthur Rackham, illustrator, Sir William Huggins, pioneer astronomer, Sir John Seeley, imperial historian, Bramwell Booth, of the Salvation Army, Sir F. G. Hopkins, Nobel Prize winner and discoverer of vitamins, Lord Chalmers, Under-Secretary for Ireland, Earl of Oxford (H. H. Asquith), E. S. Montague, who was in Asquith's cabinet, C. E. Montague, author, Cecil Roth, historian, Michael Joseph, publisher, James Leasor, and Michael Brearley, cricketer and university don.

8.

THE VICTORIAN SCHOOLS

FROM 1839 to 1899 there were numerous commissions and enquiries, and acts, on education in general and the public schools in particular. The momentum had been generated by Lord Brougham in the previous period, the spokesman for much public discontent. In 1816 he had gained a general commission of enquiry into endowed charities, many of which had become a scandal, and which included, of course, many of the schools. The resulting enquiries lasted for some twenty years and resulted in some reform. This led to the establishment of the Charity Commission in 1853 and the royal commissions and acts of the eighteen-sixties, which re-wrote the statutes of many of the old schools, freeing them at last from outdated conditions. The Clarendon Commission of 1861 looked into nine 'Certain Public Schools', as a result of public agitation, and found them all wanting (only one, Rugby, was teaching science, and that just started). It found that the original statutes had become restrictive in the extreme. The Endowed Schools Inquiry Commission of 1864–68 made searching inquiries into the old schools. It was stated that: 'The number of scholars who were obtaining the sort of education in Latin and Greek contemplated by the founders was very small . . . the general instruction in other subjects was found to be very worthless.' The Public Schools Act of 1868 dealt with Winchester, Eton, Shrewsbury, Westminster, Rugby, Harrow and Charterhouse, and revised their constitutions, but not that of St. Paul's. In 1869 the remaining endowed schools came up for examination, and were the subject of slow inquiry by Special Commissioners. In 1874 the matter was transferred to the Charity Commissioners, and it was transferred to the Board of Education in 1899. Almost every old school was thus examined and revised at least once during the century.

Parallel to this reform for the endowed schools was the slow but inevitable establishment of a state system of education, which began in 1832 when the Whig Government placed on the estimates a sum of £20,000 for education. The movement was for long hindered by religious controversy, but during the eighteen-forties many old grammar schools became elementary schools, abandoning their rigidly classical tradition. W. E. Forster's Act of 1870 recognised the responsibility of the state in certain circumstances for primary education, of state aid in the case of poor parents, and of the need for compulsory education.* (By 1886 only 38,000 votes were made by illiterates.) The Bryce Commission on Secondary Education of 1895 reported that there were 1,448 endowments in England subject to the Endowed Schools Acts. Nearly all these became integrated in the state secondary system in the next century, brought about by the new local government system, which allowed the raising of rates for education. Thus by the First World War there had been a complete revolution of boys' secondary education. The old schools of the start of the nineteenth century were either state or independent; the latter were the independent grammar schools and the 'public' schools, i.e. those not privately owned but not state controlled either. The growth of these independent schools was due to the expansion of the new middle class, the increase in value of some of the endowments, new methods of financing new schools, and the Oxford Movement and the opposing Evangelical Movement.

In Scotland, the Royal Commission of 1864, named after its chairman, the Duke of Argyll, investigated and reported on Scottish education. It discovered that £42,000 were paid in fees for secondary education; one in 250 had some form of higher education (as compared to one in 1,300 in England). An act of 1872 brought compulsory primary education, and school control from Church to state; eleven of the old endowed grammar schools opted out. The Argyll Commission had thought highly of the independent schools; it found that at the Scottish schools the hours were about twice as long as at Eton or Winchester.

*

The honour of being the first major Victorian foundation lies between Liverpool and Cheltenham colleges. Liverpool was founded first, but Cheltenham opened first.

Liverpool College was founded in 1840, after 'friends of the

---

* Forster was brother-in-law to Arnold of Rugby's son, Matthew, who, apart from poet and author, was one of the leading authorities on education in the country.

established Church', mostly merchants and clergymen, had met in order to found a Church of England school in Liverpool, where Catholic children were already provided for. One of the chief instigators was Robertson Gladstone, elder brother of William Ewart Gladstone, who, like their father, Sir John Gladstone, became a vice-president (the Gladstone family retain an interest in the college). The Stanley family became patrons of the school and the Earl of Derby is still president of the council. The college was stated quite clearly to be for 'the middle classes of society'. The Liverpool Collegiate Institution, as it was first known, was almost aggressively Anglican, in answer to the Roman Catholic and non-conformist foundations that had recently been set up. The college was planned in three parts; the lower to provide clerks for the offices of merchants in booming Liverpool, the upper to prepare for the universities. The former section later became Liverpool Collegiate School, a modern grammar school, and the latter became the Liverpool College of today, a public school mainly for day-boys, but with a few boarders. It was intended, at first, to provide higher education as well, along the lines of the Royal Belfast Academical Institution. The lower and middle sections were taken over by Liverpool corporation in 1907, but the college was reorganised and remains a school for boys from seven to eighteen, the lower school being integral, as the founders had intended, and not a separate preparatory department as at most schools.*

Hele's School, Exeter, like King William's and City of London, was also founded from an old benefaction, in this case that of Eliza Hele, dating from 1632. It was opened in 1840, for the education of the sons of tradesmen, inn-keepers and warehousemen of the city of Exeter. Another Devon school, Shebbear College, at Beaworthy, midway between Okehampton and Bideford, was founded in the following year (1841). It is now controlled by the Board of Management for Methodist Residential Schools.

Cheltenham College was an amalgamation of several private schools in the area, formed by a group of schoolmasters and parents

---

* Old Liverpoolians: Richard le Gallienne, the Nineties writer, Sir Charles Petrie, historian, Lord Evans, Physician to the Queen, Lord Russell of Liverpool, the Rt. Rev. Bishop R. W. Stopford, Maurice Davidson, authority on lung cancer, Raymond Postgate, Ernest Newman, music critic, W. Stewart, headmaster of Brighton and Haileybury, Ken Cranston, England cricketer, and Rex Harrison.

of the town. It was opened under Dr. Alfred Phillips, on 29 July 1841, with 146 boys. It was, according to its constitution, 'established for the purpose of providing an efficient course of education for the sons of gentlemen, comprising religious and moral instruction, in strict conformity with the principles of the established church; history, geography, mathematics, and with other branches of knowledge as it may be found practicable and advantageous to introduce'. Most of the pupils were sons of retired colonial servants who had settled in the area. Cheltenham was a 'Proprietary School', a popular movement in the mid-nineteenth century. Several of the new Victorian foundations went through this phase. There were 650 shares, each share entitling the holder to nominate one pupil (usually, of course, held by the parent). If the proprietors failed to nominate pupils, then the governors could do so. Fees were paid, as in the other schools. Cheltenham had Classical, Military and Junior Departments. It soon became one of the leading schools for supplying pupils to the military seminaries at Sandhurst and Woolwich. Sanskrit and Hindustani were taught in the Military Department. By 1877 there were 676 boys, 222 of them day-boys. Of the total, 110 were in the junior school. Cheltenham, clearly, was a great success. By 1913 the numbers were 585, with 125 day-boys. Since those days it has been deliberate policy to restrict the numbers to 450. Before the First World War there was a 'Special boarding house for Hebrew boys', as at Clifton. There were changes in the government of the college in 1862 and 1894. It is now governed by a council of life and ordinary members. Sir Maurice Bowra, the Oxford classicist, was at Cheltenham just before the First World War: 'Not only were we locked up in the evenings and allowed very little time for ourselves, but we were forbidden to talk to boys in other houses except in our form-rooms, and even in our own house society was practically restricted to contemporaries. There was no art, no handicraft, no music, no acting, no dancing with the girls from the Ladies' College, and only very occasionally a lecture.' Bowra was on the classical side, which was small 'in comparison with the large and highly efficient military side'. Cheltenham retains its great tradition for public service; it is stated that: 'the instilling of a sense of service to the community remains one of the main educational aims'. Old Cheltonians include Earl Loveburn, Lord Chancellor 1905–12, Viscount Morley, Viscount Lee (who presented Chequers to the nation), William Lecky, the historian, the first Lords Melchett and

Hodson, Field-marshal Sir John Dill, C.I.G.S., General Sir A. G. Cunningham, Montgomery's predecessor commanding the Eighth Army, Lieut.-General Sir John 'Pasha' Glubb, G. O. Simms, Primate of All Ireland, Frederick Corfield, M.P., author T. H. White, classicist J. V. Luce, J. P. W. Mallalieu, M.P., cricketers Duleepsinhji, E. D. R. Eagar and E. M. Wellings, squash champion Jonah Barrington, and Rugby international R. D. Hearne. There is a long-standing connection with Trinity College, Dublin (Lecky, Simms, Luce, Barrington and Hearne all went to on that university). Cheltenham has the curious distinction of having schooled one of the greatest thriller writers and one of the greatest of real spies: respectively Cyril McNeile ('Sapper'), author of that famous public-school hero Bulldog Drummond, and Sir C. M. V. Gubbins, the famous war-time 'M' of the S.O.E.

Eltham College was founded in 1842, for the sons of missionaries, at Blackheath. Missionary work was, of course, one of the great Victorian pre-occupations. Gradually the college opened its doors to others, particularly after it moved to its present site at Eltham in 1912. Today a quarter of the boys are boarders, some of them Foundationers, and four of the governing body are still nominated by the Baptist Missionary Society and the Congregational Council for World Mission. Lord Brockway is an old boy.

Wellington School, in Somerset, not to be confused with the more famous college of the same name in Berkshire, was also founded in 1842. Like Loretto and Cheltenham, it began life as a private school, but was reorganised under the Charitable Trusts Acts in 1906 and 1908, with an independent governing body. About half the boys are now boarders. Another Somerset school, Queen's College, Taunton, was founded in the following year. Queen's began in a part of Taunton Castle; it moved to a site on the edge of the town in 1847. Queen's, Taunton, is one of the schools controlled by the Methodist Conference.*

St. Columba's College, at Rathfarnham, near Dublin, is the only Headmasters' Conference school in the Republic of Ireland. It was, like Liverpool College, very much part of the Evangelical Movement, founded by the Rev. William Sewell, who, with Canon Woodard and W. E. Gladstone, was one of the great public school founders of the Victoria era. Sewell, a member of the Oxford Movement,

---

* Viscount Watkinson, a cabinet minister from 1957 to 1962, and Lord Widgery, Lord Chief Justice, are distinguished old boys.

was intent on religious propaganda. A High Church Anglican, he was Professor of Moral Philosophy at Oxford. A Wykehamist, Sewell was a great admirer of Winchester. In 1835 he had stood for the headmastership of his old school and had lost it to Moberly by one vote. In 1840 he spent the long vacation in Ireland, during which he became 'distressed beyond measure' at the decay in the Irish Church. He decided that what Ireland needed was a major public school, and with a group of Irish friends he founded St. Columba's at a house called Stackallan, Co. Meath, in 1843. It was based entirely on Sewell's ideas. The school was to be run on the collegiate system, like a sort of junior Oxford college. There was some dissension when the staff discovered that they were expected to observe religious fasts in a literal manner. The atmosphere was to be that of a happy family, the staff taking the stance of elder brothers to the pupils. For a year or two Sewell's way continued, but eventually it broke down and a more normal boarding-school routine came about. The Irish language was taught, so that products of the school would be better able to lead the Irish peasantry. According to one historian: 'St. Columba's was intended to be, and for a time seems really to have been, a homelike and happy institution. There were four schools in England or Ireland at that time of which this could be said.' However, there was a financial crisis in 1845 and this, together with the Fasting Statute of the college, led to the severing of Sewell's connection with St. Columba's. The college began a new life, with less demanding governors, in Co. Dublin in 1849.*

Marlborough College had a rather different background from that of Cheltenham. Whereas the latter was unashamedly upper class, Marlborough was founded, in 1843, for the sons of the poorer professional classes and clergy. The founders secured for the new school the premises of the Castle Inn, a well-known hostelry on the Bath Road. There are remains of a castle in the grounds. Two years later Marlborough was incorporated by royal charter (there have been additional charters in 1853 and in 1958). The college is now governed by a council consisting of twelve Anglican clergymen and twelve laymen. A feature of Marlborough was that boys ate in a communal dining-hall, not in their houses as was the custom else-

* Marshal of the R.A.F. Sir Dermot Boyle, Brian Faulkner, Nicholas Massergh, novelist William Trevor, author Monk Gibbon and the cricketer C. S. Marriott are among the old boys.

where; this had obvious economic advantages, and was soon copied at many new schools, being known as 'the hostel system'. One early Marlburian wrote of the result with some distaste: 'The sickening smell of tea, boiled in new tin cans, was quite enough for me. Henceforward I became a strict abstainer, and during the eight-and-a-half years I remained at school I invariably quenched my thirst at the college pump. Nor did the beer, which subsequently was dealt out at dinner, in any way alter my predilection for the pump. . . . I failed to appreciate its stale, flat look. . . . Beside the tea, which I declined to drink, bread and butter was provided, but in such limited supply that everyone was clamorous for more, and as there was no bell or other means of communication with the pantry, some hungry forward boy began to stamp his feet, an example which was quickly followed by us all. . . . "Waste not want not" is certainly a good motto to impress on those who are over-burdened with this world's goods; but at Marlborough College, when I was there, opportunity of having anything to waste so seldom happened that the aphorism might fairly have been regarded as a dead letter, or one which did not demand much notice. Those in authority, however, thought otherwise; and some time before we were dismissed from hall, a careful scrutiny of all our plates was made . . . hunger had made my neighbour reckless, and he demanded a second slice; and then the dreaded Inspector stood before him. . . . The master eyed his victim for some moments, which, though they may have been pleasant enough to him, were agony to the wretched boy; and at length, pulling out the well-known pocket book, he said, "Come to my desk when the school bell rings and I will cane you".' Conditions were notorious. According to Sir Cyril Norwood, headmaster 1916–25, by 1850 it had 'become a school which took a new boy, a child of eight years of age, tied him to a bench in the Upper School where there were throngs of boys present, and branded him with an anchor on the forearm by means of a red-hot poker'. In 1851 there was a rebellion.

Despite this lack of order, Marlborough, after a few decades, was thriving. This it owed largely to the Rev. G. E. L. Cotton, headmaster 1852–58, who had been a master at Rugby under Arnold. (Cotton, who was responsible for establishing the system of compulsory games, left Marlborough to become Bishop of Calcutta, and was drowned in the Ganges.) He turned the school from what has been described as a 'rebellious mob' into a leading public school.

By 1877 there were over five hundred boys: by 1913, over six hundred. During the nineteenth century a form of proprietorship, like that at Cheltenham, was carried out; pupils were admitted on the nomination of a life governor or a donor; a donation of £50 entitled a potential parent to a life-governorship, and every time he wished to enter another boy he could do so by paying another £50. By 1914 Marlborough had become one of the great schools of the nation. Under the headmastership of John Dancy, 1961–72, previously headmaster of Lancing, Marlborough was in the van in answering the critics of the public schools, and was one of, if not the first, to introduce girls (to the sixth form). Dancy said: 'Marlborough remains a boys' school, but I am convinced it's a much better boys' school for having some girls in it.' Under Dancy, Marlborough pioneered the business-studies A Level course. (Other early schools to join this course were Sevenoaks, Radley, Hele's and Harrow.) Siegfried Sassoon wrote of his experience at Marlborough: 'Public schools haven't time to worry about the artistic temperament or people with latent abilities of which they themselves are unaware. . . . I departed, thinking only of cricket matches in the holidays, and wearing an old Marlburian tie, which for me was neither more nor less than a badge of emancipation from an educational experience that I found moderately pleasant but mentally unprofitable.'*

The present headmaster of Marlborough is Roger Wykeham Ellis, who was previously head of Rossall, the next school to have been founded. This was another 'proprietary school', founded in 1844. It was founded for similar reasons to Marlborough, for the sons of clergy and laymen of modest means who sought a modern as well as a classical education. It was intended, rather grandly, that it should be the 'Northern Church of England Public School'. The instigator, remarkably enough, was one Vantini, a Corsican entre-

* Old boys: William Morris, one of the first pupils, Field-Marshal Sir Henry Wilson, Anthony Hope, Clive Bell, Lord Goddard, economist E. A. G. Robinson, Prof. Ellis Waterhouse, Lord Fisher of Lambeth, Lord Butler, Lord Hunt and Sir Francis Chichester, Marshal of the R.A.F. Sir Charles Elsworthy, Sir Robert Thompson, anti-insurgent expert in S.E. Asia, Lord Fraser of Lonsdale, T. C. Worsley, historian Keith Feiling, Rt. Rev. J. A. T. Robinson (former Bishop of Woolwich), John Parker, Labour M.P. since 1945, Peter Kirk, M.P., General Sir Charles Keightley, Sir R. Bodley Scott, physician to H.M. the Queen, James Mason, Beverley Nichols, whose first book was a public-school novel, and poets Charles Sorley, Sir John Betjeman and Louis MacNeice.

preneur, who had been Napoleon's courier and who had settled in England; its founder was the vicar of Fleetwood, the Rev. St. Vincent Beechey; and its home was that of Sir Peter Hesketh Fleetwood, whose family had owned and lived in Rossall Hall since 1583. Fleetwood had started the town of his own name, but in so doing he had spent all his reserves and was happy to sell his house to the school in 1852. The Hall was in an exposed position just off the sands, near Fleetwood. The first captain of the school later wrote: 'The choosing of the site was often held up to ridicule . . . but to us, who could bear the winds and brunt the storm, it gave a hardening strength which has braced us up for life.' From the start Rossall had financial difficulties, and was seldom free of them for long. It was rescued late in the nineteenth century by Dr. H. A. James, 1875–86, later headmaster of Cheltenham and Rugby, and one of the leading figures in public-school education at the turn of the century. James found 237 pupils at Rossall and left it with 335. James later wrote, in 1926: 'I have always thought that the best work of my life was done in those eleven years at Rossall.' Like Cheltenham, Rossall had a special Military Department, and its Corps was the first to be enrolled by an English public school (in February 1860). Rossall declined again in the nineteen-thirties, and was only two-thirds full in 1932; this was due to the general depression, which affected so many public schools, rather than to any failure on the school's part, although its financial affairs were not always wisely handled. Like St. Bees, its old boys helped it through the difficult times. As the school history has said: 'Rossall has spent lavishly in prosperity and been so ill-prepared for adversity that on at least three occasions the school has nearly gone under.' However, Rossall fully recovered after the war, and it now caters for five hundred boys. Patrick Campbell saw it first as 'a low huddle of red-brick buildings, elevated here and there by a Gothic tower. A concrete fortification rose near the sea-wall, presumably the baths, spoken so highly of in the prospectus'.*

Brighton College is another school which almost faded away in the nineteen-thirties. It owed its existence to a meeting held in Brighton on 7 July 1845, at which 'it seemed desirable and

* Old Rossallians: Lord Sydenham, soldier, Lord Lugard, imperialist, Lord Stamfordham, private secretary to Queen Victoria and George V, Sir Thomas Beecham, Lieut.-General Sir Thomas Hulton, G.O.C., Burma, 1942, Sir David Brown, industrialist, and author Leslie Charteris.

practicable to establish a College at Brighton on Church of England principles for the education of sons of noblemen and gentlemen'. Advice was sought from Cheltenham; the council were told by the honorary secretary of that school: 'Had we admitted tradesmen in any instance, we must have done so almost without limit, and in the confined circle of shops in Cheltenham we should have had the sons of gentlemen shaking hands perhaps with school-fellows behind the counter.' Such thoughts were different from those that had inspired the founders of, say, Winchester and St. Paul's in previous centuries. The Victorian public schools, from Cheltenham on, were not without their snobberies, and it is this class-consciousness which distinguished them from their predecessors. Brighton College opened in 1847 with forty-seven boys, a number which had risen to 126 by the end of the first year. But the college did not thrive as had been hoped. It moved to its present site in 1849 and expanded under the Rev. John Griffith, 1856–71. It suffered from keen rivalry with Brighton Grammar School, founded in 1859, also on proprietary lines. The grammar school was founded as a day school, 'without necessity of sending boys from under supporters' own care', one of the few proprietary schools which took this line; nevertheless, it was soon taking boarders (and still does). It had an unusually broad curriculum, including German, French, arithmetic, book-keeping, science, navigation, history and geography. By 1907 there were 350 pupils, fifty of them boarders.* Meanwhile Brighton College was in heavy debt. The Phoenix Fire Office took over the consolidated debt of £45,000 in 1891. The Phoenix Company soon virtually owned the college, which was obliged to contract, and a number of boarding houses were closed down in the eighteen-nineties. Brighton was kept alive under Canon W. R. Rodgers, 1906–33, who had been educated at King William's and Trinity, Dublin, and who had previously revitalised King's, Grantham; under Dawson, Grantham had grown from five boarders and thirty-three day-boys to 120 boarders and 127 day-boys in eight years. Under Dawson, Brighton College was bought back from the Phoenix in 1909. However, it later got into debt with the Eagle Star, and the school nearly collapsed in the late thirties owing to its being only two-thirds full. Boarding houses were again closed. By 1940 there were only 135 boys in the school, but there was a rapid recovery after the war, when the Regency Building Society became the

* Aubrey Beardsley and Sir Charles B. Cochran were students.

college's main creditor. There are now nearly four hundred boys, about half of them boarders.*

Founded in the same year as Brighton were Leeds Modern and Wesley College, Dublin. Alan Bennett, author of one of the classic school plays, *Forty Years On*, was at Leeds Modern. Wesley College was at first titled 'The Wesleyan Classical and Commercial School'. It became co-educational in 1912. George Bernard Shaw is its most famous pupil. He was 'a source of idleness in others, distracting them from their studies by interminable comic stories'. He was 'generally near or at the bottom of the class'. Wesley is in the unfortunate position of receiving the greatest caning any school has suffered in English literature, and that from its most distinguished former pupil. Shaw credited none of his culture and his intellect to his school, on the contrary: 'My schooling did me a great deal of harm and no good whatever: it was simply dragging a child's soul through the dirt. . . . None of my schoolmasters really cared a rap whether I learnt my lessons or not, provided my father paid my schooling bill, the collection of which was the real object of the school . . . in order to get expelled, it was necessary to commit a crime of such atrocity that the parents of other boys would have threatened to remove their sons sooner than allow them to be schoolfellows with the delinquent. . . . The masters must have hated the school much more than the boys did . . . these poor schoolmasters, with their small salaries and large classes, were as much prisoners as we were. I was taught lying, dishonourable submission to tyranny, dirty stories. . . . And if I had been a boarder at an English public school instead of a day boy at an Irish one, I might have had to add to these, deeper shames still.' It is only fair to add that Shaw was an acidulous critic of the entire educational system, and not just his own school.

The following year, 1846, saw the foundation of Glasgow Academy, which was to be to Glasgow what the Edinburgh Academy already was to that city. It resulted from a meeting of leading citizens in the Star Hotel, George Square, on 8 May 1845. It was intended for middle-class boys, who were 'earnestly recommended' to undertake

---

* Old boys: Sir Sydney Roberts, Vice-Chancellor of Cambridge University, Lieut.-General Sir Francis Tucker, of the Burma campaign, Air Marshal Sir J. H. Edwardes Jones, Sir Vivian Fuchs, the explorer, actors Miles Malleson, George Sanders and Michael Hordern, and writers L. A. G. Strong, Christopher Hassall and Michael Roberts.

the general course rather than a strictly classical one. The new buildings were opened in 1847. The academy took a long time before it rivalled the eminence of the Edinburgh one, but between 1861 and 1869 the numbers rose from 381 to 793. Lord Reith, first director-general of the B.B.C., was at the academy. 'Once I had been flogged with great vigour, and the tears, though few, were obvious. Some weeks later, in Cadet Corps uniform, I offended again but not enough for flogging; the beak concerned (name suppressed but not forgotten) cashed in on it. "I would flog you again," he said, "but it would be ignominious for a soldier in full uniform to be seen weeping." I still regret not giving the retort which strained for utterance: "Go ahead, you cad, and see if I cry this time." There was much variation in straps—length, breadth, thickness, flexibility and number of fingers. . . . Snubs's invitation and action were unique: "Come oot here, ma lad, and Ah'll gie ye a taste o' ma strahp".' Since 1920 the school has been controlled by the Glasgow Academy War Memorial Trust, formed in memory of the academicals who had given their lives in the First World War.*

Ratcliffe College, Leicestershire, was opened in 1847, having been founded three years previously. The new buildings were the gift of Lady Mary Arundell of Wardour. It is a Roman Catholic foundation, run by members of the Rosminian Order. Taunton School was founded in 1847, and remained a small local establishment until the end of the century. It became widely known under Dr. Whittaker, 1899–1922, and since then has become one of the leading schools in the West Country. Old boys include J. C. White, captain of M.C.C., who played for England over a period of ten years, and author and professor J. M. Roberts.

With the foundation of St. Peter's College, Radley, also in 1847, we return to the formidable Rev. William Sewell. Convinced of the success of his experiment in Ireland, Sewell now determined to establish a similar school in England, based on his own and the Oxford Movement's ideas. It was to be modelled on St. Columba's, with a Warden (as the headmaster at both places is still known), Fellows and, of course, a strict Fasting Rule. Sewell declared: 'Our college should never degenerate into a speculation for amassing

* Former pupils: James Pryde, the artist, Sir James Barrie (his brother Alexander was a teacher there) and James Bridie, Lord Lindsay, Master of Balliol, Air Chief Marshal Sir George Pirie, the philosopher J. H. Muirhead, Sir Hugh Fraser, and John French, the rugby football international.

money.' A lease was taken on Radley Hall, near Oxford; R. C. Singleton, a fervent admirer of Sewell, from Trinity, Dublin, who had been the first warden of St. Columba's, was appointed Warden; and the college opened with three boys in 1847. Two of these won scholarships to Oxford and obtained first-class honours. At the end of the next three years the roll was thirty-six, seventy-two and eighty-four. Thus Radley gradually expanded. The boys rose at 6.0 and went to bed at 9.0 It was a hardy life, and Sewell, who was against unnecessary 'stuffing', seems to have seen to it that the boys were always under-fed and hungry. Bulbs, flowers, acorns, were taken from the park and 'eagerly devoured'. Financial difficulties obliged Sewell to take up the Wardenship himself, which he did from 1853 to 1861, but although his teaching seems to have been good, his financial expertise was not. After a meeting of creditors in London, Sewell resigned. The school was taken over by a pious business-man and politician, J. G. Hubbard, later Lord Addington, under whom the freehold was purchased in 1889 for £13,000. Addington died a few weeks later and Radley passed into the hands of trustees. Under Wardens H. L. Thompson and T. Field, Radley gradually settled down as one of the major schools. By the First World War the numbers had risen to over two hundred. Radley's park now extends to seven hundred acres.*

Another school with an evangelical background is Trinity College, Glenalmond. Like Liverpool, this school largely owes its existence to Gladstone. He believed a school was necessary to support the Church of Scotland, as Sewell had tried to support the Church of Ireland. Gladstone and his friends declared that the new school was 'designed to embrace objects not yet obtainable in any public foundation in Scotland, viz. the combination of General Education with Domestic Discipline and Systematic Religious Instruction'. The school was also to provide 'a sound Clerical Education to young men destined for Holy Orders'. The scheme had the active support of the Bishops of Scotland, who still elect the Warden, and was to include a theological college (which was separated in 1876). Gladstone and his father, Sir John, personally selected the superb site, on the right bank of the Almond in Perthshire. A grandiose plan, based on a quadrangle, was approved, and work was sufficiently

---

* Old Radleans: Sir George Mallaby, Lord Shackleton, Lieut.-General Sir William Oliver, Sir Leslie Scarman, Sir Allan Noble, Sir Edward Howard, Lord Mayor, F. H. Curtis-Bennett, Q.C., and author Christopher Hibbert.

advanced for the school to open with fourteen boys in 1847. The first pupil to arrive was Lord Henry Kear, afterwards Lord Lothian, Secretary for Scotland. The Warden was the Rev. Charles Wordsworth, who had been Gladstone's tutor at Oxford. Under the Rev. John Hannah, 1854–70, the school expanded greatly, but at the cost of incurring debts. As Hannah said, 'the college was virtually mortgaged to its Council and its friends'. The first Corps in Scotland was formed at Glenalmond in 1875. Glenalmond was saved by the Wardenship of the Rev. J. H. Shrine, 1888–1902, who had been a master at Uppingham under Thring. Numbers under Shrine rose from sixty to 140. Today they are 360. As at Liverpool, the Gladstone family have retained an interest in Glenalmond until recent times. Old boys include Sir John Gilmour, Home Secretary, Sir Ninian Cowper, architect, and Admiral Sir William James. The novelist Bruce Marshall, who was at Glenalmond, wrote one of the best of all modern public-school novels, *George Brown's Schooldays*, set in 1912. Marshall describes Brown's first morning at school: 'It was morning again, with a new cold stretch of day high above his cubicle and invisible feet carrying a clanging bell along beneath the rafters. . . . He was standing dismally in the middle of the floor wondering what to do about washing when he heard his name called and looked up to see the Bruiser grinning down from the partition. . . . Rough hands seized Brown and propelled him towards the bath. The boy cried out with pain as his toe was stubbed against a rib of the wooden planking which did duty for a bath mat, but nobody paid any attention. First his head was dipped in the filthy water and held down. While his head was under water, Henson slid in the bath and crashed his feet against the boy's face. . . . "I'll teach the young weed to have fug in his ears," the Bruiser said, yanking Brown's head out of the water by the hair and crashing his cake of soap down on the boy's head. Soon a thick froth covered Brown's hair . . . and a hundred fingers seemed to thrust it down into his ears, round his neck, up into his nostrils and upwards and downwards into his eyes until he was all of him sore and stinging . . . the Bruiser mocked as he plunged the boy's head back into the bath again and held it down while more fellows got in and kicked his face. Suddenly a bell began to ring out drearily, churlishly. Brown's head was immediately released. . . . With his waistcoat buttons undone and tying his tie as he went, he joined the torrent of boys that went rushing along the dormitory and down the steep stone staircase . . . the prefect began to recite. Brown Quartus was in time for his first roll call.'

*

As a founder of great schools, the Rev. Nathaniel Woodard could hardly have differed more from his predecessors Wykeham and Colet. He was every inch a Victorian. The son of an Essex squire, he did not have any formal schooling until he entered Hertford College, Oxford, where he was influenced by the Oxford Movement. At the age of thirty-five, in 1846, he became curate of Shoreham in Sussex. Dissatisfied at the lack of schooling in the area, Woodard, aged thirty-seven, started a local school, grandly entitled Shoreham Grammar School and Collegiate Institution, in 1848. It was a success, and in the three converted houses of the school he began to take boarders. Across the churchyard was another establishment, called the Protestant Grammar School, in rivalry to Woodard's Oxford High Churchism, which had been founded by W. H. Harper in 1842. This is the existing Shoreham Grammar School, still independent, built up under S. Gregory-Taylor, 1894–1930.

Woodard, like Sewell, was obsessed with the idea of Anglican public-school education. The ideas of Arnold of Rugby, who had died in 1842, were well known and had reached a very sympathetic audience in the imperial climate of the mid-Victorian middle class. A number of young men came down from Oxford to help Woodard. In 1849 he formed the Society of St. Nicholas College, Shoreham. The seventeen members of the society were all in holy orders. Woodard was no less class-conscious than his contemporaries, and this, with his evangelism and his ability to influence people, especially in respect of financial support, was one of his main characteristics. Woodard, embarrassed by the continuing flow of pupils to his small school, met with much support in London, especially from Gladstone. About this time he visited Radley, where he met Sewell, and heard the latter's latest plans to found free or inexpensive schools for the poor on the expected profits of Radley. He split his Shoreham school into St. Mary's Grammar School, a day school for the middle class, and St. Nicholas's Grammar School, a boarding school for the sons of professional men and 'gentlemen of limited means'. He decided to make St. Nicholas's his school for the upper class, based on Winchester. In 1849 he began another boarding school at Shoreham, St. John's, for the sons of 'tradesmen, farmers, clerks', etc.

This was to be the middle school, with St. Mary's for the poorer classes. Throughout his remarkable career as a founder of public schools, Woodard, although evidently not a snob in his social relations, was a great student of the classes; he particularly liked to sub-divide the middle class into further compartments, and his schools were all class-designated with such finely drawn distinction that his administrators found it difficult to keep to the guide-lines and perhaps even to recognise them. Gradually the religious hierarchy by which his future complex of schools was governed took on almost Puritan characteristics.

With his remarkable talent for raising funds, which he achieved by presenting the obligation as a duty rather than as charity, Woodard began work on a school building for St. John's behind Brighton, at the village of Hurstpierpoint. This was a collegiate edifice, as were all the Woodard schools, of considerable merit (and an answer to those who say that the Victorian schools contributed little architecturally). The transfer of St. John's from Shoreham to Hurstpierpoint took place in 1850, and the new buildings there were occupied in 1853.

Woodard now turned his attention to Shoreham again. Hurstpierpoint had cost £35,000. For St. Nicholas's and St. Mary's, now combined, for which he had selected a commanding site at Lancing, he required even more. Soon work was begun on the new school, which was to have a vast chapel, the religious centre of the whole Woodard movement. Today, Lancing Chapel is one of the most easily recognisable landmarks on the whole south coast of England, and it is a striking memorial to Woodard's work. Like Hurstpierpoint, Lancing was designed along the lines of an Oxford or Cambridge college. The move to Lancing was made in 1857. The setting was magnificent, on a spur of the Downs, so were the plans for the mostly uncompleted buildings, but, according to the school history, 'The sanitary—or insanitary—arrangements would have disgraced a mediaeval hovel. All old boys of the time speak of them with nausea.' Like Hurstpierpoint, the school was soon doing well, although Woodard had some difficulty in calming fears about his High Church attitude (for years it was rumoured that boys at Lancing were expected to make confession). At Lancing itself, order was made from chaos under the headmastership of R. E. Sanderson, 1862–89. There was a financial crisis and falling numbers at the turn of the century, and when closure seemed possible Lancing was saved by its second great headmaster, B. H. Tower, 1902–9, an old boy. He insisted that, for the first time, the headmaster should have control over the school chaplain. The most famous old boy is Evelyn Waugh.* He recreated brilliantly, if briefly, the public school ambience in his *Scott-King's Modern Europe*: 'In 1946 Scott-King had been classical master at Grantchester for twenty-one years. He was himself a Grantchesterian and had returned straight from the university after failing for a fellowship. There he had remained, growing slightly bald and slightly corpulent, known to generations of boys first as "Scottie", then of late years, while barely middle-aged, as "old Scottie"; a school "institution", whose precise and slightly nasal lamentations of modern decadence were widely parodied.'

By the time of the move to Lancing, Nathaniel Woodard had given up his curacy at Shoreham and he was devoting all his energies, and indeed the remainder of his life, to the setting up of a public-school system that would spread over not just Sussex, but all of England. For the time being, we leave him.

*

Llandovery College, an interesting contrast to the Woodard schools and the most distinctly Welsh of the public schools, was founded by Thomas Phillips in 1848, particularly for young men studying for the ministry in the principality. The founder provided for twenty free scholars, natives of the diocese of St. David's or of Llandaff, and in this respect his foundation was more like that of previous centuries than of the Victorian era. Phillips insisted on the Welsh language being taught, and Welsh history; this qualification is honoured today, and boys who cannot speak Welsh are taught the language in their first terms. The Royal Wolverhampton School was founded in 1850 by John Lees for orphan children from all parts of England. In 1850 it moved to its present site with about twenty pupils. After it began to take boys who were not orphans, the Royal Wolverhampton expanded. Queen Victoria granted the prefix 'Royal' in 1900, and the school has received no less than six royal visits.

It can be seen that various motives were responsible for the rise

* Others: Lord Sankey, Lord Chancellor, Bishop Huddleston, Sir Humphrey Trevelyan, Peter Pears, Roger Fulford, Stuart Cloete, James Morris, Tom Driberg, Christopher Hampton, playwright. Lancing is the leading squash rackets school.

of these new schools. Cheltenham had come into being to serve the children of retired servants of the Empire; Marlborough aimed at economy and a religious education; Rossall was associated with the development of a new seaside resort; Radley and Lancing were due to the religious revivalism of the Oxford Movement. Another such was St. Andrew's College, Bradfield, founded by the Rev. Thomas Stevens, rector of Bradfield and lord of the manor. The rectorship had been in the hands of Stevens's family for some generations, and on his father's death he restored the parish church in some style. Stevens considered that the local population were not able to provide a choir suitable for his grand new church, and he opened a school partly for this purpose in 1850. He started with six boys, but by 1852 there were thirty-two. Stevens, who took the closest control himself, modelled the school, like Radley, on the original Winchester model rather than on Winchester through the Rugby of Arnold. The school grew around the old manor house. It was very much a church school: 'for the encouragement of religious and useful learning and for the careful education of boys as loving children of the Church of England'. There was a rapid succession of headmasters, owing to Stevens's inability to delegate even the most minor of decisions. R. E. Sanderson left the post for the headship of Lancing as has already been noted. In 1880 the headmaster and half the staff resigned, owing to non-payment of salaries—'disloyalty', said Stevens. The concern was declared bankrupt, with debts of £160,000. The founder resigned, the rectory was sequestered, the manor and its lands sold. But the thirteen acres of the college had been placed in a trust, and thus the foundation, like Marlborough and Radley, survived—just. By 1886 the school had recovered, and from that date made steady progress. The thirteen acres have become 185. Bradfield was the first school regularly to perform a play in Greek, a tradition which has become a well-known feature of the college.*

One school which has kept to its nineteenth-century religious foundation more than most is St. John's, Leatherhead. This was founded in 1851, at Clapton, in north-east London, as the St. John's Foundation School. It was for the education of poor sons of the clergy, who (unlike St. Edmund's) had to be living. In 1872 it

* Old Bradfieldians: Admiral of the Fleet Lord Fraser, Naval C.-in-C. Pacific, 1944–46, Air Chief Marshal Sir C. Courtney, John Hadfield, anthologist, Ian Hunter.

moved to its present site at Leatherhead, and began to enlarge by taking the sons of laymen. The school grew around an impressive, partly cloistered, quadrangle. St. John's further expanded before the Second World War, but of the 340 boys, about a hundred are still Foundationers, paying fees from only £45 p.a. About ten per cent. of Old Johnians are ordained. Victoria College, Jersey, was founded in the same year to give that island a public school (Guernsey having had its ancient grammar school since Elizabeth). It was founded in commemoration of a visit of Queen Victoria to the island.*

In the mid-century, professional people as well as clergymen began to seek a public-school education, but were deterred by the cost. Epsom College, at first known as the Royal Medical Benevolent College, was founded by John Propert in 1853, primarily for the orphans of doctors. Later it took in the sons of living doctors, and eventually of laymen. Epsom College, which the school was named from 1903, retained a strong medical bias, although there was a normal curriculum. Between 1855 and 1884 there were 1,781 entries; of these, 1,528 were the sons of medical men, and 587 went on to become doctors themselves. Epsom, however, did not become a major school until the headmastership of the Rev. T. N. H. Smith-Pearse, 1889–1914, who, as it happened, was a confirmed classicist (although the precursor of the medical sixth already existed). Under Smith-Pearse the number of boys rose from about 130 to 280. During the nineteen-thirties, against the national trend, Epsom prospered; by 1939 there were 474 boys. The curriculum was widened between the wars to include more science and preparation for medical education.†

Daniel Stewart's College, Edinburgh, was a more traditional foundation, like Llandovery, and not particularly Victorian in foundation. Stewart was an official in the Court of Exchequer, Edinburgh; starting life as a crofter's son, he ended it with £40,000, which he had obtained despite a modest salary of £80 p.a. He died in 1814, and after provision for his family he left his money and property 'for the relief, maintenance and education of Poor Boys of the name of Stewart, of the name of MacFarlane, and of any other

---

* Sir Seymour Hicks and actor Kenneth More are old boys.

† Old boys include, apart from many famous physicians, two artists, Graham Sutherland and John Piper, Kenneth Nair, Shakespearean scholar, that literary man of medicine, Francis Brett-Young, and author Derek Lambert.

name, residing in the city of Edinburgh or suburbs thereof, including the town of Leith, the children of deserving parents whose circumstances in life do not enable them suitably to support and educate their children at other Schools'. The management was left to the Merchant Company of Edinburgh (it still largely is). The death of Stewart's niece in 1845 left the way open for the 'hospital', the value of the estate having risen to £80,000'. The school opened in 1855 with fifty boys (three of them Stewarts and two MacFarlanes). The Argyll Commission reported unfavourably on Stewart's, as it did on the other school administered by the Merchant Company, George Watson's. 'It appears to us that the cost of education in hospitals is larger than it ought to be.' It was decided, therefore, that better use could be made of Daniel Stewart's if it ceased to be a Christ's Hospital type of school and became a fee-paying day school for middle-class parents of modest means. For a long time in the twentieth century numbers did not reach what they had been at the end of the nineteenth (over 750), owing to the rivalry of new free, or cheaper, secondary day schools. This transformation was made in 1870. (The same happened to George Watson's.) The Endowed Institutions (Scotland) Act, 1869, provided the freedom for this change. Further slight changes were made, as in other Scottish schools, after the commission of Lord Balfour of Burleigh, set up by the Educational Endowments (Scotland) Act, 1882. The Scottish Education Department appeared in 1888, and periodical inspection was introduced. Further reforms were made after the Earl of Elgin's committee, set up by the Education Endowments (Scotland) Act, 1928.*

In London, there was a spate of foundations at this time. St. Joseph's, a Catholic school, was founded at Clapham in 1855, moving to Beulah Hill, Norwood, later. Godolphin School was founded by the legacy of William Godolphin, who had been ambassador to Spain in the seventeenth century. His Will had provided relief for poor people, including children, but in 1852 the Charity Commissioners, investigating the endowment, thought it would be better employed for wholly educational purposes. The Godolphin School opened in Hammersmith in 1856. In its day it was a well-known boys' school, attended by, among others, W. B. Yeats and Dr. L. S. Jameson, of the Raid. But after St. Paul's moved into the area, and with keen rivalry from Latymer Upper, it began to decline.

* Most famous former pupil: Sir William Russell Flint.

In 1900 Godolphin School was closed. With help from the Latymer trust, the school re-opened as a girls' day school, the Godolphin and Latymer, in 1905. The Stationers' School, now in Hornsey, was founded by that Company in 1858, mainly for sons of liverymen and freemen of the Company. It used to be off Fleet Street.

During the eighteen-fifties the Rev. Nathaniel Woodard had not been idle. With Lancing and Hurstpierpoint struggling along, he had not forgotten the third part of his plan: a school for the sons of parents of even more modest means than those of Hurstpierpoint. This school opened at the old buildings in Shoreham in 1858. It was his intention to build for this, somewhere in Sussex, a really vast new school—'Mr. Woodard's Great Eastern', as Gladstone, still interested, called it, a reference to the largest steamship of the day. The school was planned for a thousand boys. Woodard intended to build other schools like this all around England, one or two every year for the next half-century. This plan was too ambitious altogether, even for the remarkable Woodard, incredibly adept as he was at raising funds. The Oxford Movement clergymen, noblemen, Sussex landowners, all subscribed to the latest appeal. A site was purchased at Ardingly. Once again a very fine example of school architecture was erected, superbly set in the Sussex hills and fields. St. Saviour's moved to the new buildings in 1870. During the eighteen-eighties Ardingly flourished, but its continued success was largely due to a succession of Woodard's old boys who returned to the school as dedicated staff. The three-tiered social system of Woodard's Sussex schools did not survive (today there is not much more than £50 annually in fees between Lancing and the two others). But Woodard did struggle to keep Ardingly the cheapest of the three, never permitting the minimum annual fee to rise above fifteen guineas in his lifetime, and applying a means test. Nor did Ardingly become the huge school envisaged; it remained small. During the nineteen-thirties this lack of numbers became critical. In 1933 there were only 186 boys in the school, which was losing money every year. It revived under the Rev. E. C. Crosse, 1933–46, who had been headmaster of Christ's College, Christchurch, New Zealand. By the outbreak of war numbers had risen to 333, which is the approximate size of the present senior school. Woodard, having completed his scheme for Sussex, now turned his attention north.

*

Another small school which has had its difficulties is West Buckland, near Barnstaple, in Devon. This was founded in 1858 by the Rev. J. L. Brereton, the local rector. Brereton, who gained the support of the Earl of Fortescue, member of the most influential of Devon families, had been at Rugby under Arnold, and was a great admirer of that system. He wanted to provide an Arnoldian education at reasonable cost. After three years in temporary buildings, the school moved to its present site, and new buildings, in 1861, 650 feet high, and facing across to Dartmoor. West Buckland was re-organised in 1909, and is now Direct Grant.

Four great Roman Catholic schools were founded between 1859 and 1861: Oratory, Belmont Abbey, Blackrock and Beaumont. John Henry Newman, the leader of the Oxford Movement, which had so influenced Sewell and Woodard, had been received into the Roman Catholic Church in 1845. He had helped establish the London Oratory, with its associated school, and then he went to live at Edgbaston, near Birmingham. Here he founded a school in 1859, connected with the Birmingham Oratory. Newman, who had been at Oriel College only two years after Arnold, was impressed by the public-school idea, and he had been encouraged to found the Oratory School by a group of Catholic laymen, headed by the historian Sir John (later Lord) Acton, who wanted a Catholic public school for the sons of gentlemen not necessarily intended for the priesthood. Newman had originally intended a seminary for the priesthood—'the Eton of the Oratory', as he said, 'where the Fathers would turn with warm associations of boyhood'. But this idea was abandoned and the Oratory School emerged as quite a different place. The first headmaster and his deputy were Wykehamists, and the school was built up on Winchester lines, claiming to be a more typical public school than the other Catholic foundations. The Oratory School opened on 2 May 1859. Newman took a close interest in its development. It moved, to Caversham Park, near Reading, in 1922, and again, to nearby Woodcote, in 1942. The Oratory, unlike most Roman Catholic schools, was and is administered by laymen.* In 1931 it was taken from the control of the Birmingham Oratory and put under the control of a governing body under the chairmanship of an old boy, the first Viscount Fitzalan.

* Old boys: Duke of Norfolk, Lord Lothian, Ambassador to the U.S., 1939–40, Hilaire Belloc, Sir William Teeling, Simon Elwes, portrait painter, Michael Levey, art critic.

Belmont Abbey, near Hereford, founded in the same year, was the main training school for the English Benedictines and was part of the monastery (raised to an abbey in 1920). It did not become a lay school until 1926. Blackrock College, Dublin, was founded in 1860 by the French Holy Ghost Fathers, whose European methods of teaching were soon enjoying great academic success and reputation. Beaumont College, almost as an answer to the Oratory School, was founded two years later, in 1861, by the Jesuits, settling in Warren Hastings's old house near Windsor, which for seven years had been the home of the English Jesuit Novices, who had now moved to Roehampton. After twelve months there were fifty boys. The staff were largely priests. Queen Victoria, who otherwise showed little interest in the public schools, visited Beaumont three times. In the nineteen-sixties, despite great indignation among old boys, Beaumont was closed by the Society of Jesus, the remaining boys transferring to Stonyhurst. The famous architectural family of Gilbert Scott all went to Beaumont. St. Augustine's, Westgate, was founded by the Benedictines in 1865, near the spot where St. Augustine landed in England. In 1917 it was closed on account of the Zeppelin raids. It did not re-open until 1953.

During the eighteen-sixties and seventies new public schools were founded almost every month. Birkenhead School, in a growing community, was founded in 1860. It provided a full modern education. F. E. Smith, later Lord Birkenhead, was educated there. Weymouth College, Dorset, once a well-known public school, was founded in 1863 'by a small but select body of churchmen' under the Rev. T. A. L. Greaves, the local rector, a 'protagonist of pronounced Evangelicalism'. By the early nineteen-thirties its numbers were less than two hundred and it was one of the major fatal casualties of that decade. Bloxham School, near Banbury, was founded by the Rev. P. R. Egerton. Egerton had purchased it, for £1,550, from a former master of Woodard's at Shoreham. He opened it with one day-boy in 1860, the staff being himself and an elderly housekeeper. The first boarder, who joined later that year, remained at Bloxham until 1936, as boy, master and bursar, possibly a unique record. The school gradually grew under Egerton. In 1896 he handed over the school to the Woodard Foundation as a free gift. By a curious coincidence, another school later acquired by the Woodard Foundation was also founded in 1860. This was King's, Tynemouth, which joined the Woodard group in 1959. It is the only day public school in the group. Coleraine Academical Institution was opened in 1860 (a grammar school had been in existence previously). William Ellis School, Highgate, dates from 1862. St. Clement Dane's opened in 1862 as a 'commercial grammar' school, having been founded under an order of the Court of Chancery, 1844. Tettenhall College, near Wolverhampton, was founded in 1863 by local nonconformists.

*

Three of the greatest public schools in the country were founded at this time, almost together: Wellington, Clifton and Haileybury, each with its own character. Wellington College was built, conveniently near Sandhurst, as the result of a public subscription in memory of the Duke of Wellington. Lord Derby had discussed the project with Queen Victoria on the day the news of Wellington's death was received at Balmoral. The name of the college had been decided at a meeting of principal subscribers at Buckingham Palace under the chairmanship of Prince Albert. The royal family had contributed £3,655. So Wellington College was well connected. Originally it was intended that the foundation should be for the sons of deceased officers of the Army and of the East India Company's army, but by the time the school opened, in 1859, the East India Company's army was no more, and non-Foundationers were admitted also. Since then the royal charter has been amended to permit the sons of deceased officers of the Royal Navy, the Royal Marines and the R.A.F. to benefit from it. No school could have had a more impressive list of backers. The Queen associated herself with it as 'Visitor' (an association which succeeding monarchs have maintained). The Prince of Wales was President. The Earl of Derby, who had already been associated with the founding of several public schools in the north, became Vice-President. *Ex-officio* governors were the Commander-in-Chief of the Army, the Secretary of State for War, the Archbishop of Canterbury and the Duke of Wellington (the last two governorships survive). Disraeli was at one time a governor. The school was a success. By 1877 there were three hundred boys, twenty of them Foundationers. This was partly due to the fact that Wellington concentrated on the modern side more than any leading school at that time. Modern subjects were 'encouraged in the same way as classical studies are encouraged, and to allow proficiency in them to advance a boy in the school'. By 1913 there were nearly five hundred boys (there are now 660). Wellington introduced a compromise between the old house system and the hostel system. The enormous dormitories, nearly forty yards long, were partitioned off into small study-bedrooms. Over the years three separate houses have also grown up.

From the start it was recognised that Wellington would be a military school. In 1891 the cadets going to Sandhurst were mainly from the following schools:

Wellington	37
Eton	29
Clifton	19
Marlborough	16
Harrow	16
Haileybury	14
Charterhouse	14
Cheltenham	12
I.S.C.	11
Bedford	11

For many years, with only Cheltenham and Haileybury to rival it sustainedly, Wellington supplied numerous cadets to the military colleges. Of the 10,700 Wellingtonians from 1859 to 1948, 1,300 'died for their country'. In the nineteen-twenties there was a rumour that the Master, F. B. Malim, was discouraging boys from entering the Army, a rumour which caused some outrage. Malim wrote to Lord Derby (the family have maintained its connection): 'I do not think there is anything to which I could plead Not Guilty with a clearer conscience.' But the rumour persisted, although statistics disproved it. Of the 182 Victoria Crosses awarded in the Second World War, five were won by Wellingtonians. In recent years, however, the military tradition has suddenly waned. Of the candidates awarded places at the Royal Military Academy, Sandhurst, in September 1970, only two were from Wellington (and only two from Haileybury, and one from Cheltenham). Of the eighty-nine cadets on the passing-out list at Sandhurst in December 1970, twenty-three were from grammar schools and only two from Wellington. In the passing-out list of April, 1972, there was only one from Wellington. Of the sixty-three cadets passing out of Mons, the other officer-training school, twenty-five were from grammar schools and only one was from Wellington.* This can be compared with the period

* *Daily Telegraph*: 19.12.70.

1945–53, when Wellington, far and away the leading school, sent 254 cadets to Sandhurst (the next seven schools being in this order: Eton, Marlborough, Sherborne, Winchester, Cheltenham, Hailey-bury and Bedford).* By 1961 the gap was still wide:

Wellington	54
Haileybury	21
Eton	20
Ampleforth	17
Marlborough	16
Downside	15
Rugby	12
Cheltenham	11
Sherborne	11
Bedford	10†

It is since the late nineteen-sixties that Wellington has lost its traditional lead. There are said to be some discernible types produced by a few schools, as seen above, and Cheltonians and Wellingtonians once had the reputation of being ruddy-faced men with trim military moustaches and shooting-sticks. Not all the boys were necessarily cut out for a military life, and some such have since complained bitterly of their experience at Wellington, including the actor Robert Morley. Harold Nicolson wrote in 1942: 'I am just back from Wellington College. . . . It was strange to be back at school. The sight of the two towers above the pine-trees brought a wave of depression followed by a wave of exhilaration. My old sadness that hung like mist among the bracken suddenly settled down on me again: and then I realised that it was over and could never return, and my heart sung hymns at heaven's gate. I must have been *very* unhappy there for the mood to return to me after forty years.'‡ Wellington and St. Paul's are the only two schools which were

---

* *The Times*: 4.2.53.

† Intakes to Sandhurst, 1891 and 1961: Sampson, *Anatomy of Britain*.

‡ Other O.W.s: Field-Marshal Sir Gerald Templer, General Sir Geoffrey Baker (both Chiefs of the General Staff), General Sir Ian Hamilton, General Sir M. Stopford, V. F. W. Cavendish-Bentinck, head of Intelligence in the War, General Sir Richard O'Connor, Lieut.-General Sir Ian Jacob, Major-General Sir Harry Tuzo, Marshal of the R.A.F. Sir J. Salmond, Air Chief Marshal Sir Donald Evans, Sir Tyrone Guthrie, Algernon Blackwood and John Masters, authors, Michael Howard, military historian, Sir Rudolph Peters, biochemist, C. R. Boxer, historian, P. Gordon Walker, M.P., Desmond Curran, psychiatrist, David Caute, historian.

founder members of the Rugby Union (the Old Pauline Rugby Football Club was founded as early as 1872).

Clifton College was founded because of the need felt in Bristol for a local public school. Bristol Grammar School had been empty since 1829, though the headmaster, with his Negro servant, continued to draw his salary. A group of Bristol professional and merchant people met on 5 April 1860, and decided to found a public school along the lines of Rugby. A small school was started in temporary buildings in 1861, while building took place on the site chosen in the suburb of Clifton, beside the zoo. The first buildings were designed by Charles Hansom, brother of the inventor of the hansom cab, who went on to build Malvern and Kelly College. The Rev. John Percival, a junior assistant master at Rugby, was chosen as headmaster, 1862–79. Percival was by no means a slavish adherent to Arnold's principles. It was largely due to him that Clifton achieved early success, although beset with financial difficulties, and its proud liberal tone. He chose an excellent staff, and Clifton almost immediately showed academic distinction, as well as joining the ranks of those schools which supplied the colonial and military services. Like Wellington, there was no shying away from the demands for a modern education. In a piece of symbolism that would not have impressed Arnold, the chapel was opened in the same year as the laboratories. Another aspect of Clifton's tone was that it was closely linked to the city of Bristol, having, unusually for a major public school, always had a large number of day-boys. Percival, having put Clifton on its feet, went on to become President of Trinity College, Oxford, and then returned to Rugby as headmaster, 1887–95, where he rescued that school from a bad patch. 'Town Boys' at Clifton were organised into separate houses, under housemasters, so as to integrate them more fully into the life of the school. At other schools, like Rugby, this integration had been found extremely difficult. Clifton's answer to the problem was widely copied elsewhere. As a later headmaster of Clifton put it: 'Day-boys may almost be described as boarders boarding in their parents' homes.' Percival also founded a Jewish house at Clifton, where boys could practise the Jewish faith and customs, instead of just being exempted from Anglican ones as at other public schools, and Clifton has consequently had a long association with the Anglo-Jewish community. Of all the Victorian public schools, Clifton has probably produced a more varied and distinguished list of great men than any other school. Its record in this respect, in little over a century, is quite remarkable.*

Haileybury, founded in 1862, began in a unique way. The great buildings of the East India Company College, near Hertford, had been vacant since December 1857, when the college was closed. The East India College had brought considerable prosperity to Hertford, and especially to the village of Hertford Heath, where a community relying on the college for its livelihood, not least the five public houses, had risen over the years. At length some leading land-owners and business men of the neighbourhood, led by Stephen Austin, who had been the college's printer, formed themselves into a board to found a new public school, for which the buildings, designed and built for educational purposes, seemed ideally suited.† This seems partly to have been for the protection of the livelihood of those in the area. They bought the property, for £18,000, from the speculative land company that had acquired it.

Haileybury is synonymous with India. The school, starting with fifty-four boys, grew fast, and under the Rev. E. H. Bradby, 1868–83, who had been a master at Harrow, it joined the ranks of the major public schools. The rapid rise of Haileybury was due mostly to its inheritance from the East India Company. Expansion was not limited, as at so many of the Victorian schools, by building and the raising of money for new buildings. Moreover, it was more than acceptable to many families which had a connection with India and which regretted the end of the old 'John Company'. (This connec-tion with service in India was maintained until recent times.) Traditions, also were ready made. New boys at Haileybury are still called 'Guv'nors', after the system of nomination of students in the Company's day. A reputation for a somewhat spartan, tough regime,

* Among former pupils were Earl Haig, Field-Marshal Lord Birdwood, Francis Younghusband, the explorer of Tibet, Sir Henry Newbolt, Sir Arthur Quiller-Couch, Lord (Hore-) Belisha, Viscount Caldecote, Lord Chief Justice, Roger Fry, Lieut.-General Sir Frederick Morgan, planner of D-Day, Major-General Sir Percy Hobart, father of the tank corps, Sir Roy Feddon, aviation engineer, Lord Milverton, colonial administrator, I. A. Richards, Sir Nevill Mott, J. E. McTaggart, philosopher, Joyce Cary, Frederick Boas, Shakespearean scholar, Sir Bernard Waley-Cohen, Sir Michael Redgrave, Trevor Howard, John Biggs-Davison, M.P.

†The magnificent terrace, and fine quadrangle, reputed to be the largest in England, were by William Wilkins, also responsible for Downing College, Cambridge. Wilkins had been headmaster of the Perse School, 1804–06.

for which the old East India College was well known, lasted until at least the Second World War. One Haileyburian of the 'eighties recalled: 'There is no doubt that the feeding was its poor point. We knew every midday what dinner was coming on the table, the same every Monday, and another every Tuesday, and so on, but always the same breakfast, nothing but bread in squares and butter which was often rancid. We used to say if any butter was left on a plate the 'tobies' [servants] collected it and put it back for next day's meal. Tea: the same, bread and butter only. Of course we had our own private store, on shelves in the Hall, until it ran out, before half-term usually. None the less, we were strong and happy and proud of our school. . . . I know the training was good for us, for after I had taken my degree I was offered £150 a year as tutor to the six boys of an M.F.H. and I had to find my own lodgings and feed myself, waiting for my first quarter's salary. I lived for six weeks on a half-penny arrowroot biscuit a day and water, as I only had enough to pay my landlady, and I felt that as my father had sent me to Hailey-bury and Cambridge I ought to do for myself.'

Haileybury became a services school from the start. Its Corps was the senior one in the country, and for many years at annual camps it was given the place of honour in the camp lines. Between the foundation of the school and 1946 one in eleven old boys lost his life in battle. After the formation of the R.A.F. it had for a long time a closer connection with that service than any other school. Marshal of the R.A.F. Sir John Slessor has written: 'At a big Royal Air Force conference at Old Sarum in 1948 there were no less than seven Haileyburians: Clement Attlee, then Prime Minister, and six senior R.A.F. officers who had been at Haileybury together in 1912 —three Commanders-in-Chief, the Commandant of the Imperial Defence College, the Chairman of the Ordnance Board and H. M A. Day, who so distinguished himself as senior British officer in P.O.W. camps in the late war. Three years later we had a majority of Haileyburians on the Air Council—the Under Secretary of State, the Chief and Deputy Chief of the Air Staff and the Air Member for Supply and Organisation.'

The Second World War was a difficult time for Haileybury and, because of this, it amalgamated in 1942 with the Imperial Service College, another military school, which was in an even more perilous condition, its numbers being down to 120. The amalgamation, under Canon E. F. Bonhote, was the subject of a leader in *The Times*.

The two schools were closely connected. In 1874, one of the Haileybury housemasters, Cornell Price, had left to help found the United
Services College at Westward Ho!, taking twelve Haileybury boys
with him. In 1912 it had moved to Windsor, merging with St. Mark's
School there, to become the U.S.C. Rudyard Kipling was at the
United Services College and had written of it in perhaps the most
famous of all school stories, *Stalky and Co.*, dedicated to Cornell
Price. He gives the military feel of the old U.S.C.: 'It was winter and
bitter cold of mornings. Consequently Stalky and Beetle . . . drowsed
till the last moment before turning out to call-over in the gas-lit
gymnasium. It followed that they were often late; and since every
unpunctuality earned them a black mark, and since three black
marks a week meant defaulters' drill, equally it followed that they
spent hours under the Sergeant's hand. Foxy drilled the defaulters
with all the pomp of his old parade-ground.' In his *Land and Sea
Tales*, Kipling wrote: 'It was a good place for a school, and the
school considered itself the finest in the world, excepting perhaps
Haileybury, because it was modelled on Haileybury lines and our
caps were Haileybury colours.' One intriguing fact about the U.S.C.,
recorded by Kipling, is that the Army Class were allowed to smoke
pipes.

Like Tonbridge, Haileybury has had its bad patch in the twentieth
century, but it has been second to none in recent decades; under the
headmasterships of C. P. C. Smith, 1948–63,* formerly Warden of
Glenalmond, and William Stewart, Master since 1963. Like Winchester, Haileybury has a radical tradition. In the famous 1945
Parliament, the number of Haileyburians was only exceeded by
Etonians and Wykehamists. They included Clement Attlee, Sir
Ungoed-Thomas, Solicitor-General, Lord Burntwood, Geoffrey de
Freitas, and Christopher Mayhew. Like Clifton, Haileybury's list of
famous men, more impressive than some schools three times as old,
is remarkable.†

*

* From a famous educational family; son of George Smith, head of Merchiston
and Dulwich, and brother-in-law of R. Groves, Master of Dulwich.
  † Apart from those mentioned: Viscount Allenby, Sir Henry MacMahon,
Sir Reginald Blomfield, architect, Erskine Childers, H. N. Ridley, founder of the
Malayan rubber industry, General Sir A. J. Godley, Lionel Curtis, Air Chief

The last of the schools founded as a direct result of the Oxford Movement was St. Edward's, in the home of the movement itself. It was founded by the Rev. Thomas Chamberlain, in 1863, at 29 New Inn Hall Street, Oxford. Chamberlain, a don at Christ Church, and a follower of Keble and Newman, took little interest in the school after its foundation. After three years the number of boys had risen to forty-nine, all boarders, and this was about capacity. Under the Rev. A. B. Simeon, 1869, St. Edward's moved to its present site on the outskirts of the city and expanded despite the same sort of accusations of Romanism as had been levelled at the Woodard schools. The *Oxford Guardian* indignantly reported: 'It would seem but fair that parents should fully comprehend the religious proclivities of teachers, who at the recent laying of the foundation stone of the School Chapel by the Bishop, in their ceremonial appointments simply plagiarised Rome. . . . The whole ceremony . . . seemed to the outsider nothing if not Roman . . . [we] have little sympathy for such partisans as those who have created St. Edward's School.' Like so many Victorian schools with ambitious building programmes St. Edward's was beset with mortgage problems. For years its survival was in the balance. But Simeon, like so many of his contemporaries, over-rode the financial problems and kept his school alive. Simeon, a relative of George Moberly of Winchester, resigned in 1892, overburdened with worries. 'While quite prepared to allow that I may have certain qualities, that have been useful in building up the school, it does not follow that I am the right man under the present circumstances.' After Simeon, St. Edward's nearly collapsed, and in 1919 the council applied to the Woodard Society to join the Woodard schools. The provost of Lancing replied: 'We held our Chapter meeting on Saturday at Lancing and decided unanimously to take you over.' This association helped St. Edward's to survive a difficult time, but it left the group in 1927. It further expanded under

Marshal Sir R. Brooke-Popham, one of the founders of the R.A.F., Air Chief Marshal Sir T. Leigh Mallory, Air Chief Marshal Sir B. E. Baker, Marshal of the R.A.F. Sir W. Dickson, Air Chief Marshal Sir A. P. M. Sanders, Admiral Sir A. Lewis, Lord Rennell of Rodd, Lord Oaksey, the judge at Nuremberg, Lord Radcliffe, Lord Alport, Colonel J. P. Carne, V.C., of the Gloucestershire Regiment in Korea (I.S.C.), G. V. Stephenson, one of the most capped players in Rugby, Hugh Williams, author of *The Grass Is Greener*, Rex Whistler, Nevill Coghill, B. L. Hallward, H. M. of Clifton and Vice-Chancellor of Nottingham University, historians Bonamy Dobrée and Denis Mack Smith, Sir Gilbert Longden, M.P., Stirling Moss, Michael Bonallack.

the Rev. E. H. Kendall, and has grown to a school of 520 boys, about fifty of them day-boys.*

Cranleigh School was founded in 1865, but it has a very different background from that of St. Edward's. The intention was to establish a leading public school in Surrey, and the buildings were subscribed to by many leading Surrey inhabitants. The site was presented by Lord Ashcombe. It remains very much a county school, and *ex-officio* members of the council include the Bishop of Guildford, the Archdeacon of Surrey, the Chairman of the Surrey Quarter Sessions, and the Chairman of the Surrey County Council. By 1877 there were 175 boys and seven masters: there are now some 420. Cranleigh has an estate of 275 acres.† Another county school is Framlingham, founded in 1864 as the memorial of the County of Suffolk to Prince Albert. It, too was established by local public subscription. It began as the Albert Middle Class College and was intended for three hundred boys. Setting out to provide a good education at a modest price, it has maintained its object better than most. Boarding fees have always been among the most reasonable in the country. The Lord Lieutenant of Suffolk is still President of the corporation.‡ Methodist College, Belfast, the largest school in Ireland, was founded in 1865. Its aim was to provide for the education of boys irrespective of religious persuasion, but giving priority to the sons of Methodist clergymen. In 1885 the Endowments (Ireland) Act divided the funds between the school and the theological department, which caused great difficulty. But Methodist survived and now has nearly two thousand pupils.

The greatest foundation of 1865 was Malvern College. There is something more peculiarly Victorian about Malvern, apart even from its appearance, than any other school. It was founded through the efforts of two brothers called Burrow, who bottled the famous Malvern waters. Supported by their rich former employers, Messrs. Lea and Perrin, of the Worcestershire Sauce, they canvassed the

---

* Among distinguished old boys are Kenneth Grahame, author of *The Wind in the Willows*, Lord Olivier, Sir Geoffrey de Havilland, Group-Captain Douglas Bader, Guy Gibson, V.C., John Davies, M.P., writers Robert Gittings and Tom Hopkinson, Peter Cranmer, Captain of Warwickshire at cricket and English Rugby international.

† Major-General Sir C. Townshend, of Kent, Sewell Stokes, and E. W. Swanton were pupils.

‡ Old boys include Sir Alfred Munnings, Lord Harvey (formerly Sir Arthur Vere Harvey), and Sir Frederick Minter.

idea of a school for Malvern like Cheltenham College. In 1862 they founded a company for that purpose. The prospectus declared: 'That the town of Malvern, from its bracing air, gravelly soil, pure water and convenient access by Railway, is well adapted for an undertaking of this nature.' A number of suitably eminent men were brought together to form a council, including Earl Beauchamp, a member of the Oxford Movement, and J. W. Lea of the sauce family; both men poured money into the new school. The Earls Beauchamp have continued their connection. The proprietary company was of five hundred shares, each one entitling the holder to a place at the school. Malvern College opened in 1865 with twenty-four boys, eleven of them day-boys. The tuition fees were £25 p.a., the boarding fees £60. There were the customary financial difficulties, and it was not till the headmastership of the Rev. W. Grundy, 1885–91, that Malvern began to gain a wide reputation. Grundy had been headmaster of Warwick School, which he had found almost dead with eight pupils; in less than three years he had raised its numbers to seventy boarders and fifty-four day-boys. Under Grundy numbers at Malvern rose from 188 to 323, partly due to the introduction of an Army Class and book-keeping and commerce; but there was room for another two hundred boys. Malvern came slowly to its full strength. Between the world wars it acquired the reputation of a 'Games School', somewhat unjustifiably as there were perhaps even more obvious cases of schools where games seemed to be all-important. The Malvern cricket eleven of 1922 contained six future first-class players. The old boys won the Arthur Dunn Cup, an association football competition, in 1924, 1925, 1926 and 1928. C. S. Lewis, a boy at Malvern just before the First World War, wrote: 'The truth is that organised and compulsory games had, in my day, banished the element of play from school life almost entirely. There was no time to play (in the proper sense of the word). The rivalry was too fierce, the prizes too glittering, the "hell of failure" too severe.'

Between 1903 and 1912 the Old Malvernian Society began acquiring the shares of the college; by 1912 it had acquired 492 of the 574 shares, and a new constitution came into force that year. Michael Arlen, author of *The Green Hat*, like Lewis, did not much care for Malvern. In his novel *Piracy*, he wrote: 'The difference between a College Prefect and a House Prefect is that a Coll Pree can do what he likes everywhere, and a House Pree can do what he likes in his House. Inferiors can do what they like in their studies, more or less. Fags can't do what they like anywhere.'*

Trent College, at Long Eaton, in Derbyshire, was founded in 1866 by the Church Association, and was intended as an answer to the Oxford Movement schools, particularly those of Nathaniel Woodard. The foundation stone was laid by the seventh Duke of Devonshire, and the dukes have retained their connection with the school, the present duke being President of the governors, as he is of Eastbourne College, founded in the following year—the Devonshire family also being closely connected with that school. The seventh duke had enjoyed a brilliant academic career at Cambridge and was not impressed by Newman's followers. He was one of the founders of Eastbourne, a good example of a school which has thrived since the end of the Second World War. Eastbourne ended the war with 120 boys and a debt of £120,000. By 1964 the debt had been paid off and many new buildings and facilities had been added. There are now over six hundred boys and the college is engaged on an ambitious development programme, which will result in virtually every boy having a 'bed-sitter'.†

Kelly College, Tavistock, although on a smaller scale, became at one time to the Royal Navy what Wellington was to the Army. It was founded in 1867 by Admiral Benedictus Marwood Kelly. Kelly had fought the French and had been engaged in running down slave traders on the African coast. His wife had died a year after they were married and his grief at having no children prompted him to found a school. It was intended primarily for his branch of the Kelly family and for sons of Naval officers. He lived in near penury while he was planning the school, which was founded under the terms of his Will. He left £150,000 for the school. Kelly College was not able to open until ten years later. Today about twenty per cent of the boys are the sons of Naval officers.‡ Another West Country school, Monkton

---

* Other Malvernians: Lord Malvern, first prime minister of Rhodesia, Admiral of the Fleet Sir Varyl Begg, General Sir Nevil Brownjohn, Sir John Wheeler-Bennett, J. E. Meade, economist, Christmas Humphreys, Q.C., Raymond Mortimer, R. E. Foster, captain of England at football and cricket, F. T. Mann, another England cricket captain, and England cricketers E. R. T. Holmes and G. B. Legge.

† Old boys: Lord Tenby, Home Secretary, Air Chief Marshal Sir John Baker, Admiral of the Fleet Sir U. Willis, Sir Hugh Casson, Prof. A. A. Luce, logician, Woodrow Wyatt, M.P.

‡ Old boys: Dr. Mervyn Stockwood, Basil Davidson, Africanist.

17a. Glenalmond

17b. Lancing, 1856

18a. Wellington, 1882

18b. Clifton

19a. Haileybury, 1900

19b. Fettes, 1876

20a.   Stowe

20b.   Canford

Combe, near Bath, was founded in the following year by the Rev. F. Pocock. He educated a few boys, mostly for Holy Orders or missionary work. Monkton Combe became a more important school under the Rev. R. G. Bryan, who had been a pupil at Rugby under Arnold; but it retained its clerical association for many years, and 'the services are in the Evangelical tradition of the Church of England with which the school has always been associated'. Bishop's Stortford College, Hertfordshire, was entirely different. It harked back to the setting-up of nonconformist schools at the start of the century, and was founded in 1868 by nonconformists in East Anglia for boys whose parents were of that persuasion. Since 1904 it has educated members of all Protestant denominations.*

By now, 1868, Nathaniel Woodard had founded his first school in the north. This was 'St. Chad's Middle School', at Denstone, Staffordshire. It was meant to be for the north what Hurstpierpoint was in Sussex, i.e. a school for the middle-income group of the middle class. The site had been offered him by an admirer, Sir Percival Heywood, two years previously; he had also offered Woodard £1,000 towards construction. A worthy companion to the Sussex schools was built, costing in the end £100,000, built around two open quadrangles. Denstone opened in 1873 with accommodation for two hundred boys, soon increased to a maximum of four hundred. The fees were thirty-four guineas a year. By 1890 the number of boys was 245. Woodard, despite continuing opposition, kept on doggedly raising funds. There was considerable discussion about the merits of Denstone as compared to the opposing and evangelical Trent College.

*

The report of the Public Schools Commission of 1868 gave the following leaders among the grammar and public schools, which had gained awards at Oxford and Cambridge:

	No. of students with open awards	No. of students at Oxford and Cambridge
Rugby	24	109
Merchant Taylors'	14	27
Manchester G.S.	13	21
Eton	12	161

* Edward Crankshaw, 'Sovietologist', and Sir Dick Goldsmith White, past head of the Secret Service were pupils.

	No. of students with open awards	No. of students at Oxford and Cambridge
Repton	10	36
Winchester	10	74
Harrow	9	107
Uppingham	9	35
Charterhouse	8	20
Shrewsbury	8	35
Bradfield	5	20
King Edward's, Birmingham	4	18

*

The year 1869 is important in the history of the public schools as it saw the first gathering of headmasters, to be known as the Headmasters' Conference. It was on 2 March 1869, in London. The meeting was at the suggestion of and organised by Dr. John Mitchinson, head of King's, Canterbury, to discuss the implications of the Endowed Schools Bill of that year. Of the headmasters present, Edward Thring was easily the most forceful. He had not been keen on the meeting, and Mitchinson had been obliged to beg him to attend. But afterwards Thring wrote in his diary: 'Much pleased at having gone.' Thring was so delighted that he proposed such a meeting should be an annual event, and that the next one should take place at Uppingham in December of the same year. Sixty-six headmasters were invited, but only ten were present and nine sent their apologies.* The schools represented at this historic meeting were:

> Bromsgrove
> Liverpool Coll.
> Bury St. Edmund's
> King's, Canterbury
> Oakham
> Repton
> Richmond G.S., Yorks
> Sherborne
> Tonbridge
> Uppingham

* The schools sending apologies were Dulwich, Durham, Highgate, Ipswich, Christ's Hospital, City of London, Magdalen College School, Marlborough and St. Peter's, York.

The following year thirty-five headmasters met, this time at Sherborne. The third conference was held at Highgate School, in 1871, when fifty attended. Those present were always by invitation. Thring was the main personality in making the conference an annual event. By 1872, seventy-one headmasters were present (q.v. Appendix 3). In 1886 a closer association was initiated, implying 'membership' (i.e. not just invitation year by year). The object was always, in Thring's words, to 'annually assemble at some school to watch over, discuss and study school questions'. Today the membership is on three main considerations: the degree of independence; the number of boys aged over thirteen; the proportionate size of the sixth form. State schools are admitted.

*

The number of Catholic schools was added to in 1869 by the foundation of St. George's College, first at Croydon then, from 1884, in Weybridge. The school is governed by the Josephite Fathers. It is stated that 'the centre of the school life is in the Chapel'. The High School, Dublin, was founded as a Protestant institution in 1870 as a curious result of the Will of Erasmus Smith. Smith had died over a century-and-a-half previously, and for many years the treasurers of his charitable endowment had not drawn their honorary fees. It was on the money saved by this that the High School was founded. It was, at first, a classical school. It is still stated that 'in accepting entries preference is given to boys of Protestant denominations'.

Fettes College was founded as the result of the Will of Sir William Fettes (1750–1836), who was twice Lord Provost of Edinburgh. Fettes himself had been educated at the Royal High School. In a trust settlement of 1830 he left over £170,000, mainly in property, 'for the maintenance, education and outfit of young persons whose parents have either died without leaving sufficient funds for the purpose or who, from innocent misfortune during their lives, are unable to give suitable education to their children'. It was an expression, unusual for the time, worthy of Colet, for free or nearly free secondary education. The trustees, however, found Fettes's instructions 'somewhat vague'. They decided to use the money to set up a public school for the middle and upper classes, for whom, it was said, there was little opportunity in Edinburgh. But some free places were to be provided. Fettes's money, in fact, was used to provide Edinburgh with a prestige public school. Impressive buildings were constructed on the founder's estate, less than two miles from Princes Street. The school opened in 1870. In 1886 the Commissioners examined the scheme and hardly altered it. In respect of the founder's wishes, about five Foundation places are offered annually to boys who need assistance, in some cases even covering all the fees. R. H. Bruce Lockhart, in his *Memoirs of a British Agent*, wrote that at Fettes he 'spent five years in the worship of athleticism'.*

Dover College, which opened in 1871 with the object of giving a public school education at a moderate cost, had an unusual advantage. The fine and important buildings of the Priory of St. Martin were available, and so the school had from the start the appearance and atmosphere of an ancient foundation. The school hall was once the magnificent Norman refectory. Dover was a proprietary school until 1923, when it was acquired by the old boys in memory of their fellows who had died in the First World War. A. D. C. Peterson, headmaster of Adams Grammar School 1946–52, was headmaster 1954–57, during which time he achieved a great reputation for the school and for himself as an educationist.† Newcastle under Lyme High School was founded in 1874, as was Huish's Grammar School, Taunton, founded on an endowment of Richard Huish, of 1615.

In 1871 the ancient universities were at last opened to persons of every religious denomination. This was the reason for the foundation of another Methodist school, The Leys, at Cambridge. It was founded, in 1875, by a group of Methodist laymen (Kingswood still being restricted to the sons of clergymen). The Leys opened with sixteen boys. Denominational barriers have always been strictly avoided, and the school progressed steadily under the Rev. W. F. Moulton, 1875–98. Since its foundation there have only been five headmasters. The Leys is magnificently set in sixty acres less than half a mile from the centre of Cambridge. 'The policy of the Governors is to maintain the school at a size which combines economic running, a stimulating sixth form and the intimacy of the school as a unit. This intimacy has characterised The Leys since its

* Old boys include: Viscount Simon, Lord Norwood, Lord President of Scotland 1935–47, Lord Drumalbyn, Ian Macleod, Selwyn Lloyd, Sir Knox Cunningham, Sir Alexander Glen, Sir Michael Fraser, poet Norman Cameron, Ian Hunter, festival impresario, and G. P. S. Macpherson, financier and Rugby footballer.

† Viscount Maugham, Sir Frederick Ashton, Richard Aldington, Air Marshal Sir L. Darvall, commandant of the N.A.T.O. Defence College, Paris, were pupils.

foundation.' James Hilton, author of one of the most famous of all school books, *Good-bye Mr. Chips*, was at The Leys. The book is about what was acceptable as one of the types of public-school master: loyal, kindly and hiding a basically sensitive nature behind a woolly exterior: 'His dream had been to get a headship eventually, or at any rate a senior mastership in a really first-class school; it was only gradually, after repeated trials and failures, that he realised the inadequacy of his qualifications. His degree, for instance, was not particularly good, and his discipline, though good enough and improving, was not absolutely reliable under all conditions. He had no private means and no family connections of any importance. About 1880, after he had been at Brookfield a decade, he began to recognise that the odds were heavily against his being able to better himself by moving elsewhere; but about that time also, the possibility of staying where he was began to fill a comfortable niche in his mind. At forty he was rooted, settled and quite happy. At fifty he was the doyen of the staff. At sixty, under a new and youthful Head, he *was* Brookfield; the guest of honour at Old Brookfieldian dinners, the court of appeal in all matters affecting Brookfield history and traditions.'* Another Methodist school, Ashville College, at Harrogate, was founded two years later. It amalgamated with Elmfield College, York, in 1932.

The Grocers' Company's School was founded in 1876, and was handed over to the London County Council in 1906. Plymouth College was founded in 1877, the aim being to provide for the West Country a new public school based on 'the spirit and methods which at Rugby had given new life to the Public School system'. It began as a private company, but became a Direct Grant school in 1909. In 1896 Plymouth amalgamated with Mannamead School, founded in 1854. In April 1970, the governors announced that in the event of the Direct Grant system being abolished, Plymouth College would be maintained as an independent school. The governing body includes a representative of Exeter College, Oxford, the Bishop of Plymouth, the Flag Officer, Plymouth, the Vice-Chancellor of Exeter University, and several councillors. Oxford High School, now the (City of) Oxford School, was founded in 1878. T. E. Lawrence, John Drinkwater and Lord Salter were educated there.

* Others: Sir John Clapham, economic historian, Lord Rank, Lord Stamp, bacteriologist, F. R. Brown, who played cricket for England 1931–51, Sir Percy Rugg, editor Alastair Burnet.

Simon Langton Grammar School, Canterbury, was founded in the same year on an earlier foundation of 1575. It was for 110 boys and 110 girls.

By now the idea of the limited company proprietary school had moved to Scotland, and Kelvinside Academy was founded in 1877, in Glasgow. The school was built at a cost of nearly £22,000, which was more than the sum subscribed, and Kelvinside was in debt from the start. Competition with Glasgow Academy was disadvantageous for both schools (at first it had been thought that the Glasgow Academy was to be handed over to the corporation, thus providing a gap for private education, but this did not materialise). During the eighteen-eighties the staff had to agree to salary reductions. In 1915 the school was called upon to realise its overdraft, and was only able to do so through the guarantees of twenty old boys. By 1919 the debt was £46,000. Kelvinside followed the example of Glasgow Academy, in similar troubles, and the former pupils raised the money to buy the school, in memory of those who had been killed in the war. The old company was wound up in 1923, and since then the board of governors has mostly consisted of Academicals. Between 1913 and 1923 the numbers increased from 137 to 314, and the upper school now has four hundred boys. St. Lawrence College, Ramsgate, was founded in 1879 as an evangelical school, and incorporated in 1892. It was brought to success, through a difficult time, under the headmastership of Canon Ronald Perfect, 1938–69, himself an old boy and an England hockey international (St. Lawrence had also had a reputation at that sport). St. Lawrence, which started with four boys, now stands in an estate of 150 acres. A special house, for boys aged eleven to thirteen, was opened in 1965 for boys whose parents had sought to by-pass the preparatory school system and had been at state primary schools. The acceptability of this idea to parents may be judged by the fact that within two years the house was full (this was in addition to St. Lawrence's own preparatory school). Truro School was founded in the same year. In 1904 it came under the direct control of the Methodist Church, in accordance with the expansionist policy of the Board of Management for Methodist boarding schools. Since then the day-boy side has been greatly expanded.

The indefatigable Nathaniel Woodard had now moved himself north, where he had been appointed Dean of Manchester, on Gladstone's recommendation. He considered himself well placed to found a companion school to Denstone, which was, as has been seen, a 'middle school'. The next move was to establish a 'lower school', a second Ardingly, for the sons of Manchester men. The scheme, as usual, was grandiose: an enormous building for a thousand boys, boarding at fifteen guineas a year. A suitable site was offered by Lord Brownlow, on his estate at Ellesmere in Shropshire. Woodard always insisted on a perfect site for his schools. The foundation stone of 'St. Oswald's School' was laid in 1879. The school opened in 1884 with eighty-one boarders. As usual, work on the buildings was incomplete, although some £20,000 had been spent. With the great cities of the north not far away, Ellesmere was a more immediate success than Ardingly had been. After two years the numbers had risen to 173. But expansion depended on the raising of further funds, which proved difficult to get. There was no room for a thousand boys—170 remained about the maximum for the remainder of the century—and the fee was eighteen guineas, three higher than at Ardingly. The chapel was not opened till 1928. Like many Woodard schools, Ellesmere did not come into its own until well into the twentieth century. In the same year as the foundation of Ellesmere, Woodard bought King's, Taunton.

Another school was founded in Shropshire in the same year— Wrekin College. This was the personal foundation of Sir John Bayley. It ran into difficulties, but remained under Bayley's control until 1920, when he retired. Since then the school has been under a board of governors. The popular demand, by the vast middle class, for public schools was growing all the time. Foundations came one after the other. They were due to the interest of the Methodists in boarding education, to the activities of the Charity Commissioners, and to individual efforts to join in the swim either for profit, for religious purposes (although these were less than in previous decades), or to put into practice educational theories. Culford School was founded in 1881, as the East Anglian School, at Bury St. Edmunds. In 1904 it was bought by the Board of Management of the Methodist schools and moved to Calford Hall, formerly the seat of the Earls Cadogan, in 1935, when its name was changed. Wycliffe College, in Gloucestershire, was yet another private foundation, founded by G. W. Sibley in 1882. It came under a board of governors in 1931 and had a mildly progressive tinge. The novelist Peter Forster recalls it as 'a minor public school in the West Country with a reputation for sensible eccentricity'. Barnard Castle

School, Co. Durham, was the result of the Charity Commissioners putting to better use old endowments, those of Benjamin Flounders and John Balliol, founder of the Oxford college, Dean Close School, Cheltenham, was founded in 1884 in memory of Dr. Francis Close, who had been rector of Cheltenham, 1826–56. It was stated to be evangelical in purpose. The majority of life governors are clergymen. Dean Close was one of the first public schools to admit girls to the sixth form. Seaford College was founded at that town in the same year, and moved to Petworth in 1945. Kent College, Canterbuty, founded in 1885, was taken over by the Methodist schools, like Truro, Ashville and Culford; in the case of Kent College, this was in 1920. Rydal School, 1885, founded by T. B. Osborn, was taken over by the Methodist Conference in 1910.

Kingham Hill School, near Chipping Norton, was founded in 1886, by C. E. B. Young, for those for whom a boarding education was believed to be essential. Young controlled the school in every detail until he died in 1928. The school aimed to provide a basis for boys with disturbed backgrounds. The trust owns a thousand acres of magnificent Cotswold countryside, with seven separate boarding-houses. Kingham Hill still honours its foundation by providing a high standard of boarding education at a very moderate cost (£300 per annum in 1972). William Hulme's Grammar School, Manchester, was founded in 1887 under the endowment of that name. St. Dunstan's, Catford, in south-east London, founded in 1888, was the successor to the parish school of St. Dunstan-in-the-East, which had been absorbed by the Greencoat School by 1709. As the City had ceased to become a residential area, the parish had fallen into decline and the educational funds had accumulated unused. The Court of Chancery decided the money should be used in some other part of London. The new school of St. Dunstan's was thus built and endowed on land that had belonged to St. Dunstan's church since 1632. Boarders were taken at first, but from 1898 only day-boys were admitted. Sexey's School, Bruton, Somerset, derives from the Charity Commissioners arranging for the endowment of Hugh Sexey, 1619, to be used for a school. It opened in 1891, with fifteen boys, as 'Sexey's Trade School'. It came under county control in 1948, but since then the boarding side has continued to develop.

In 1889 Abbotsholme School, Derbyshire, was founded by Dr. Cecil Reddie. This was the first of those public schools which were determined to find a new approach to boys' boarding education. The curriculum was to be wider, interdenominational, more balanced and more individual attention given. Reddie ran the school himself for many years. In 1913 he wrote: 'The school does not undertake to prepare boys for competitive exams, owing to the fact that these exams require specialisation too much at the expense of a more broadly educative curriculum. . . . There is no modern side, and no classical side, and, therefore, no one-sidedness. A liberal education is regarded as not having sides, but the continuous and related surface of a sphere. When the boy has travelled over this surface he may show what more specialised work he is best suited for.' Abbotsholme signalled the beginning of the end of the strict adherence to Arnoldian tradition. Already F. W. Walker, at St. Paul's, was declaring that character-building could be left to look after itself, and his boys were walking off with awards at the universities in numbers never seen before from one school, and H. H. Almond, of Loretto, was following up the work of Thring, providing hygienic conditions and rational clothing. Abbotsholme became co-educational in 1969.*

Margate College was founded about this time. It was a private school, for the sons of gentlemen. It closed during the Second World War. It is now an athletics school.

*

There was already some doubt as to which schools could claim to be 'public schools' and which schools could not. It seemed everybody had their own ideas. In fact, there was no hard-fast definition at all. More than anything else, it was a matter of general agreement, or acceptance, as to whether one of the old foundations, 'grammar schools', or one of the new Victorian foundations was a public school. It was, indeed, a matter of reputation, always difficult to define. As there was no legal, official, or generally accepted definition, membership of the Headmasters' Conference came to be taken as something which could be used, although this itself was a selective group and usually misleading. Some authorities cast the net wide, others kept it fine. The Public Schools Act of 1868 had named seven: Eton, Harrow, Rugby, Winchester, Westminster, Shrewsbury and Charterhouse. The newcomers were pushing some of the

---

* Lytton Strachey, publisher Sir Stanley Unwin, writer Mervyn Jones were pupils.

older schools down the scale. Especially, it was considered more distinguished to be a boarding rather than a predominantly day school. A book entitled *Our Public Schools*, published in 1881, named seven:

Eton
Harrow
Winchester
Rugby
Westminster
Marlborough
Charterhouse

In 1889 the first *Public Schools Year Book* appeared. A list of the public schools had been compiled by 'three Public School men', guided by such principles as 'Does the school possess the Public School spirit? Are its pupils entitled to be called Public School men?' Armed with these curious guide-lines, it was decided that the following were the public schools:

Bedford
Boston G.S., Lincs.
Bradfield
Brighton
Charterhouse
Cheltenham
Clifton
Derby
Dover
Dulwich
Eton
Fettes
Glenalmond
Haileybury
Harrow
Hereford Catholic School
Ipswich
Lancing
Loretto
Malvern
Marlborough
Merchant Taylors', London
Portsmouth G.S.
Radley
Rossall
Rugby
St. Paul's
Sherborne
Stonyhurst
Tonbridge
Shrewsbury
Uppingham
Wellington
Westminster
Winchester
Wyggeston

In the next issue another eight were named: Henry VIII, Coventry, St. John's, Leatherhead, The Leys, Lincoln, Monmouth, Newport (Salop), St. Bees and Trent. It is noticeable that only the one 'upper' Woodard school was considered a public school, and King's, Canterbury, St. Peter's, York, Magdalen College School,

Sedbergh, Christ's Hospital, Repton, Felsted, Blundell's and Mill Hill, were not considered public schools at all. In 1899 the *Public Schools Year Book* abandoned its own judgement and listed the schools of the Headmasters' Conference, which it still does, although insisting that 'This is not to be taken as suggesting any definition of a Public School or as implying a distinction in that respect between schools whose headmasters are members of the Conference and schools whose headmasters are not.' *Whitaker's Almanack* also had its list of public schools, but gave it up for the Headmasters' Conference schools.

In 1893 *The Great Public Schools* appeared, contributed to by some of the leading educationists and schoolmasters of the day. It listed ten schools as the great schools, in the following order:

> Eton
> Harrow
> Charterhouse
> Cheltenham
> Rugby
> Clifton
> Westminster
> Marlborough
> Haileybury
> Winchester.

Four of these ten schools had been founded since the beginning of the reign.

*

By the 'nineties the rush had begun to die out, but further schools were being founded, for much the same reasons as in the 'eighties. Leighton Park School was founded in 1890, after the yearly meeting of the Society of Friends had decided there was a need for a Quaker public school in the south of England. It still reports annually to the conference. Leighton Park has long been noted for its advanced educational policy, and today it has a unique system of admission, which encourages entry from the state system.* Bishop Wordsworth's School, Salisbury, was founded in 1891. Bedales,† founded

---

* Lord Caradon, Quentin Bell, painter and art critic, Michael Foot, David Lean, Peter Cadbury, and composer Richard Rodney Bennett are among its old boys.

† Some old boys: Ivon Hitchens, Stephen Bone, Jocelyn Brooke, Malcolm MacDonald.

by J. G. Badley as a co-educational school in 1893, followed Abbots-holme down the trail of progressive education. Hymer's College, Hull, was founded in 1889 on an endowment of the Rev. John Hymer, Fellow of St. John's College, Cambridge. Wimbledon College was also founded in 1893, when the Jesuits purchased the buildings of the former Wimbledon School (1860–85). Fr. Nichol-son moved in as the first Rector with a few boys whom he had been teaching in a house in nearby Worple Road since 1888, and by 1925 the school had some 300 boys. In 1969 Wimbledon College, which had been independent until the 1944 Act, became a Catholic com-prehensive school.* Another Wimbledon school, Rutlish, was founded two years later on the endowment of William Rutlish, embroiderer to Charles I. His Will of 1687 catered 'for ever for and towards the placing of such poor children, born in Merton, appren-tices whether male or female'. By 1894 there were very few applica-tions for help, and the income from rents had become considerable. The chairman of the trustees, John Innes, was a supporter of modern education, and he instigated the foundation of the Rutlish Science School. There was considerable opposition because there was, con-trary to Rutlish's wish, no provision for girls, and the scheme did not seem to provide for the *poor* of Merton. But the school was built on a site belonging to the trustees, and was opened in 1895, with twenty-three boys. As well as modern subjects, the curriculum included electricity, shorthand and mechanics, and no Latin or Greek. In 1905 the word 'Science' was dropped from the school's name, and the fees were set at £6 to £10 per annum. By the end of that year there were 202 in the school. Under the 1944 Act Rutlish became a voluntary controlled school. It moved to new buildings in Merton Park in 1957.

Campbell College, Belfast, was founded in 1894 under the Will of H. J. Campbell. The aim was to establish in Ireland a public school of the Arnoldian type, which had not yet been done, St. Columba's having been a purely religious foundation. St. Andrew's College, Dublin, was founded in the same year, for the sons of Presbyterians, at 21, St. Stephen's Green. It later moved to more spacious premises.

Woodard was now an old man, but he had an able lieutenant in the Rev. E. C. Lowe. In 1890 Woodard accepted from the Duke of

---

* Old boys include Lieutenant-Commander Eugene Esmond, V.C., D.S.O., who led the naval air attack against the *Scharnhorst* and the *Gneisenau*, Harold French, actor and director, and Pat Reid, author of *The Colditz Story*.

Newcastle a site of 150 acres (now 310) in the Dukeries, at Worksop. This was to be for another 'lower' school. The foundation stone was laid the same year, but Woodard was too worn out to attend the ceremony. He did not live to see his third great northern school open. He died in 1891, at Henfield, Sussex, aged eighty. He was buried in Lancing Chapel. St. Cuthbert's School, Worksop, was duly opened in 1895 with twenty-five boys and four masters. In a year the number of boys was up to one hundred. The buildings were as imposing as usual: Queen Anne in style. The Gothic chapel was designed by Sir Aston Webb. The dining-hall is 132 feet long, with an enormous hammer roof.

Clayesmore School, the third of the progressive schools, was founded in 1896. Like Abbotsholme, there was a policy of broadening the curriculum beyond mere cramming for examinations. But cultural activities and manual work were added. The emphasis was on developing a boy's creative instincts. Clayesmore began at Pangbourne, Berkshire, but moved to near Blandford, in Dorset, after the First World War. In 1913 it was stated that: 'The strongest fight is made against the method of concentrating the attention of the young boy upon two or more subjects which might secure him honour and money, and closing his mind to all that is most human in history, in art, in poetry and in literature, because it will not pay in the exams. Education cannot be both broad and special at the same time.' Clayesmore retains its original principles.*

Arnold School, Blackpool, Newport High School (Mon.), St. Brendan's College, Bristol, Cardiff High School and Scarborough College were all founded in the last four years of the century. St. Brendan's, a Roman Catholic foundation, moved to new buildings in 1960. The history of Newport High, founded by the local authority in 1895, illustrates what would soon be happening to the smaller private schools all over the country. 'The opening of the Newport Intermediate sounded the death of various private schools. . . . The sons of many Newport business-men had attended these schools [at Chepstow, etc.] as boarders, and now the younger sons naturally went as day boys to the Intermediate.'

*

During the latter half of the nineteenth century the endowments of

* Prof. J. Plamenatz, political scientist, Edward Ardizzone, illustrator, and George Devine, theatrical producer are among its old boys.

money of the old schools rose in value. Income from endowments
increased as follows:

	Early 1860s	1890
Christ's Hospital	£56,000	£66,601
Dulwich	£16,839	£21,470
Bedford	£13,121	£15,192
King Edward's, Birmingham	£12,128	£33,394
St. Paul's	£9,550	£15,426
Tonbridge	£3,803	£6,114
Repton	£2,400	£3,266
Durham	£22	£3,284

The annual income of Eton from endowments in the early
eighteen-sixties was about £20,000, although this sum belonged to
the college rather than to the school as a whole.

*

In 1900 A. H. H. Maclean carried out a survey of the education of
eminent men since the start of Victoria's reign in 1837 to the Diamond Jubilee in 1897. His men were from all walks of life and were
taken from four reference sources: (i) *Men of the Reign 1837–1886*;
(ii) *The Times* principal obituaries, 1886–97; (iii) for those living in
1897, *Men of the Time* and *Who's Who*. This produced a list of 3,068
names. The percentage of those who were educated at public school
was as follows:

Government service	71%
Education	52%
Religion	29%
Law	27%
Army*	16%
Medicine	15%

The leading twenty schools which emerged for this sixty-year
period did not include any of the Victorian schools except Marlborough. Eight of them were predominantly day-schools in London:

Eton	186
Harrow	72
Rugby	60
Westminster	56
Winchester	52

* The lowness of this figure is due to the many crammers specialising in Army
entry.

Charterhouse	38
Royal High School	30
Merchant Taylors'	22
St. Paul's	17
Christ's Hospital	15
Edinburgh Academy	13
Marlborough	13
Shrewsbury	12
K.C.S.	11
City of London	10
Aberdeen G.S.	9
King Edward's, Birmingham	9
U.C.S.	8
King Edward VI, Bury St. Edmunds	7
Tonbridge	7

The leading schools in modern subjects gave a different picture; in Science: Rossall, U.C.S., Eton; and in Medicine: Royal High School, Harrow, Aberdeen G.S.

*

The death of Queen Victoria coincided with the South African War. Maclean, in another pamphlet, made an analysis of the education of the officers who served in the war. A different list emerges from the list of eminent men of the reign. By 1900 the new Victorian schools had taken over a large share of filling the posts in public and military service, at the expense of the specialised crammers and the ancient foundations. The numbers of officers who served in the war were as follows:*

Eton	1,326
Harrow	592
Wellington	521
Cheltenham	438
Marlborough	379
Charterhouse	367
Clifton	313
Haileybury	281
Winchester	274
Rugby	236
Uppingham	178

* *Public Schools and the War in South Africa*, A. H. H. Maclean.

Bedford	144
Malvern	132
St. Paul's	132
U.S.C.	116
Radley	108
Dover	103
Bradfield	93
Shrewsbury	91
Repton	90

It was noted that 36 per cent of the officers from both Cheltenham and Wellington were decorated, as compared to 23 per cent from Eton and Harrow.

9

THE TWENTIETH CENTURY

AT the beginning of the twentieth century the chance of an elementary (primary) school-child going on to secondary school was 270 to one. Nearly all of these were middle- or upper-class children. The work of the Charity Commissioners had resulted in many old free, or almost free, endowed schools becoming larger, but more expensive, public schools. The new foundations, even when the intentions had been otherwise, as that of William Fettes and Nathaniel Woodard, had ended in schools for the sons of comfortably-off fee-payers. The Education Act of 1902 led to the establishment, alongside the old endowed schools, of a large number of municipal and county secondary schools giving a modern education. Already, in 1899, the office of the Charity Commissioners dealing with schools had come under the Education Department, to form the Board of Education. By 1902 the elementary and the few existing official secondary schools all came together under local authorities; organisation and education thus became integrated. Under the 1902 Act the L.E.A.s were provided with the power to 'consider the educational needs of their area and take such steps as seem to them desirable, after consultation with the Board of Education, to *supply* or *aid* the supply of education other than elementary, and to promote the general co-ordination of all forms of education'. New 'Grammar Schools' were built, at ratepayers' expense, and old ones were helped from the rates, losing some autonomy. The term 'grammar' school had by now lost its original meaning and referred to an official, or officially-supported, secondary school that provided more than a purely modern or technical education (except in some cases, where independent schools proudly retained 'Grammar School' in their titles, such as Manchester; others, like Bedford, more conveniently dropped the appellation early in the century).

Predictably, there was some trouble over the teaching of religion in the new schools, particularly in Wales, and some nonconformists refused to pay their education rate on the grounds that the schools were denominational. The Education Act of 1902 was the cause of long and bitter controversy in its day, although, compared to Foster's Act, it is comparatively forgotten. It was a brilliant and far-reaching measure: the work primarily of Arthur Balfour and Sir Robert Morant. Morant was permanent secretary at the Board 1903–11, and entirely remodelled it. The compulsory school age, however, was twelve, and it was not raised to fourteen until H. A. L. Fisher's Act of 1918. In Scotland, where opportunities for secondary education were greater, there had been compulsory attendance to fourteen since 1901. The Scottish Education Act of 1918 gave education authorities similar rights to those in England and Wales. The relevant act in Northern Ireland was in 1923. The Direct Grant system, by which some schools accepted state aid in return for free places, which undoubtedly bolstered up many a school, was introduced in 1919.* After Foster's Act, secondary schools appeared thick and fast. By 1930 one child in every eight went on to secondary education.

Some of these new council schools, in middle-class areas, were inclined to base themselves to some extent on the public schools, and enjoyed a good reputation very early; Leamington College (1902), for instance,† which began as Leamington Municipal School, Chatham House, and Hereford High School (1912).

At the same time the need for special interests in education was high-lighted, and three Roman Catholic public schools were founded. St. Benedict's, Ealing, was founded in 1902 by Albert H. E. Ford to provide a traditional Benedictine education in London. Douai School, near Reading, having been expelled from France, found a ready home in England. St. John's College, Southsea, was founded by the De la Salle brothers in 1908. Two old novitiates, Belmont Abbey, dating from 1859, and Prior Park, dating from 1830, were converted to public schools in the nineteen-twenties. St. Boniface's, Plymouth, opened in 1931 on premises that had been used on and off for Catholic education since 1884. It opened with 142 boys, fifteen of them boarders (today: 430, seventy of them boarders). St. Peter's, Bournemouth, began in 1936 as a prep. school, becoming a day and boarding public school in 1947. St. Bede's, Manchester, was established earlier.

* In 1968 there were 36,083 boys at H.M.C. Direct Grant schools, 5,821 of them being boarders.

† Sir Bernard Spilsbury and Sir Frank Whittle were educated there.

By the First World War it was clear that the boom of founding new public schools was over. Although the country was at present too class-ridden for the upper classes to send their children to the new council schools, most of which could only be expected to be inferior educationally for a long time to come, the numbers of public school places was probably quite a bit higher than the demand for them. Many of the private schools closed as a result of the act, however, and one public school, Bath College (1857) had to close in 1909. By this time it was still far from clear what was meant by a public school, although the Education Act of 1902, with its subsidies, had helped. If a school accepted funds from official sources, it was thought not to be a public school. Thus some of the old endowed schools which had been accepted without question as public schools, and had been members of the Headmasters' Conference, no longer were either. This very much strengthened a feeling already existing that day schools were not to be termed public schools. This notion had begun in 1860, with a judgement in court concerning Bristol Grammar School, which had wanted to take boarders, but was refused; the judge had given the impression that the public schools were all boarding schools and that they were for the upper classes. This feeling continued until after the First World War. Schools such as Dulwich and St. Paul's, which took boarders but were primarily day schools, suffered in prestige (if in nothing else). When the Public Schools Club was formed in Albemarle Street in 1909, membership was confined to the old boys of twenty-four schools, all of them boarding, and not including Dulwich, Manchester, Merchant Taylors' and St. Paul's. The products of such great schools were anxious to know why they could not join a club for the public schools, and the membership was later extended. Sometimes it was a matter of little more than luck whether an old grammar school became a 'public school': the choice of headmaster. The obscure village school at Oundle, for instance, was being turned into a leading school at this time by Sanderson. The public, even the politicians, were thoroughly confused as to what precisely a public school was, but where it was more clear which was one and which the other, as at Bristol, the rivalry was fierce, although seldom, alas, on the sporting field. But after another fifty years Bristol again seemed to be accepted as a public school.

*

The state entered into the public school system in 1907 with the opening of the new Royal Naval College, at Dartmouth (a junior wing had existed at Osborne since 1903; it closed in 1921). This was one of the reforms being brought about at that time in the Royal Navy. The aim was 'a naval public school'. Previous training, on H.M.S. *Britannia*, at Dartmouth since 1863, had been almost exclusively navigational. Boys went to Dartmouth after a year or two at public school, or direct from cramming establishments. For many years Dartmouth was a member of the Headmasters' Conference. After the Second World War the Army entered a similar field with the establishment of Welbeck College, in 1953: 'an all-boarding six-form college' of 150 boys who, armed with a scientific education, went on to the Royal Military Academy, Sandhurst. The Duke of York's Royal Military School, at Dover, had long been in existence as an Army charity run by the Royal Army Educational Corps.

King Edward VII School, Lytham, was founded in 1908 on ancient endowments. There is a King Edward VII Grammar School at Sheffield. Langley School, Norwich, opened in 1910 as Norwich High School, in competition to the grammar school. In 1946 it moved to Langley Hall, the home of the Beauchamp family, and changed its name. Lord Wandsworth College, near Basingstoke, was founded in 1912 under an endowment of a former Liberal M.P. of that name, who possessed considerable property in London. Strathallan School, Perthshire, was founded in the same year by H. Riley, who continued to run it until his death in 1942. Another Scottish school, Keil, was founded three years later, under bequests of the Mackinnon family, for the education of 'Highland lads', and has taken on the characteristics of a public school. Pangbourne College, formerly the Nautical College, was founded in 1917 by Sir Thomas Devitt as a naval establishment. In 1931 the school passed from family control to a board of governors and the curriculum was changed to provide for a general education, but the headmaster was known as the Captain Superintendent until 1969.* Ryde School, Isle of Wight, was founded in 1921. The best of the County Grammar Schools was probably Raynes Park County Grammar School, founded in 1935. John Garrett was the first headmaster.

The pre-Great War years saw an expansion in progressive

* Old boys: Admiral Sir Frank Hopkins, Atlantic rower John Ridgway, Beverley Cross, playwright.

education. Sanderson at Oundle, Almond at Loretto, Rouse at the Perse, Howson at Gresham's, Alexander Devine at Clayesmore, Reddie at Abbotsholme, J. H. Badley at Bedales, were all working in new fields in their own ways, with Olive of Dauntsey's soon after and, later and even more advanced, the co-educational Dartington Hall. Almond prefects sat in his study sucking pipes discussing education. Some of these headmasters called their boys by their first names. St. George's, Harpenden, opened as a co-educational school in 1907. Bembridge School, Isle of Wight, was founded in 1919 by J. H. Whitehouse; arts and crafts were to the fore in the curriculum.* Rendcomb College, at Cirencester, was endowed in 1920 by one of the Wills tobacco family, who retain an interest in the school. Rendcomb was consciously opposed to the games cult of the day, and it has remained small as a deliberate act of policy. It took about fifty per cent of its intake from council schools. The influence of these new schools, and new ideas, was slow to spread. Many schools remained strictly traditional until 1939, with the emphasis on games, Latin, cold baths and corporal punishment. At Haileybury, as late as 1906, the library was kept locked, only sixth-formers having a key; other boys visited it at set hours with a master present.

*

On 18 July 1911, a remarkable event in the story of the public schools took place. All the Woodard schools met at Lancing, as the Rev. Nathaniel had always envisaged they would do. His great chapel, indeed, had been built for that purpose. The Archbishop of Canterbury was present, together with thirteen bishops. A great procession—each school with its banner to the fore—took place: boys from Hurstpierpoint, Lancing, Ardingly, Bloxham, Denstone, Ellesmere, King's, Taunton, Worksop; girls from Woodard schools at Bognor, Bromley, Bangor and Scarborough. A witness wrote: 'In its splendour and dignity it was impressive in the extreme—Bishops in scarlet, Provosts in rich capes, the Lancing Chapter in their blue mantles, the banners, and last, but not least, the representatives of the girls' schools in white and wearing veils. And then the choir and orchestra, with its drums, at times like thunder—the brilliant trumpets in the gallery—all combined to lift up the whole scene, and

---

* Former pupils: Sir Frank Milton, London Chief Magistrate, Desmond Donnelly, Robin Day, Sir Dingle Foot.

kindle the imagination into thoughts too deep for words.' How Woodard would have enjoyed this religious festival of youth!

*

The First World War decimated the Edwardian generation of public-school men to an almost unbelievable extent. Since the decline of the military crammers it had become accepted that young officers were from the public schools, although under conscription this broke down towards the end of the war; and the death-rate of junior officers was, of course, notoriously high. Of the boys entered at Haileybury between 1905 and 1912, about one-third were killed in action. Figures from only two other schools are enough to reveal the extent of the tragedy: 687 Carthusians lost their lives; out of the 2,833 Malvernians who served, 457 died. Those who survived, and some of those who did not, wrote memorable accounts of the death of a generation. Some of them, like Rupert Brooke, are famous: others totally forgotten. Paul Jones was head boy of Dulwich when the war began, and was awarded the Brackenbury Scholarship at Balliol College, Oxford, the first Dulwich boy ever to win a history scholarship at Balliol. He played in the Dulwich XV for three seasons and was captain in 1914–15, when Dulwich had one of the best seasons it had ever had, beating Haileybury, St. Paul's, Bedford, Merchant Taylors' and Sherbourne (at that time a regular fixture). At the school sports in 1915 he won the mile, the half-mile and the steeplechase. A month later he joined the Army, and was killed in action in 1917. In 1916 he wrote: 'The glamour had decidedly worn off. Oh, if we could but get through the Boche lines! As things are at present, there is no thrill and not much scope for initiative. It is just a sordid affair of mud, shell-holes, corpses, grime and filth. Even in billets the thing remains intensely dull and un-inspiring. One just lives, eats, drinks, sleeps, and all apparently to no purpose. The monotony is excessive. . . . If we are to win this war it will only be through gigantic efforts and great sacrifices. It is the chief virtue of the public school system that it teaches one to make sacrifices willingly for the sake of *esprit de corps*. Well, clearly, if the public school men hold back, the others will not follow.'

Schools whose products received the most knighthoods or higher honours in the services in the First World War were as follows:

Eton	35
Wellington	24

Marlborough	17
Cheltenham	14
Harrow	14
Winchester	13
Charterhouse	11
Clifton	11
Haileybury	8

Dulwich, Edinburgh Academy, Rugby, St. Paul's and Westminster had six each. Of the schools whose old boys won the Victoria Cross, the following were the leaders:*

Eton	13
Harrow	8
Cheltenham	6
Clifton	5
Dulwich	5
Wellington	5
Haileybury	4
Rugby	4
Uppingham	4
Winchester	4

*

After the Great War the public schools entered a phase of great prosperity. Owing to the part their products had played in the war, their reputation had never been higher. Those educated elsewhere who had been commissioned wished to send their sons to such schools. So did a great new class of what was condescendingly called the *nouveaux riches*. Despite the losses in the war, the male population had increased by over a million between 1911 and 1921, and more people than ever before were prepared to make the sacrifice of paying school fees for secondary education. This took place despite a new school of thought, which was highly critical of established ways, and in particular of the public schools: books such as Alec Waugh's *The Loom of Youth*, Robert Graves's *Goodbye to All That*, H. G. Wells's *Joan and Peter*, C. E. Montague's *Rough Justice*, and Somerset Maugham's *Of Human Bondage* (which had appeared in the war) were some of them. *Sinister Street* had already set the scene in 1913.

* Both tables: *Public Schools and the Great War*, A. H. H. Maclean.

The pressure on the existing public schools was so great that the founding of new schools seemed, to some, imperative. One of these was E. H. Montauban, proprietor of a famous preparatory school in Hampstead, The Hall. Montauban was a member of the council of the Association of Preparatory Schools (later the I.A.P.S.), and as such he knew that all the great schools were full up for many years to come. Parents at his own school were pressing him and complaining about the lack of places at the public schools. To Montauban it was obvious that there was room for at least one new school, and the sooner the better. He took the idea to the association, suggesting that the prep. schools themselves should finance a new school. At the same time, in 1921, the magnificent Stowe House, at Buckingham, home of the last of the Dukes of Buckingham, came on the market. Montauban realised immediately that this was the right sort of place, although, it seems, more from the point of view of grandeur than of practicality. The mansion was sold privately, with a surrounding estate, for the incredibly cheap price of £35,000. The new owner agreed to hand over the house to Montauban's scheme providing a suitable endowment for financing the school could be raised. Montauban, working through the I.A.P.S., went about the task. He came in for considerable opposition, particularly from *The Times* and from Lyttleton, headmaster of Eton, both of whom declared that there were enough places already and that a new school would either not last long or would severely damage the existing ones. For Montauban had always made it clear that he was interested only in a great new public school—'one of the first half-dozen', as he put it—not a minor one. An association of parents for Stowe was formed in 1932, and two months later The Provisional Committee for Stowe was formed. It included three leading headmasters, including Sanderson. Architects were instructed for the necessary alterations, and a headmaster appointed. Sufficient funds had been raised, and it was announced that Stowe School would open in September 1923. It owed its existence to one man: Montauban.

To celebrate the opening, a dinner was held at the Central Hotel, Marylebone. The new headmaster made a provocative speech, belittling Clifton and Haileybury and claiming that Stowe was going to be a major school. He also hinted that while he was not going to be progressive, he did not intend to stick blindly to every old tradition of public school education. His name was J. F. Roxburgh, a former housemaster at Lancing, and he was the ideal man for the task. Roxburgh knew exactly the right path to tread, and he built Stowe into a leading school, accepted as such, with modern ideas but not too different to put off potential parents. For the public-school parents did not want too much progressive education (the progressive schools were lagging behind in the general expansion), but were well aware that improvements were overdue. This was the background to Roxburgh's policy, and whether the school would have survived under any other is doubtful. He was one of the ablest headmasters in the long history of the public schools. By the time he retired, in 1949, Stowe was fully established, perhaps even in the 'first six', as Montauban had predicted. In a very short time Stowe produced a remarkable list of distinguished sons.* Tradition and age, it seemed, were not as necessary to public school education as had been claimed.

Canford School, in Dorset, came into being because of the sale of another great mansion, Canford Manor, which mainly dated from the plans of Sir Charles Barry in 1843, although a part of the medi-aeval manor remains (most of the old building having been pulled down in 1763). Lord Wimborne sold it in 1922 and the school was opened the following year. Although run on more traditional lines, it, too, was successful, growing under the headmastership of Sir Cyril Norwood's son-in-law, the Rev. C. B. Canning, 1928–47. Canning had been a housemaster at Marlborough under Norwood. Canford possesses one of the few Royal Tennis courts in the country. The next headmaster was J. W. S. Hardie, 1947–61, a hockey international from St. Lawrence, who had been a headmaster in the West Indies.

The next four schools to be founded were all more progressive than the tentatively advanced Stowe and the almost uncompromis-ingly traditional Canford. Frensham Heights, 1925, was co-educational and designed to concentrate on each individual. Bryanston, 1928, was less progressive than many, but somewhat more daring than Stowe. Bryanston, near Blandford, a neo-Georgian mansion of 1897 by Norman Shaw, was the home of Viscount Portman. Its foundation was due to J. G. Jeffreys, who

---

* Prince Rainier, Lord Annan, Lord Taylor of Harlow, Lord Kennet (Way-land Young), Sir Tufton Beamish, M.P., Group-Captain L. Cheshire, V.C., actor David Niven, P. B. 'Laddy' Lucas, fighter pilot, M.P. and golfer, poet John Cornford, and authors Lawrence Whistler, James Reeves, Anthony West, Frank Tuohy and John Gale.

found support for the sort of modern public school he wanted to establish. 'First and foremost the School stresses the need for recognizing the boy as an individual.' Jeffreys was followed by T. F. Coade, 1932–59, who pioneered many educational reforms at Bryanston and who brought the school to its present size and reputation.* Gordonstoun School was founded in 1934, as a far more hearty sort of place, by Kurt Hahn, a German educationist who had left Germany under the Hitler regime. Hahn's idea was to find a middle position between those who concentrated on the individual and those who retained the traditional idea of training for 'service' at the expense of the individual. He believed that progressive ideas could still be used for the purpose of turning out those who would 'serve the community'. He wrote: 'I will call the three views of education the Ionian view, the Spartan view, the Platonic view. . . . Those who hold the first view believe that the individual ought to be nurtured and humoured regardless of the interests of the community. . . . According to the second view the individual may and should be neglected for the benefit of the state. . . . The third, the Platonic view, is that any nation is a slovenly guardian of its own interests if it does not do all it can to make the individual citizen discover his own powers: and further, that the individual becomes a cripple from his or her own point of view if he is not qualified by education to serve the community.' Hahn, like several of his predecessors, probably took too simplistic a view of the traditional public schools, about which he knew little. Thring had already made much the same point. And the stress which Hahn put on the importance of character-building had been considered the strength of the public schools since Arnold's time. It turned out that Hahn's system amounted to a very considerable amount of rock-climbing, arduous rescue work, sailing and the like, and various rules which were based more on mutual trust than was customary. By 1939 the numbers had risen to 135. During the war Gordonstoun was evacuated to Wales, where it played a part in the founding of the first Outward Bound School. The Duke of Edinburgh and the Prince of Wales were both at Gordonstoun.†

* Stephen Rhys, musician, scientist Frederick Sanger, author Richard Mason, journalist N. Tomalin, and A. R. D. Wright, headmaster of Shrewsbury are among the old boys.

† Others: Prof. W. Hayman, mathematician, Winthrop Young, educationist, Lord Beaumont, Mark Arnold Foster, journalist.

One of the features of Gordonstoun was that the fees should be paid on a scale, those who could afford it paying more than those who could not. This also is a feature of Millfield, founded in Somerset by R. J. O. Meyer in 1935. Meyer, known as 'Boss' to staff and pupils alike, had little experience of public schools apart from his years at Haileybury. He had previously been a cotton-broker and a private tutor in India. Millfield was a great success, particularly after the war. The success was based on the personality of the founder and the good ratio of pupils to teachers. The school was not overburdened with progressive ideas, the accent being on hard work and plenty of games, and Millfield gained a formidable reputation at sport unequalled in the country. It was typical of Meyer that the aim of Millfield was quite bluntly stated to be 'the most efficient teaching organization in the world'. There are nearly one thousand pupils, of whom a third are girls. In 1971 Meyer was succeeded as headmaster by C. R. M. Atkinson, who, like Meyer, had been a captain of Somerset at cricket. The publicity Millfield has received should not detract from a proper appreciation of it as one of the most important schools to be founded in Britain for at least a hundred years.

During the financial slump of the nineteen-thirties, as Lyttleton had predicted, the boom in public-school education fell away and many schools found it a very difficult time. Weymouth College was obliged to close, Brighton, Rossall and St. Bees only just survived, and U.S.C. had to amalgamate in 1942. Nevertheless, the public schools were at the peak of their influence, although many books and plays of the era ridiculed the 'old public school-boy', caricaturising him with monocle and spats, tongue-tied, his old-school tie his most precious article of clothing. During the half-century, 1886–1936, of the 208 cabinet ministers, 115 had been educated at public school, the leading schools being:

Eton	50
Harrow	23
Rugby	11
Winchester	6
Cheltenham	5*

The Second World War completely demolished the belief that satisfactory officers in the armed forces came only from the public schools. The war itself disrupted public-school education, especi-

---

* *Winchester and The Public School Elite*, T. J. H. Bishop, R. Wilkinson.

ally in the case of the boarding schools. For one reason or another many schools were evacuated. Often their buildings were required by the authorities. In many cases schools were hosts to those ousted: Harrow received Malvern, Shrewsbury had Cheltenham, Dulwich went to Tonbridge, Mill Hill to St. Bees, Lancing to Denstone and Ellesmere, Kingswood to Uppingham, Westminster to Hurstpierpoint, Oratory to Downside, City of London to Marlborough, Eastbourne to Radley, Mercers' to Collyer's. At the end of the war numbers had dropped considerably, and many schools were in a poor state financially and otherwise. Eastbourne only just survived the war, and Margate College did not. In an effort to combat the difficulties of the war, the Association of Governing Bodies of Public Schools was formed in 1941. But, although less dramatically than after the First World War, numbers soon picked up and, although fees had to be increased, the public schools once more had long waiting-lists. The chief characteristic of the post-war years has been the steady rise in fees. Four schools—Beaumont, Chard, Mercers' and Sebright—have closed.

Under R. A. Butler, preparations were made for a revised educational system after the war, and to study what part the public schools should play a committee was set up under Lord Fleming. The public schools were defined as those which belonged to the Headmasters' Conference and the Governing Bodies Association, which, as the committee later pointed out, was an unsatisfactory definition; this covered 188 schools. The Fleming Report suggested that those public schools already in receipt of public funds could be easily assimilated in the state system; those that were quite independent should take twenty-five per cent of their intake from the state primary schools. Some schools, notably of course Christ's Hospital, had been taking boys from the state system for a long time. The idea was by no means a new one, and it had little success. Local authorities turned out to be more reluctant than the schools. In recent years, however, more positive steps have been made in this direction at some schools. For the schools which had been receiving public funds, several alternatives were available under the 1944 Act: (1) to go over completely to L.E.A. control; (2) to become maintained by the L.E.A. but reserving certain control while receiving no fees from day pupils (Voluntary Aided and Voluntary Controlled); (3) to receive a Direct Grant from the Ministry of Education, providing a certain percentage of free places, and fees scaled in accordance with a parent's income; (4) to go completely independent. Voluntary Aided schools have two-thirds of the governors appointed independently and one-third by the L.E.A., appoint their own teachers and maintain the exterior of the buildings. Voluntary Controlled schools have two thirds of the governors appointed by the L.E.A. and one-third independently. Under this system several old foundations, like Cranbrook, Voluntary Aided, and Sir Roger Manwood's, Voluntary Controlled, have thrived as never before, greatly to the benefit of the community, both locally and at large.

A few new schools were founded, showing confidence in the independent sector: Carmel College, for Jewish boys, in 1948; Austin Friars, Roman Catholic, in 1951; Grenville College, Bideford, also founded in 1954; Shiplake, 1959; Rannock, Perthshire, 1959; and Redice, Andover, 1961. Worth School, 1959, was originally a preparatory school for Downside, which had begun in 1933. In 1951 the state entered the field in a more direct way than ever with the establishment of Wymondham College, Norfolk, run as a co-educational boarding-school by the L.E.A., as is Ottershaw School, Surrey.

The great virtue of the post-war system, from Butler's Act, was its diversity and variety, something which has usually appealed to the British. But not to all of them, and because the public schools were considered to be perpetuators of the class-system (which they may have been over half a century previously) there were suggestions to do away with them in one way or another, usually by financial pressure or integration. These schemes got nowhere and some of the most outspoken critics sent their children to them. In 1964 a Labour Government came to power and set about re-organising secondary education along comprehensive lines (some counties had already begun the process).* In 1965 yet another Public Schools Commission, under Sir John Newsom, was set up, this time 'to advise on the best way of integrating the public schools with the state system of education'. The terms of reference were the same as the Fleming Commission's: Headmasters' Conference and Governing Bodies Association. The Commission reported in July 1968. Its recommendations were sensible, moderate, constructive, and presented a compromise: many boarding schools should offer at least half their

* By 1972 there were 1,370 comprehensive schools, with 41% of the secondary school children enrolled.

places to financially assisted pupils, who could benefit from boarding education, about eighty thousand places; the public schools should accept more children of lower standards; and that 'aided' status should be encouraged by the formation of a central body, which would be more acceptable than the L.E.A. As for the present, co-education should be more widely introduced, beating and fagging abolished, and financial and tax loopholes that helped the paying of boarding fees should be ended. About the main suggestions, nothing whatever was done. At this time the public sector was already supporting the independent schools to the extent of some twenty thousand places either wholly or partly paid for.

New subjects include computer training, in which Eton, Harrow and Royal Liberty have all taken a lead. Over 250 schools compete annually in a computer game, run by the Institute of Chartered Accountants. The first three winners were all public schools: Downside, Cheltenham and Cranbrook. The public schools, led by Marlborough, pioneered the business-studies A-level course. Oundle has initiated a new approach to history at O-level.

What the future holds is uncertain, but certainly there will be change. One thing seems likely: the public schools will survive financial pressure, for the most striking aspect of their history is that they have seldom been without financial difficulties but have always survived. There have been five schools which have been essential to forming what we know as the public schools today: Winchester, Eton, St. Paul's, Rugby and Uppingham. It would be interesting to know what the sixth will be when it is added to the list in twenty-five years' time. Millfield, perhaps, if the private sector is to thrive. Or Cranbrook, if the state takes a more active part. As for the wishes of the schoolboy himself, our best writer on childhood, Forrest Reid, should have the final words: 'There is nothing, perhaps, quite so conventional, in his own queer way, as the average schoolboy.'

APPENDICES

1. Landmarks in the History of the Public Schools.
2. Partly Independent Schools: Direct Grant Schools.
    Voluntary Aided Schools.
    Voluntary Controlled Boarding Schools.
    Grant-Aided Schools, Scotland.
3. The Headmasters' Conference: 1873.
    Chairmen 1945–72.
4. Fees: 1876–1972.
5. Related Schools.
6. The Public Schools Academically.
7. The Public Schools and the Nobel Prize.
8. The Public Schools in the Twentieth-Century Establishment.

Appendix 1: Landmarks in the History of the Public Schools

598	Augustine founds Canterbury cathedral, and Latin school soon after.
1382	William of Wykeham founds school at Winchester.
1440	Henry VI follows his example at Eton.
c. 1500	Printed Latin textbooks appear, based on the methods of Magdalen College School.
1509	Colet founds St. Paul's, model for future schools.
1536	Suppression of monasteries, and schools associated with them, begins.
1545	Suppression of chantries, colleges, and other foundations: many schools close, some re-founded afterwards independent of religious foundations.
1552–3	New schools founded or re-founded. Many schools a mixture of free scholars (local) and fee-payers, headmasters and ushers arranging boarding themselves.
1700–90	Grammar schools decline, owing to abuse of endowments and classical emphasis
1768–1818	Boys in certain old schools rebel against conditions.
1793	Return of Catholic pupils from Europe.
c. 1795	Rival establishments, offering boarding education, have appeared.
c. 1800	Widespread scepticism about the grammar schools.
1818	Lord Brougham's Act passed authorising commissioners to enquire into and report on educational endowments. Some schools required to improve.
1827	Arnold becomes headmaster of Rugby and formulates modern public school.
1836	The Charity Commissioners inspect endowed schools.
1840	Grammar Schools Act gives schools power to teach subjects other than those stipulated in statutes, but excludes the best-known public schools from its provisions.
1853	Thring becomes headmaster of Uppingham and improves conditions.
1861	Royal Commission set up to report on nine selected schools.
1862	H. H. Almond becomes headmaster of Loretto and advocates humanising schools.
1864	Royal Commission to enquire into all other endowed schools, with power to appoint inspectors.
1868	Public Schools Act alters constitutions of seven of the nine schools.
1869	Endowed Schools Act requires other old schools to change their statutes; work of overseeing this to be done by En-

	dowed Schools Commission, later (1874) taken over by Charity Commissioners; transferred to Board of Education, 1899; many free places go.
1869	First meeting of the Headmasters' Conference.
1892	Sanderson becomes headmaster of Oundle and leads change-over to modern curriculum, giving emphasis to technical and scientific subjects.
1900	G. W. S. Howson becomes headmaster at Gresham's, and removes Greek from curriculum.
1902	W. H. D. Rouse becomes headmaster of The Perse, and pioneers modern teaching.
1902	Balfour's Education Act brings in state secondary education.
1919	Direct Grant System introduced.
1919	G. W. Olive becomes headmaster of Dauntsey's and liberalises education.
c. 1935	Some smaller public schools near bankruptcy.
1944	Report of Commission on the Public Schools, under Lord Fleming, advocates some integration with state system.
1944	R. A. Butler's Education Act introduces Voluntary Aided and Voluntary Controlled schools.
1965	Public Schools Commission, under Sir John Newsom, to advise on integration of 'public schools with the state system of education'.

Appendix 2: Partly Independent Schools

(i) THE DIRECT GRANT SCHOOLS FOR BOYS:
ENGLAND AND WALES

Abingdon (b)
Alleyn's
Arnold (b)
Ashville (b)
Bablake
Bancroft's
Barnard Castle
Bedford Modern (b)
Birkenhead (b)
Bolton
Bradford G.S.
Brentwood (b)
Bristol Cathedral Sch.
Bristol G.S.
Bury G.S.
Caterham (b)
* Catholic, Preston
Culford (b)
Dame Allan's
Dauntsey's (b)
* De la Salle, Salford
* De la Salle, Sheffield
Eltham (b)
Exeter (b)
Framlingham (b)
Haberdashers' Aske's, Elstree (b)
Hereford Cathedral Sch. (b)
Hulme G.S.
Hymer's
Kent (b)
Kimbolton (b)
King Edward VII, Lytham
King Edward's, Bath
King Edward's, Birmingham
King Henry VIII, Coventry
King's, Chester
King's, Worcester
Kingston G.S.

Latymer Upper
Leeds G.S.
Loughborough G.S. (b)
Magdalen College Sch. (b)
Manchester G.S.
Merchant Taylors', Crosby (b)
Monmouth (b)
Norwich (b)
Oakham (b)
Perse (b)
Plymouth (b)
Pocklington (b)
Portsmouth G.S.
Queen Elizabeth's, Blackburn
Queen Elizabeth's, Bristol (b)
Queen Elizabeth's, Wakefield (b)
R.G.S., Newcastle
St. Alban's
* St. Anselm's, Birkenhead
* St. Bede's, Manchester (b)
* St. Boniface's, Plymouth (b)
* St. Brendan's, Bristol
* St. Cuthbert's, Newcastle
* St. Edward's, Liverpool
* St. Francis Xavier's, Liverpool
* St. John's, Southsea (b)
* St. Joseph's, Blackpool (b)
* St. Joseph's, Stoke on Trent
* St. Mary's, Blackburn (b)
* St. Mary's, Crosby
* St. Michael's, Leeds
Shebbear (b)
Stamford (b)
Stockport G.S.
* Thornleigh, Bolton
Truro (b)
Wellington, Somerset (b)
West Buckland (b)

* Roman Catholic   (b) Boarders

* West Park GS., St. Helens
William Hulme's G.S.
Woodbridge (b)

Woodhouse Grove (b)
* Xavierian, Manchester

In 1970 twenty-one of the Direct Grant schools had over 70% Local Education Authority free or reserved places, the top being St. Michael's, Leeds, with 99%. Of these twenty-one schools, seventeen were Roman Catholic. Only two Direct Grant Schools had less than 10% free or reserved places: West Buckland (8%) and Kent (3%).

(ii) VOLUNTARY AIDED BOYS' SCHOOLS: ENGLAND AND WALES

Adam's G.S., Newport (Salop) (b)
Churcher's (b)
Cranbrook (b)
Hardye's (b)
H.M.S. Conway (b)
King's, Peterborough (b)
Liverpool Blue-Coat (b)

Newcastle under Lyme High
R.G.S., Lancaster (b)
R.G.S., Worcester (b)
St. Bartholomew's, Newbury
St. George's, Harpenden (b)
St. Olave's and St. Saviour's
* Salesian, Chertsey
Wolverhampton G.S.

(iii) VOLUNTARY CONTROLLED BOYS' OR CO-ED.
PART-BOARDING SCHOOLS

King's, Grantham (b)
Lincoln (b)
De Aston, Market Rasen (b)
King Edward VII, King's Lynn (b)
Paston, North Walsam (b)
Magdalen College School, Brackley (b)
Southwell Minster G.S. (b)
Lord Williams G.S., Thame (b)
Lulow G.S. (b)
Adams' G.S. (Salop) (b)
Sir John Talbot's G.S., Whitchurch (b)
Sexey's (b)
Crewkerne (b)
Ilminster G.S. (b)
King Edward VI, Bury St. Edmunds (b)
King Edward's, Aston (b)

Bishop Vesey's G.S. (b)
Heversham G.S. (b)
Marlborough G.S. (b)
Harley Castle G.S. (b)
Old Swinford Hospital, Stourbridge (b)
Bridlington (b)
Sir William Turner's, Coatham (b)
Richmond G.S. (Yorks) (b)
Ermysted's G.S. (Yorks) (b)
Archbishop Holgate's (b)
King Alfred's, Wantage (b)
Royal Latin, Buckingham (b)
R.G.S., High Wycombe (b)
Keswick (b)
Buxton College (b)
Shaftesbury G.S. (b)
King Edward VI, Chelmsford (b)
R.G.S., Colchester (b)

Brighton, Hove and Sussex G.S. (b)

King Edward VI, Louth (b)

Caistor G.S. (b)

Brigg G.S. (b)

Ashby-de-la-Zouch G.S.

Earl's Colne G.S. (b)

Palmer's (b)

Peter Symonds'

Sir Roger Manwood's (b)

Hutton G.S. (b)

Kirkham G.S. (b)

(iv) GRANT-AIDED BOYS' OR CO-ED. VOLUNTARY SCHOOLS: SCOTLAND

Daniel Stewart's

Dollar Academy (b)

George Heriot's

George Watson's

Hutcheson's

Kelvinside Academy

Melville (b)

Morrison's (b)

Robert Gordon's (b)

* St. Aloysius, Glasgow.

Appendix 3: Headmasters' Conference

(i) MEMBERS 1873 (ATTENDED OR INVITED)

Abingdon
Bedford
Berkhamsted
King Edward's, Birmingham
Bishop's Stortford
Blackheath
Blundell's
Bradfield
Brentwood
Brewood
Brighton
Bromsgrove
Bury St. Edmunds
Charterhouse
Cheltenham
Christ's Hospital
Clifton
Cowbridge
Cranbrook
Derby
Dulwich
Durham
Eastbourne
Elizabeth College, Guernsey
Epsom
Eton
Felsted
Giggleswick
Guildford R.G.S.
Haileybury
Harrow
Hereford C.S.
Highgate
Ipswich
King's, Canterbury

King's, Ely
King's, Rochester
King's, Worcester
King William's Coll.
Lancaster R.G.S.
Lancing
Leeds
Liverpool
Magdalen Coll. Sch.
Malvern
Manchester
Marlborough
Merchant Taylors'
Mill Hill
Monmouth
Norwich
Oakham
Oscott (R.C.)
Oswestry
Perse
Radley
Reading
Repton
Richmond (Yorks)
Rossall
Rugby
Sherborne
Shrewsbury
Sutton Valence
Tonbridge
Uppingham
Wellington
Westminster
Winchester
Wolverhampton G.S.
Victoria Coll.

(ii) CHAIRMEN: 1945-72

J. F. Wolfenden (Sir J. Wolfenden)	Shrewsbury
P. H. B. Lyon	Rugby
G. C. Turner	Charterhouse
R. Birley (Sir R. Birley)	Eton
E. James (Lord James)	Manchester G.S.
W. Hamilton	Westminster
H. D. P. Lee (Sir D. Lee)	Winchester
C. P. C. Smith	Haileybury
D. R. Wigram	Monkton Combe
D. D. Lindsay	Malvern
T. E. B. Howorth	St. Paul's
J. Mackay	Bristol G.S.
A. R. D. Wright	Shrewsbury
F. H. Shaw	K.C.S.

Appendix 4

BOARDING FEES

	1876 £	1896 £	1913 £	1922 £	1932 £	1956 £	1972 £
Bedford	–	78	89	150	130	255	654
Blundell's	–	–	84	150	137	270	705
Bradfield	105	95	95	145	158	284	801
Charterhouse	84	–	116	150	175	315	795
Cheltenham	72	85	108	–	162	328	780
Dulwich	60	84	88	135	150	270	636
Eton	144	–	167	230	230	360	861
Felsted	56	56	88	–	116	282	660
Haileybury	–	80	84	130	150	288	765
Harrow	–	–	153	216	216	360	759
Highgate	–	84	85	–	130	216	666
King's, Canterbury	–	78	86	99	135	285	702
Lancing	90	85	111	150	174	285	780
Malvern	–	93	98	156	165	297	726
Marlborough	70	80	91	145	185	321	768
Oundle	45	75	100	150	180	315	798
Radley	–	–	115	175	185	330	780
Repton	–	88	117	168	168	291	795
Rossall	65	74	93	–	145	300	708
Rugby	95	–	126	174	201	351	780
Sherborne	–	109	96	165	165	279	798
Shrewsbury	80	100	111	180	180	320	750
Tonbridge	–	93	111	141	141	269	741
Uppingham	75	110	119	183	186	327	696
Wellington	110	–	114	175	175	294	789
Westminster	95	–	102	129	165	310	780
Winchester	105	–	127	210	200	354	867

Appendix 5: Related Schools

(i) A number of schools of early foundation, which became increasingly
for fee-payers in the nineteenth century, were obliged by the Charity
Commissioners or other authorities to establish, on the same foundation,
schools primarily for local pupils, or to provide a modern education.

Old Foundation	*Modern Foundation*
Bedford	Bedford Modern
Dulwich	Alleyn's
Harrow	John Lyon
Oundle	Laxton G.S.
Rugby	Lawrence Sheriff
Tonbridge	Judd
Whitgift	Trinity

(ii) SCHOOLS CONNECTED WITH MERCHANT COMPANIES

Aldenham	Brewers
Bancroft's	Drapers
Dauntsey's	Mercers
Collyer's	Mercers
Colston's	Merchant Venturers (Bristol)
Cooper's	Coopers
Daniel Stewart's	Company of Merchants (Edinburgh)
George Watson's	Company of Merchants (Edinburgh)
Gresham's	Fishmongers
Haberdashers' Aske's	Haberdashers
Judd	Skinners
Merchant Taylors'	Merchant Taylors
Monmouth	Haberdashers
Norwich	Dyers
Oundle	Grocers
Owen's	Brewers
Skinners'	Skinners
St. Paul's	Mercers
Sevenoaks	Tobacco Pipemakers and Blenders
Tonbridge	Skinners
Stationers	Stationers

(iii) PUBLIC SCHOOLS MANAGED BY THE CHURCH OF ENGLAND

Dean Close	King's, Ely
Durham	King's, Rochester
King's, Canterbury	

(iv) PUBLIC SCHOOLS WHICH ARE CHURCH OF ENGLAND CHOIR SCHOOLS

Hereford Cathedral School
King's, Ely
King's, Gloucester
King's, Peterborough
King's, Rochester

King's, Worcester
Magdalen College School
Truro Cathedral School
Wells Cathedral School

(v) BOYS' PUBLIC SCHOOLS CONTROLLED BY THE WOODARD FOUNDATION

Ardingly
Bloxham
Denstone
Ellesmere
Grenville
Hurstpierpoint

King's, Taunton
King's, Tynemouth
Lancing
St. Edward's (1919–27)
Worksop

(vi) ENGLISH SCHOOLS CONTROLLED BY THE SOCIETY OF FRIENDS

Ackworth
Bootham
Leighton Park

Sidcot
Friends' School, Grt. Ayton
Friends' School, Saffron Walden

(vii) PUBLIC SCHOOLS CONTROLLED BY THE METHODIST CONFERENCE

Ashville
Culford
Kent College
Kingswood
The Leys
Methodist, Belfast

Queen's, Taunton
Rydal
Shebbear
Truro
Wesley, Dublin
Woodhouse Grove

(viii) ROMAN CATHOLIC PUBLIC SCHOOLS IN ENGLAND

Ampleforth
Austin Friars
Belmont Abbey
Cotton
Douai
Downside

Benedictine
Austin Friars
Benedictine
Diocese of Birmingham
Benedictine
Benedictine

Mount St. Mary's	Society of Jesus
Oratory	Lay
Prior Park	Christian Brothers
Ratcliffe	Rosminian
St. Augustine's	Benedictine
St. Benedict's	Benedictine
St. Boniface's	Christian Brothers
St. Edmund's, Ware	Benedictine
St. Francis Xavier's	Society of Jesus
St. George's, Weybridge	Josephite
St. Peter's, Bournemouth	De la Salle
St. John's, Southsea	De la Salle
Stonyhurst	Society of Jesus
Worth	Benedictine

(ix) UNITED WESTMINSTER SCHOOLS

Emanuel	St. Margaret's Hospital
Emery Hill's G.S.	Sutton Valence
Palmer's	Westminster City

Appendix 6: The Public Schools Academically

(i) OPEN AWARDS TO OXFORD AND CAMBRIDGE, ALL SCHOOLS: LEADING SCHOOLS*

1954/5	1957/61	1960/2	1964/5	1965/6	with no. of boys†
Manchester G.S.	Manchester G.S.	Manchester G.S.	Manchester G.S.	Manchester G.S.	1,400
St. Paul's	Dulwich	Dulwich	Dulwich	Dulwich	1,500
Bristol G.S.	Winchester	Winchester	Winchester	K.C.S.	580
Winchester	St. Paul's	St. Paul's	St. Paul's	Winchester	525
King Edward's	Bradford G.S.	Bradford G.S.	Bradford G.S.	King's, Canterbury	682
Bradford G.S.	Rugby	King's, Canterbury	Rugby	Marlborough	820
Downside	Bristol G.S.	Rugby	Christ's Hospital	St. Paul's	650
Marlborough	King's, Canterbury	Bristol G.S.	Eton	Westminster	449
Dulwich	Marlborough	Marlborough	King Edward's	Bristol G.S.	1,200
Christ's Hospital	Downside	Eton	City of London	Eton	1,190

* The *Daily Telegraph*.
† These figures apply to the schools listed in the 1965/6 column.

(ii) LEADING SCHOOLS ON ESTIMATED PERCENTAGE OF BOYS ENTERING OXFORD AND CAMBRIDGE*

1864–67	1955
Shrewsbury (50%)	Rugby (57%)
Winchester	Winchester (57%)
Rugby	Marlborough
Harrow	Westminster
Repton	Clifton
Eton	Charterhouse
Bradfield	Shrewsbury
Westminster	Ampleforth
Bromsgrove	Eton
Radley	Downside
St. Paul's	Harrow
Charterhouse	Tonbridge
Uppingham	U.C.S.
Marlborough	Oundle
Brighton	Whitgift

(iii) LEADING INDEPENDENT BOARDING SCHOOLS ON NUMBER OF A-LEVEL PASSES PER 100 BOYS IN THE SCHOOL: 1961/2†

Ampleforth	Rugby
Epsom	Kingswood
Winchester	Downside
Oundle	St. John's
Marlborough	Westminster
Radley	Tonbridge
Wycliffe	Rossall
Bootham	

(iv) NUMBER OF SUBJECTS PASSED AT A-LEVEL: 1970‡

	Comprehensive	Direct Grant and Independent Day	Independent Boarding
	%	%	%
Three subjects	34	56	59
Four subjects	5	12	13
Five subjects	0	2	4

* *Winchester and the Public School Elite*, T. J. H. Bishop, R. Wilkinson.
† *Where?*, Advisory Centre of Education, February 1964.
‡ *Schools Council Sixth Form Survey*, Vol. III.

Appendix 7: Nobel Prize Winners from the Public Schools to 1971

Medicine:	A. V. Hill	Blundell's
	Sir F. G. Hopkins	City of London
	E. D. Adrian	Westminster
	Sir H. H. Dale	The Leys
	P. B. Medawar	Marlborough
	J. H. C. Crick	Mill Hill
	M. H. F. Wilkins	King Edward's, Birmingham
	A. L. Hodgkin	Gresham's
	A. F. Huxley	Westminster
Peace:	Sir A. Chamberlain	Rugby
	Viscount Cecil	Eton
	P. Noel-Baker	Bootham
Literature:	R. Kipling	U.S.C.
	W. B. Yeats	Dublin High Sch.
	J. Galsworthy	Harrow
	Sir W. Churchill	Harrow
	S. Beckett	Portora
Physics:	W. H. Bragg	King William's
	G. P. Thomson	Perse
	C. G. Borkla	Liverpool Inst.
	P. M. S. Blackett	Dartmouth
	C. F. Powell	Judd
	E. T. S. Walton	Methodist, Belfast
Chemistry:	Sir W. Ramsay	Glasgow Academy
	F. Soddy	Eastbourne
	F. W. Aston	Malvern
	A. Horden	Tettenhall
	A. J. P. Martin	Bedford
	R. L. M. Synge	Winchester
	F. Sanger	Bryanston
	J. C. Kendrew	Clifton
	R. Norrish	Perse
	D. H. Borton	Tonbridge

In the same period there were thirty-one British awards from other schools. An Australian public school, St. Peter's, Adelaide, has produced two Nobel Prize winners: W. L. Bragg (Physics 1915) and Sir H. W. Florey (Medicine 1945).

Appendix 8: The Public Schools in the Twentieth-Century Establishment

(i) ARCHBISHOPS OF CANTERBURY AND YORK

W. D. Maclagan	Royal High School
F. Temple	Blundell's
R. T. Davidson	Harrow
C. G. Lang	—
W. Temple	Rugby
C. F. Garbett	Portsmouth G.S.
G. F. Fisher	Marlborough
A. M. Ramsey	Repton
F. D. Coggan	Merchant Taylors'

(ii) SPEAKERS OF THE HOUSE OF COMMONS

W. C. Gully	—
J. W. Lowther	Eton
J. H. Whitley	Clifton
E. A. FitzRoy	Eton
D. Clifton Brown	Eton
W. S. Morrison	George Watson's
Sir H. Hylton-Foster	Eton
H. M. King	—
J. S. B. Lloyd	Fettes

(iii) PRIME MINSTERS

Marquess of Salisbury	Eton
A. J. Balfour	Eton
Sir H. Campbell-Bannerman	Glasgow High Sch.
H. H. Asquith	City of London
D. Lloyd George	—
A. Bonar Law	Glasgow High Sch.
S. Baldwin	Harrow
J. R. MacDonald	—
N. Chamberlain	Rugby
W. L. S. Churchill	Harrow
C. R. Attlee	Haileybury
Sir A. Eden	Eton
H. Macmillan	Eton
Sir A. Douglas-Home	Eton
J. H. Wilson	—
E. R. G. Heath	—

(iv) LORD CHANCELLORS

Halsbury	—
Loveburn	Cheltenham
Haldane	Edinburgh Academy
Buckmaster	Aldenham
Birkenhead	Birkenhead
Cave	Merchant Taylors'
Hailsham	Eton
Sankey	Lancing
Maugham	Dover
Caldecote	Clifton
Simon	Fettes
Jowitt	Marlborough
Simonds	Winchester
Kilmuir	George Watson's
Dilhorne	Eton
Gardiner	Harrow
Hailsham	Eton

(v) LORD CHIEF JUSTICES OF ENGLAND

Alverstone	Charterhouse
Reading	U.C.S.
Trevethin	Mill Hill
Hewart	Manchester G.S.
Caldecote	Clifton
Goddard	Marlborough
Parker	Rugby
Widgery	Queen's, Taunton

(vi) VICEROYS OF INDIA

Curzon	Eton
Minto	Eton
Hardinge	Harrow
Chelmsford	Winchester
Reading	U.C.S.
Irwin	Eton
Willingdon	Eton
Linlithgow	Eton
Wavell	Winchester
Mountbatten	Dartmouth

(vii) SECRETARIES OF STATE FOR FOREIGN AFFAIRS

Lord Lansdowne	Eton
Sir Edward Grey	Winchester
A. Balfour	Eton
Lord Curzon	Eton
Sir A. Chamberlain	Rugby
A. Henderson	—
Lord Reading	U.C.S.
Sir J. Simon	Fettes
Sir S. Hoare	Harrow
A. Eden	Eton
Lord Halifax	Eton
E. Bevin	—
H. Morrison	—
H. Macmillan	Eton
J. S. B. Lloyd	Fettes
Lord Home	Eton
R. A. Butler	Marlborough
P. G. Walker	Wellington
M. Stewart	Christ's Hospital
G. Brown	—

(viii) CHANCELLORS OF THE EXCHEQUER

Sir M. E. Hicks Beach	Eton
C. T. Ritchie	City of London
A. Chamberlain	Rugby
H. Asquith	City of London
D. Lloyd George	—
R. McKenna	K.C.S.
A. Bonar Law	Glasgow High Sch.
Sir R. Horne	George Watson's
S. Baldwin	Harrow
N. Chamberlain	Rugby
P. Snowden	—
W. L. S. Churchill	Harrow
Sir J. Simon	Fettes
Sir K. Wood	—
Sir J. Anderson	George Watson's
H. Dalton	Eton
Sir S. Cripps	Winchester
H. T. N. Gaitskell	Winchester
R. A. Butler	Marlborough

H. Macmillan	Eton
P. Thorneycroft	Eton
D. Heathcote-Amory	Eton
J. S. B. Lloyd	Fettes
R. Maudling	Merchant Taylors'
L. J. Callaghan	—
R. H. Jenkins	—
A. Barber	—

(ix) SECRETARIES OF STATE FOR HOME AFFAIRS

Sir H. W. Ridley	Harrow
C. T. Ritchie	City of London
A. Akers-Douglas	Eton
H. J. Gladstone	Eton
W. L. S. Churchill	Harrow
R. McKenna	K.C.S.
Sir J. Simon	Fettes
Sir H. Samuel	U.C.S.
E. Shortt	Durham
W. C. Bridgeman	Eton
J. R. Clynes	—
Sir W. Joynson-Hicks	Merchant Taylors'
Sir J. Gilmour	Glenalmond
Sir S. Hoare	Harrow
Sir J. Anderson	George Watson's
H. Morrison	—
Sir D. Somervell	Harrow
J. Chuter Ede	—
Sir D. Maxwell-Fyfe	George Watson's
G. Lloyd George	Eastbourne
R. A. Butler	Marlborough
H. Brooke	Marlbough
Sir F. Soskice	St. Paul's
R. Jenkins	—
J. Callaghan	—
R. Maudling	Merchant Taylors'

(x) SECRETARIES OF STATE FOR SCOTLAND

Lord Balfour of Burleigh	Eton
A. G. Murray	Harrow
Linlithgow	Eton
Lord Pentland	Wellington

T. M'Kinnon Wood	Mill Hill
H. Tennant	—
R. Munro	—
Lord Novar	—
W. Adamson	—
Sir J. Gilmour	Glenalmond
Sir A. Sinclair	Eton
Sir G. Collins	Dartmouth
W. Elliott	Glasgow Academy
D. J. Colville	Charterhouse
A. E. Brown	—
T. Johnston	—
Lord Rosebery	Eton
J. Westwood	—
A. Woodburn	—
R. McNeil	—
J. Stuart	Eton
J. S. Maclay	Winchester
M. Noble	Eton
W. Ross	Ayr Academy
G. Campbell	Wellington

(xi) PRESIDENTS OF THE BOARD OF EDUCATION, MINISTERS OF EDUCATION

Duke of Devonshire	—
Marquess of Londonderry	Eton
A. Birrell	—
R. McKenna	K.C.S.
W. Runciman	—
J. Pease	—
A. Henderson	—
H. A. L. Fisher	Winchester
E. F. L. Wood	Eton
Sir C. P. Trevelyan	Harrow
H. B. Lees-Smith	Aldenham
Sir D. Maclean	Carmarthen G.S.
O. Stanley	Eton
Lord Stanhope	Eton
Lord de la Warr	Eton
H. Ramsbotham	Uppingham
R. A. Butler	Marlborough
R. K. Law	Shrewsbury
Miss E. C. Wilkinson	—

G. Tomlinson	—
Miss F. Horsbrugh	—
Lord Hailsham	Eton
G. W. Lloyd	Harrow
Sir D. Eccles	Winchester
Sir E. Boyle	Eton
M. Stewart	Christ's Hospital
A. Crosland	Highgate
P. G. Walker	Wellington
E. W. Short	—
Mrs. M. Thatcher	—

(xii) CHIEF SECRETARIES FOR IRELAND

G. W. Balfour	Eton
G. Wyndham	Eton
J. Bryce	Glasgow High Sch.
A. Birrell	—
H. Duke	—
E. Shortt	Durham
I. Macpherson	George Watson's
Sir H. Greenwood	—

(xiii) PRIME MINISTERS OF NORTHERN IRELAND

Sir J. Craig	Merchiston Castle
J. M. Andrews	Royal Acad. Instit.
Lord Brookeborough	Winchester
T. M. O'Neill	Eton
J. D. Chichester-Clark	Eton
B. Faulkner	St. Columba's

(xiv) FIRST SEA LORDS

Lord W. Kerr	Radley
Sir J. A. Fisher	—
Sir A. K. Wilson	Dartmouth
Sir F. Bridgeman	Dartmouth
L. A. Mountbatten (Prince Louis)	—
Sir J. Jellicoe	Dartmouth
Sir R. E. Wemyss	Dartmouth
Earl Beatty	Kilkenny
Sir C. E. Madder	Dartmouth

Sir F. L. Field	Dartmouth
Lord Chatfield	Dartmouth
Sir D. Pound	Dartmouth
Sir A. Cunningham	Edinburgh Academy
Sir J. Cunningham	Dartmouth
Lord Fraser	Bradfield
Sir R. McGrigor	Dartmouth
Earl Mountbatten	Dartmouth
Sir Caspar John	Dartmouth
Sir D. Luce	Dartmouth
Sir V. Begg	Malvern
Sir M. Le Fanu	—
Sir P. Hill-Norton	Dartmouth
Sir M. Pollock	Dartmouth

(H.M.S. *Britannia* = Dartmouth; the schools were attended before Dartmouth)

(xv) CHIEFS OF THE GENERAL STAFF

Lord Roberts (C.-in-C.)	Eton
Sir N. G. Lyttleton	Eton
Sir W. G. Nicholson	—
Sir J. French	—
Sir C. Douglas	—
Sir A. J. Murray	Cheltenham
Sir W. Robertson	
Sir H. Wilson	Marlborough
Lord Cavan	Eton
Sir G. F. Milne	
Sir A. Montgomery-Massingberd	Charterhouse
Sir C. J. Deverell	Bedford
Lord Gort	Harrow
Sir W. E. Ironside	Tonbridge
Sir J. Dill	Cheltenham
Sir A. Brooke	—
Lord Montgomery	St. Paul's
Sir W. Slim	King Edward's, Birmingham
Sir S. Harding	—
Sir G. Templer	Wellington
Sir F. Festing	Winchester
Sir R. Hull	Charterhouse
Sir J. Cassels	Rugby
Sir G. H. Baker	Wellington
Sir M. Carver	Winchester

(xvi) CHIEFS OF THE AIR STAFF

Sir H. Trenchard	—
Sir J. Salmond	Wellington
Sir E. L. Ellington	Clifton
Sir C. Newall	Bedford
Sir C. Portal	Winchester
Lord Tedder	Whitgift
Sir J. Slessor	Haileybury
Sir W. Dickson	Haileybury
Sir D. Boyle	St. Columba's
Sir T. Pike	Bedford
Sir C. Elworthy	Marlborough
Sir J. Grandy	U.C.S.
Sir D. Spotswood	—

(xvii) PERMANENT SECRETARIES TO THE TREASURY AND HEADS OF THE HOME CIVIL SERVICE

Sir F. Mowatt	Winchester
Sir E. W. Hamilton	Eton
Sir G. H. Murray	Harrow
Sir R. Chalmers	City of London
Sir T. Heath	Clifton
Sir J. S. Bradbury	Manchester G.S.
Sir W. Fisher	Winchester
Sir H. J. Wilson	—
Sir R. V. N. Hopkins	King Edward's, Birmingham
Sir E. Bridges	Eton
Sir N. Brook	Wolverhampton G.S.
Sir R. Makins	Winchester
Sir F. Lee	Brentwood
Sir W. Armstrong	—
Sir L. Helsby	Sedbergh
Sir D. Allen	—

(xviii) PRESIDENTS OF THE ROYAL SOCIETY

Sir W. Huggins	City of London
Lord Rayleigh	—
Sir A. Geikie	Royal High School
Sir W. Crookes	—
Sir J. J. Thomson	—
Sir C. S. Sherrington	—

Lord Rutherford	—
Sir F. G. Hopkins	City of London
Sir W. H. Bragg	King William's
Sir H. H. Dale	The Leys
Sir R. Robinson	—
Lord Adrian	Westminster
Sir C. Hinshelwood	—
Lord Florey	—
Lord Blackett	Dartmouth
Prof. A. Hodgkin	Gresham's

(xix) PRESIDENTS OF THE ROYAL COLLEGE OF SURGEONS OF ENGLAND

Sir W. MacCormac	Royal Acad., Instit.
Sir H. C. Howse	U.C.S.
Sir J. Tweedy	—
Sir H. Morris	Epsom
Sir H. T. Butlin	—
Sir R. J. Godlee	—
Sir Watson Cheyne	Aberdeen G. S.
Sir G. H. Makins	—
Sir A. A. Bowlby	Durham
Sir J. Bland-Sutton	—
Lord Moynihan	Christ's Hospital
Sir H. J. Waring	—
Sir C. Wallace	Haileybury
Sir H. Lett	Marlborough
Sir A. Webb-Johnson	—
Sir C. Wakeley	Dulwich
Sir H. Platt	—
Sir J. Paterson Ross	Christ's College, Finchley
Sir A. Porritt	—
Sir R. Brock	Christ's Hospital
Sir H. Atkins	Rugby
Sir T. Sellors	Loretto

(xx) PRESIDENTS OF THE ROYAL ACADEMY

Sir F. J. Poynter	Ipswich
Sir A. Webb	—
Sir F. Dicksee	—
Sir W. Llewellyn	—
Sir E. Lutyens	—

Sir A. Munnings	Framlingham
Sir G. Kelly	Eton
Sir A. E. Richardson	—
Sir C. Wheeler	—
Sir T. Monnington	—

(xx) POETS LAUREATE

Alfred Austen	Stonyhurst
Robert Bridges	Eton
John Masefield	—
C. Day Lewis	Sherborne
Sir John Betjeman	Marlborough

(xxii) DIRECTORS GENERAL OF THE B.B.C.

Lord Reith	Gresham's
F. W. Ogilvie	Clifton
Sir C. Graves	Gresham's
R. W. Foot	Winchester
Sir W. Haley	Victoria College
Sir I. Jacob	Wellington
Sir H. C. Greene	Berkhamsted
C. Curran	—

(xxiii) DIRECTORS GENERAL OF THE I.T.A.

Sir R. Fraser	St. Peter's, Adelaide
B. Young	Eton

(xxiv) HEADMASTERS OF ETON

E. Warne	Eton
E. Lyttleton	Eton
C. Alington	Marlborough
Sir C. Elliott	Eton
R. Birley	Rugby
A. Chenevix-Trench	Shrewsbury
M. W. McCrum	Sherborne

(xxv) HEADMASTERS OF WINCHESTER

W. E. Fearon	Winchester
H. M. Burge	Bedford
M. J. Rendall	Harrow
A. T. P. Williams	Rossall

S. Leeson	Winchester
W. F. Oakeshott	Tonbridge
Sir D. Lee	Repton
J. L. Thorn	St. Paul's

(xxvi) PRESIDENTS OF THE FEDERATION OF BRITISH INDUSTRY AND C.B.I.

F. D. Docker	—
Sir R. Vassor-Smith	—
Sir V. Caillard	Eton
Sir W. P. Rylands	Charterhouse
O. C. Armstrong	—
Sir E. Geddes	Merchiston Castle
Lord Barnby	—
Sir M. Muspratt	Clifton
Lord Gainford	—
Lord Ebbisham	—
L. B. Lee	Eton
Sir J. Lithgow	Glasgow Academy
Sir J. G. Beharrell	—
Sir G. MacDonogh	—
Lord H. Scott	Eton
Sir T. Joseph	—
Lord Hirst	—
P. F. Bennett	King Edward's, Birmingham
Lord D. Gordon	Harrow
Sir G. Nelson	—
Sir C. Baillieu	—
Sir F. Bain	Banff Academy
Sir R. Sinclair	—
Sir A. Forbes	Rugby
Sir H. Pilkington	—
Sir G. Hayman	Wellington
Sir H. Beaver	—
W. H. McFadzean	—
Sir C. Harrison	Burnley G.S.
Sir P. Runge	Charterhouse
Sir M. Laing	St. Lawrence
Sir S. Brown	Taunton
J. Partridge	Queen Elizabeth's, Bristol

(xxvii) JOURNALISM: EDITORS

The Times

G. E. Buckle	All Hallows
G. Dawson	Eton
H. W. Stead	—
R. Barrington-Ward	Westminster
W. F. Casey	Castleknock
Sir W. Haley	Victoria College
W. Rees-Mogg	Charterhouse

The (Manchester) Guardian

C. P. Scott	—
E. Scott	Rugby
W. P. Crozier	Manchester G.S.
A. P. Wadsworth	—
A. Hetherington	Gresham's

The New Statesman (and Nation)

C. D. Sharp	St. Lawrence
K. Martin	Mill Hill
J. Freeman	Westminster
P. Johnson	Stonyhurst
R. Crossman	Winchester
A. Howard	Westminster

(xxviii) SCHOOLS WITH MOST MEN IN APPENDIX 8

Eton	57
Winchester	20
Dartmouth	17
Harrow	14
Rugby	10
Marlborough	9
Wellington	8
Charterhouse	7
George Watson's	7
Clifton	6
City of London	5
Bedford	4
Gresham's	4
Haileybury	4
Merchant Taylor's	4
U.C.S.	4
Westminster	4

Cheltenham	3
Christ's Hospital	3
Glasgow High School	3
King Edward's, Birmingham	3
Manchester G.S.	3
Mill Hill	3
St. Paul's	3

(xxix) NOTES

(a) Only three women are represented in these appointments.

(b) Absence of Roman Catholic Schools apart from Stonyhurst.

(c) Only in industry and art are public-school-educated not overwhelmingly represented.

(d) One representative from all the Woodard schools.

BIBLIOGRAPHY

The History & Register of Aldenham School, 7th ed. (Aldenham, 1938)
Allport, D. H. *Camberwell Grammar School, Wilson's* (London, 1964)
Anstey, F. *Vice Versa* (Smith Elder, 1882)
Ashcroft, R. L. *Haileybury 1908–61* (Haileybury, 1961)

Baines, J. M. and Conisbee, L. R. *The History of Hastings Grammar School* (Hastings, 1956)
Baldwin, Earl. *On England* (Penguin, 1937)
Bamford, T. W. *Rise of the Public Schools: 1837 to Present Day* (Nelson, 1967)
Banks, F. R. *The Penguin Guide to London* (Penguin, 1958)
Battersby, W. J. *St Joseph's College* (Burns & Oates, 1955)
The History of St. Stanislaus College Beaumont (Windsor, 1911)
Bell, E. A. *A History of Giggleswick School* (Leeds, 1912)
Berners, Lord *A Distant Prospect* (Constable, 1945)
Besant, Sir W. *London in the Nineteenth Century* (Black, 1909)
Besant, Sir W. *London North of the Thames* (Black, 1911)
Bishop, T. J. H. and Wilkinson, R. *Winchester and the Public School Elite* (Faber, 1967)
Blackmore, R. D. *Lorna Doone* (London, 1869)
Blanch, W. H. *Dulwich College and Edward Alleyn* (London, 1877)
Blatchley-Hennah, F. T. W. *A Short History of Sutton Valence School* (Kent Messenger, 1952)
Blumenau, R. *A History of Malvern College 1865–1965* (Malvern, 1965)
Blunden, E. *Christ's Hospital* (Christophers, 1923)
Bowra, C. M. *Memories 1898–1939* (Weidenfeld & Nicolson, 1966)
Boyd, A. K. *The History of Radley College* (Blackwell, 1948)
Brett-James, N. G. *The History of Mill Hill School* (London, 1909)
Brice, L. J. *Notes on Rutlish School* (unpublished, 1968)
Brodie, W. *Kelvinside Academy 1878–1923* (University of Glasgow, 1924)
Bryant, P. H. M. *Harrow* (Blackie, 1936)
Burgess, T. *A Guide to English Schools* (Pelican, 1969 ed.)
Buscot, W. *The History of Cotton College* (Burns & Oates, 1940)
Butler, S. *The Way of all Flesh* (Grant Richards, 1903)

Carleton, J. D. *Westminster School* (Hart-Davis, 1965)
Cavell, J. and Kennett, B. *A History of Sir Roger Manwood's School* (Cary, Adams & Mackay, 1963)
Chesterton, G. K. *Autobiography* (Hutchinson, 1936)
Churchill, W. L. S. *My Early Life* (Butterworth, 1930)
Clarke, H. L. and Weech, W. N. *History of Sedbergh School* (Sedbergh, 1925)
Centenary Essays on Clifton College (Arrowsmith, 1962)
Craig, M. *Dublin 1660–1860* (Cresset Press, 1952)
Craze, M. *A History of Felsted School* (Ipswich, 1955)
Croom-Johnson, Sir R. P. *The Origin of Stowe School* (W. S. Cowell, 1953)

Dancy, J. *The Public Schools and the Future* (Faber, 1966)
Darwin, B. *The English Public School* (Longmans, 1931)
Davis, R. *The Grammar School* (Pelican, 1967)
de Quincey, J. *Confessions of an English Opium-Eater* (John Lane, 1930)
The Derby School Register 1570–1901, ed. B. Tacchella (Derby, 1902)
The Dictionary of National Biography
Dilke, C. *Dr. Moberly's Mint-Mark* (Heinemann, 1965)
The Direct Grant School (Headmasters' Conference, 1968)
Douglas-Smith, A. E. *City of London School* (Blackwell, 1965)
Dowling, P. J. *A History of Irish Education* (Cork, 1971)
Doyle, Sir A. Conan *Memories and Adventures* (Hodder & Stoughton, 1924)
Draper, F. W. M. *Four Centuries of Merchant Taylors' School* (Oxford, 1962)
Memories of Dulwich College, by Old Alleynians (Dulwich, 1919)

Epsom College Register, with a history (ed. T. R. Thomson)

Falkiner, Sir F. R. *The Foundation of the Hospital and Free School of King Charles II* (Dublin, 1906)
Falkner, C. G. *History of Weymouth College* (London, 1937)
Farrar, F. W. *Eric, or Little by Little* (London, 1858)
Felton, H. and Harvey, J. *The English Cathedrals* (Batsford, 1950)
Forester, C. S. *Long Before Forty* (Michael Joseph, 1967)
Fry, C. B. *Life Worth Living* (Eyre & Spottiswoode, 1939)
Furness, W. *The Centenary History of Rossall School* (Gale & Polden, 2nd ed. 1946)

The Glasgow Academy: The Fist 100 Years, various (Blackie, 1946)
The Glenalmond Register, with a history (Edinburgh, 1955)
Glover, E. P. *The First Sixty Years, Newport High School* (Newport, 1957)

Gourlay, A. B. *A History of Sherborne School* (Winchester, 1951)

Graham, J. A. and Pythian, B. A. *The Manchester Grammar School 1515–1965* (Manchester University Press, 1965)

Graham, J. P. *Forty Years of Uppingham* (Macmillan, 1932)

Graves, C. *Leather Armchairs* (Cassell, 1963)

Graves, R. *Goodbye to all That* (Cape, 1929)

Gray, J. M. *A History of the Perse School* (Bowes & Bowes, 1921)

The Great Public Schools, various (Arnold, 1893)

Greene, G. ed. *The Old School* (Cape, 1934)

Grey, I. E. and Potter, W. E. *Ipswich School 1400–1950* (Ipswich, 1950)

Gruggen, G. and Keating, J. *Stonyhurst* (Kegan Paul, 1901)

Haileyburian Centenary Number (1962)

Handford, B. W. T. *Lancing* (Blackwell, 1933)

Hastling, A. H. L., Willis, W. A. and Workman, W. P. *History of Kingswood School* (London, 1898)

Heeney, B. *Mission to the Middle Classes: The Woodard Schools 1848–91* (S.P.C.K., 1969)

Hibbert, F. A. *A Short History and Description of Denstone College* (London, 1900)

Hill, R. D. *A History of St. Edward's School* (Oxford, 1962)

Hilton, J. *Good-bye, Mr. Chips* (Hodder & Stoughton, 1934)

Hollis, C. *Eton* (Hollis & Carter, 1960)

Hughes, E. A. *The Royal Naval College, Dartmouth* (London, 1950)

Hughes, T. *Tom Brown's Schooldays* (London, 1857)

Icely, H. E. M. *Bromsgrove School Through Four Centuries* (Blackwell, 1953)

Inge, B. G. ed. *Notes on the History of Blue-Coat Schools* (unpublished, 1968)

Inglis, B. ed. *John Bull's Schooldays* (Hutchinson, 1961)

Jacobs, P. M. *Registers of the Universities, Colleges and Schools of Great Britain and Ireland* (University of London, 1964)

Jameson, E. M. *Charterhouse* (Blackie, 1937)

Jamieson, J. *The Royal Belfast Academical Institution 1810–1960* (Belfast, 1959)

Jones, P. *War Letters of a Public-School Boy* (Cassell, 1918)

Joyce, J. *A Portrait of the Artist as a Young Man* (London, 1916)

Jullian, P. *Oscar Wilde* (Constable, 1969)

Kalton, G. *The Public Schools* (Longmans, 1966)

King, C. *Strictly Personal* (Weidenfeld & Nicolson, 1969)

Kipling, R. *Land and Sea Tales for Scouts and Guides* (Macmillan, 1923)

Kipling, R. *The Complete Stalky & Co.* (Macmillan, 1929)
Kirk, K. E. *The Story of the Woodard Schools* (Abingdon, 1952)

Lambert, R. *The Hothouse Society* (Weidenfeld & Nicolson, 1968)
Lambert, R. and others. *New Wine in Old Bottles* (Bell, 1968)
Lawson, J. *A Town Grammar School Through Six Centuries, Hull G.S.* (Oxford, 1963)
Leach, A. F. *English Schools at the Reformation 1546–8* (London, 1896)
Leach, A. F. *A History of Bradfield College* (Frowde, 1900)
Leamington College 1902–52, various (Leamington, 1952)
Lord Leverhulme, by his son (Allen & Unwin, 1927)
Lewis, C. H. *Kimbolton School* (Kimbolton, 1950)
Lindsay, K. *English Education* (Collins, 1941)
Lockwood, E. *The Early Days of Marlborough College* (Simkin, Marshal, 1893)
Luft, H. M. *A History of Merchant Taylors' School, Crosby* (Liverpool University Press, 1970)
Lyte, Sir H. C. Maxwell. *A History of Eton College* (London, 1911)

Mackenzie, Compton. *My Life and Times: Octave Two* (Chatto & Windus, 1963)
Mackenzie, Compton. *On Moral Courage* (Collins, 1962)
Mackenzie, Compton. *Sinister Street* (Secker, 1913)
Maclean, A. H. H. *Public Schools and the Great War* (Stanford, 1923)
Maclean, A. H. H. *Public Schools and the War in South Africa* (Stanford, 1903)
Maclean, A. H. H. *Where We Get Our Best Men* (Simkin, Marshal, 1900)
Marshall, B. *George Brown's Schooldays* (Constable, 1946)
Matthews, C. M. *Haileybury Since Roman Times* (Haileybury, 1959)
Maugham, W. S. *Of Human Bondage* (Heinemann, 1915)
Merchiston Castle School Register 1833–1929 (Edinburgh, 1930)
Mosley, L. *Curzon* (Longmans, 1960)
Mumford, A. A. *The Manchester Grammar School 1515–1915* (Longmans, 1919)
Murray, A. L. *Sebright School* (Heffer, 1954)

Newsome, D. *Godliness and Good Learning* (Murray, 1961)
Newsome, D. A. *A History of Wellington College* (Murray, 1959)
Nicolson, H. *Diaries and Letters 1939–45* (Collins, 1967)

Oakley, R. A. *A History of Oswestry School* (Seeley Service, 1964)
Ogilvie, V. *The English Public School* (Batsford, 1957)
Oldham, J. B. *A History of Shrewsbury School* (Blackwell, 1952)
Olive, G. W. *A School's Adventure.* Dauntsey's (Sylvan Press, 1951)

Ormiston, T. L. *Dulwich College Register 1619–1926* (London, 1926)
Our Public Schools (Kegan Paul, 1881)

Parker, E. *Floreat: An Eton Anthology* (Nisbet, 1923)
Paton's List of Schools (1923 onwards)
Peel, J. H. B. *Country Talk* (Hale, 1970)
Percival, A. C. *The Origins of the Headmasters' Conference* (Murray, 1969)
Perry, R. *Ardingly 1858–1946* (London, 1951)
Picciotto, C. *St. Paul's School* (Blackie, 1939)
Prospectuses, numerous
Public Schools Commission Report, 2 vols (H.M.S.O., 1968, 1970)
The Public Schools From Within, various (Sampson Low, 1906)
The Public Schools Year Book (Black, 1965–72)
Purdy, A. and Sutherland, D. *Burgess and Maclean* (Secker & Warburg, 1963)

Roberts, S. C. ed. *A History of Brighton College* (Brighton, 1957)
Rodgers, J. *The Old Public Schools of England* (Batsford, 1938)
Roe, W. N. ed. *Public Schools Cricket 1901–50* (Parrish, 1951)
Rogers, P. W. *A History of Rippon Grammar School* (Rippon, 1954)
Ross, W. C. A. *The Royal High School* (Oliver & Boyd, 1934)
Ruscoe, R. G. *Hereford High School for Boys* (Hereford, 1962)

The Story of St. Bees 1583–1939, Old St. Beghians Club (London, 1939)
Sale, G. *Four Hundred Years A School, King's, Bruton* (1950)
Sampson, A. *Anatomy of Britain* (Hodder & Stoughton, 1962)
Sassoon, S. *The Old Century* (Faber, 1938)
Schools (Truman & Knightley, 1931–1971)
Scotland, J. *The History of Scottish Education*, Vol. I (University of London, 1969)
Shaw, G. B. *Prefaces* (Odhams, 1938)
Sitwell, O. *Penny Foolish* (Macmillan, 1935)
Smith, J. H. *Churcher's College* (Manchester University Press, 1936)
Somervell, D. C. *A History of Tonbridge School* (Faber, 1947)
Snell, F. J. *Blundell's* (Hutchinson, 1928)
Stanier, R. S. *Magdalen School* (Blackwell, 1958).
Stanley, A. P. *The Life of Thomas Arnold* (New ed., 1903)
Staunton, H. *The Great Schools of England* (London, 1877)
Steven, W. *History of the High School of Edinburgh* (Edinburgh, 1849)
Strachey, L. *Eminent Victorians* (London, 1918)
Symons, K. E. *The Grammar School of King Edward VI, Bath* (Bath, 1934)

Thackeray, W. M. *The Newcomes* (London, 1853)
Thomas, A. W. *A History of Nottingham High School* (Nottingham, 1957)

Thomas, B. *Repton 1557–1957* (Batsford, 1957)

Thompson, J. *A History of Daniel Stewart's College 1855–1955* (Edinburgh, 1955)

Tristram, H. B. *Loretto School Past and Present* (Unwin, 1911)

Usher, B. ed. *Public Schools at a Glance* (The Assoc. of Standardized Knowledge, 1913)

van Zeller, Dom H. *Downside By and Large* (Sheed & Ward, 1954)

Varley, B. *The History of Stockport Grammar School* (Manchester University Press, 1957)

Victoria County Histories of England, various: London, Surrey, Sussex, Yorkshire

Vincent, W. A. L. *The Grammar Schools 1660–1714* (Murray, 1969)

Wainwright, D. *Liverpool Gentlemen* (Faber, 1960)

Walpole, Hugh, *Jeremy* (London, 1919)

Walpole, Hugh, *Jeremy at Crale* (London, 1927)

Ward, B. *History of St. Edmund's College* (Kegan, Paul, 1893)

Warner, Sir Pelham, *Lords* (Harrap, 1946)

Warner, Rex, *English Public Schools* (Collins, 1945)

Warner, R. T. *Winchester* (Bell, 1900)

Watson, F. *The Old Grammar Schools* (Cambridge, 1916)

Waugh, E. *Scott-King's Modern Europe* (Chapman & Hall, 1947)

Whitaker's Almanac (1900–72)

Whitaker's Boarding Schools (1928)

Who Was Who, Vols. I–V (Black)

Worksop College 1895–1955, various (Worksop, 1955)

INDEX